D0319525

PITTVILLE LEARNING CENTRE
Albert Road Cheltenham

UN--- ---ITY OF
--- ---SHIRE
---ER

RETHINKING HERITAGE

RETHINKING HERITAGE

CULTURES AND POLITICS IN EUROPE

EDITED BY

ROBERT SHANNAN PECKHAM

PITTVILLE LEARNING CENTRE
UNIVERSITY OF GLOUCESTERSHIRE
Albert Road, Cheltenham, GL52 3JG
Tel: (01242) 532259

I.B. TAURIS

LONDON · NEW YORK

Published in 2003 by I.B.Tauris & Co Ltd
6 Salem Road, London W2 4BU
175 Fifth Avenue, New York NY 10010
www.ibtauris.com

In the United States and Canada distributed by Palgrave Macmillan
a division of St. Martin's Press
175 Fifth Avenue, New York NY 10010

Copyright © Eleni Nakou Foundation, 2003

All rights reserved. Except for brief quotations in a review, this book,
or any part thereof, may not be reproduced, stored in or introduced
into a retrieval system, or transmitted, in any form or by any means,
electronic, mechanical, photocopying, recording or otherwise, without
the prior written permission of the publisher.

ISBN 1 86064 796 0

A full CIP record for this book is available from the British Library
A full CIP record for this book is available from the Library of Congress

Library of Congress catalog card: available

Typeset in Minion by Dexter Haven Associates, London
Printed and bound in Great Britain by MPG Books, Bodmin

CONTENTS

Part III: Placing Heritage

Part IV: The Disinheritance of Heritage

ILLUSTRATIONS

CONTRIBUTORS

Stephen Bann is Professor of the History of Art at the University of Bristol. His publications include *The True Vine: On Visual Representation in the Western Tradition* (1989), *Under the Sign: John Bargrave as Collector, Traveller, and Witness* (1994), *Paul Delaroche: History Painted* (1997) and *Parallel Lines: Printmakers, Painters and Photographers in Nineteenth-Century France* (2001). He is the editor of several volumes, including *Frankenstein, Creation, and Monstrosity* (1994).

Peter Bugge is Reader in Czech and European Studies at the University of Aarhus and the author of numerous articles on European integration.

Denis Cosgrove is the Alexander von Humboldt Professor of Geography at the University of California, Los Angeles. He is the author of *Social Formation and Symbolic Landscape* (1984), *The Palladian Landscape: Geographical Change and its Cultural Representation in Sixteenth-Century Italy* (1993) and *Apollo's Eye: A Cartographic Genealogy of the Earth in the Western Imagination* (2001). Professor Cosgrove has edited a number of volumes, including *Mappings* (1999), and co-edited *The Iconography of Landscape: Essays on the Symbolic Representation, Design and Use of Past Environments* (1988) with Stephen Daniels.

James Duncan is a University Lecturer in Geography at the University of Cambridge and a Fellow of Emmanuel College. He is the author of *The City as Text: The Politics of Landscape Interpretation in the Kandyan Kingdom* (1990), and co-author, with John Agnew, of *The Power of Place: Bringing together Geographical and Sociological Imaginations* (1989). He has co-edited the following volumes: *Writing Worlds: Discourse, Text and Metaphor in the Representation of Landscape* (1992) with Trevor Barnes, *Place/Culture/Representation* (1993) with David Ley and *Writes of Passage: Reading Travel Writing* (1999) with Derek Gregory.

Simon Gaunt is Professor of French Language and Literature at King's College, University of London. His books include *Troubadours and Irony* (1989) and *Gender and Genre in Medieval Literature* (1995). He has also co-edited *The Troubadours: An Introduction* (1999) with Sarah Kay.

Alexander Kiossev is Lecturer in the Cultural History of Modernity at the University of Sofia. He is the editor of *Post-Theory, Games, and Discursive Resistance: The Bulgarian Case* (1995) and the author of the forthcoming *Essays in Cultural History of the Transition*.

Thorkild Kjærgaard is the former Director of the Museum at Sønderborg Castle, founded in 1908. He is the author of several books, including *The Danish Revolution 1500-1800: An Ecohistorical Interpretation* (1994).

Michael Landzelius is a Visiting Research Fellow in the Department of Geography at Cambridge University. He is currently completing a politico-spatial study on Swedish World War II labour camps.

Karen Lang is Assistant Professor of Modern European Art History and Theory at the University of Southern California.

Robert Shannan Peckham has been a Research Fellow at St Catharine's College, Cambridge and a Fellow of St Peter's College, Oxford. His articles on cultural politics have appeared in numerous edited books, journals and newspapers. He is the author of *Fuel Three Thousand* (2000) and *National Histories, Natural States: Nationalism and the Politics of Place in Greece* (2001).

Donald Preziosi is Professor of Art History at the University of California, Los Angeles. His books include *The Semiotics of the Built Environment* (1979), *Rethinking Art History: Meditations on a Coy Science* (1989); he is co-author with Louise Hitchcock of *Aegean Art and Architecture* (1999) and author of *Brain of Earth's Body: Museums and the Fabrication of Modernity* (in press). He is also the editor of a critical anthology, *The Art of Art History* (1998).

Thomas Risse has recently taken up a chair at the Centre for Transatlantic Foreign and Security Policy at the Otto Suhr Institute for Political Science at the Free University of Berlin. He is the author of *Cooperation among Democracies: The European Influence on US Foreign Policy* (1995), *International Relations Theory and the End of the Cold War* (1995) with Richard Lebow and the editor of *Bringing Transnational Relations Back In: Non-State Actors, Domestic Structure and International Institutions* (1995) with Steve Smith.

Stephanos Stephanides is Associate Professor in the Department of Foreign Languages and Literatures at the University of Cyprus. He is the author of *Translating Kali's Feast: The Goddess in Indo-Caribbean Fiction* (2000) and he served as judge for the Commonwealth Writers Prize (2000). In 1989 the Society of Humanistic Anthropology of the American Anthropological Association awarded him first prize for poetry.

AbdoolKarim Vakil is Lecturer in Portuguese History at King's College, University of London.

Joachim Wolschke-Bulmahn is Professor in the History of Open Space Planning and Landscape Architecture at the University of Hanover. He is the editor of numerous books, including *The Vernacular Garden* (1993) with John Dixon Hunt, *Mughal Gardens: Sources, Places, Representations and Prospects* (1996) with James L. Wescoat and *Nature and Ideology: Natural Garden Design in the Twentieth-Century* (1997).

FOREWORD

ERIK HOLM

The momentous changes that swept through Europe during the last decade of the twentieth century contributed to the mounting sense of *fin de millénaire*. While for some these changes signalled the 'end of history,' for others they represented the dawn of a new day, or indeed a new era; a chance to shape the future instead of remaining imprisoned by the past.

The sentiment that profound change was taking place, not only in history, but in society and in human relations more generally, was also the result of developments in technology and the natural sciences. Globalization, information and communication networks dissolved borders that for generations had seemed to be historical givens. More fundamental questions were raised relating to our self-perception as part of nature and the universe. The breaking of the genetic code, for example, placed mankind face-to-face with the core of nature, if not with genesis itself. Taken to its extreme, science might enable us to take control of our own heredity, many seemed to think – or fear.

During the 1990s, 'identity' became the catchword of social, political and cultural discourse. Identity politics appeared on the academic and social agenda, along with questions of ethnicity, nationalism, multiculturalism and civil society. History, myths and realities were reconsidered, and heritage, political and cultural, was celebrated, accepted or discarded in the search for personal, ethnic or national identities.

As the very title of this volume suggests, *Rethinking Heritage: Cultures and Politics in Europe* engages with this wider debate. The essays collected here originated as papers presented at a symposium held at the European Cultural Centre of Delphi in May 2000. The focus of the discussion was on heritage considered within different European cultural and political contexts. Admittedly, we set ourselves an ambitious challenge in convening such a meeting at Delphi, the *omphalos* or navel of the classical Hellenic world, which has been so central in the formulation of Western cultural and political heritages.

However, there were other reasons for choosing Delphi as the venue. The Eleni Nakou Foundation has its own origins in Greece. It is a charity set up under the terms of the will of the late Eleni Nakou, whose life work in quality tourism left a lasting impact in Greece and particularly in Crete. Her love of the

Hellenic heritage and her enthusiastic spirit inspired the aims of the foundation, which are to establish a forum for wider appreciation of the dimensions and depth of European culture. The major means for doing so is to initiate a biennial symposium on a theme related to European culture. In 2000 we wanted to mark the tenth anniversary of the foundation by going back to Greece.

I was fortunate in 1998, through Greek friends, to meet Dr Robert Shannan Peckham of St Peter's College, Oxford, who accepted our invitation to develop the idea for a symposium on the theme of cultural heritage, to research the literature, to identify potential contributors to the debate and to organize the event. It was done in close collaboration and I was therefore partially responsible for the outcome, but Dr Peckham carried by far the largest part of the workload, and I am very grateful to him for the excellent result achieved.

As on earlier occasions, we invited a diverse group of scholars and intellectuals to address the theme, and a further number of experts to participate in the debate during the three-day meeting. I should stress that the aim of this, as of the earlier symposia, was not to follow a narrowly academic and arcanely specialist agenda. Of course, specialists were invited. But at these symposia it has always been our intention to provoke searching discussions on a wide range of cultural and political issues, and to establish a forum to promote dialogue between people who would not otherwise meet through the usual professional channels.

This was the fifth symposium on European culture organized by the Eleni Nakou Foundation. The first was held in Crete in 1992, when a group of historians, sociologists, political scientists and journalists was invited to discuss the theme 'Images of Europe.' In 1994, a second symposium was convened at the Louisiana Museum of Modern Art near Copenhagen to debate the question 'What is European in European Modern Art?' We held our third symposium in Toledo in 1996 with the theme 'Europe and Islam, Dynamics and Convergent Trends,' and in 1998 the fourth took place at Stirin Castle near Prague, where the participants discussed the question: 'Central Europe: core of the continent or periphery of the West?'

After each symposium we have published a book containing edited versions of some of the papers presented. They are not offered as records of the proceedings, but as self-contained publications in their own right covering the breadth of the discussions. I am grateful to Dr Peckham for having undertaken the heavy task of editing the present volume, which reflects these intentions so well.

Dr Erik Holm
Director, Eleni Nakou Foundation

INTRODUCTION

THE POLITICS OF HERITAGE AND PUBLIC CULTURE

ROBERT SHANNAN PECKHAM

THE HERITAGE DEBATE

Rethinking Heritage: Cultures and Politics in Europe has been conceived as an unashamedly ambitious attempt to explore notions of 'heritage' across different disciplinary and geographical spaces. It addresses the pressing questions that surround heritage as a political issue. What is the relationship between heritage and identity? What meanings does heritage have in the context of hybrid societies and within the so-called new 'politics of difference?' What happens to heritage when the concept of culture is uncoupled from the nation? What histories does heritage have? And how does the past become heritage?

For most people today 'heritage' carries two related sets of meanings. On the one hand, it is associated with tourism and with sites of historical interest that have been preserved for the nation. Heritage designates those institutions involved in the celebration, management and maintenance of material objects, landscapes, monuments and buildings that reflect the nation's past. On the other hand, it is used to describe a set of shared values and collective memories; it betokens inherited customs and a sense of accumulated communal experiences that are construed as a 'birthright' and are expressed in distinct languages and through other cultural performances.

The background to this collection of essays is an ongoing debate about heritage, which has been fuelled by anxieties that are one consequence of living in a globalized, post-colonial world where the nation-state is in a process of radical redefinition. The issues of sovereignty raised in the Danish referendum for joining the single European currency held in September 2000 underscore the connections between heritage and nation and the attendant fears of relinquishing a national identity through incorporation into a larger political and economic entity.[1]

Heritage, in fact, has been closely linked to the development of the nation-state. This is hardly surprising, considering that from at least the eighteenth century the nation-state has been the dominant form of political community within Europe. Many of the institutions through which heritage is promoted, including museums, folklore societies and other educational establishments, played a formative role in the nation-building process. To this extent, heritage signifies the politicization of culture and the mobilization of cultural forms for ideological ends.

At the beginning of the twenty-first century, many conventional assumptions about the inevitability of the nation-state are being called into question. Globalization has undermined many of those borders within which we are accustomed to define 'ourselves' and 'others.' As European societies become increasingly secular and multicultural, the concept of a monolithic, encompassing and integrative heritage becomes untenable. In Europe, the process towards economic and political integration, as well as the increasing emphasis on regional diversification and autonomy, have suggested alternative models of political community. These centripetal and centrifugal forces have raised questions about the state's role as the custodian of a collective heritage. And yet, as the outcome of the Danish referendum suggests, the nation remains a potent rallying cry in Europe today.

MUSEUMS, HERITAGE AND PUBLIC CULTURE

Museums, at least since the eighteenth century, have served to bolster, naturalize and fix national and imperial identities.[2] Given the reality of Europe's diverse society, it is not surprising that museums are proliferating at the same time as their authority is being contested. Museums provide an important index of broader cultural changes. The process of collecting that they embody – the gathering up of objects into a system of value and meaning – is central to the formation of cultural and personal identities.[3]

As an institution, the museum involves a twofold process of disconnection and reconnection. Objects and customs are lifted from the dynamic contexts in which they derived, and 'authenticity' is produced by this removal and re-integration into the static milieu of the showcase.[4] As Denis Cosgrove observes in his essay on Venice in the present volume, 'preserving the heritage fragment inescapably involves its relocation, reconstruction and re-presentation within the different landscape of the present.' The museum, it could be argued, stands as a particularly striking example of this process of 'de-territorialization' and 're-territorialization,' which is one consequence of modernity: in the showcase, objects that have been uprooted from their concrete social relations are incorporated back into new hierarchies and institutions.[5]

In contemporary Europe, where the notion of a coherent symbolic order and the legitimacy of 'grand narratives' are in decline,[6] strategies of display have become increasingly problematic.[7] Western assumptions about ways of seeing, travelling, and learning – experiences that are associated with heritage – have been called into question.[8] Museums have become expressive of larger concerns about authenticity, representation and identity.[9]

The debate about the fate of the museum has underlined two more general tendencies. The first is a drive to anchor group identity in the face of change. The second, as James Duncan points out in the present volume, is an attempt to challenge the authority of heritage sites, including museums, through innovative, self-critical curatorial practices that invite spectators to reflect upon their own position within the 'exhibitionary complex.'[10] Endeavours to demystify heritage institutions reflect what has been called 'public culture;' a new 'cosmopolitan arena' where the notion of 'culture' is defined and contested by different groups.[11] This dynamic notion of the public sphere, as a 'zone of contestation,'[12] contrasts sharply to the conventional idea of the 'public' as a 'mythical creature with invisible interests on whose behalf people claim to speak so as to disguise the self-interest of their own actions.'[13]

In the midst of upheavals there is a craving for stability, even while those same upheavals are undermining the legitimacy of the order that is sought. Although the museum is often conceived as a bastion against the instability of the present, it increasingly relies upon and promotes those same mass-market technologies from which it ostensibly shields us. The museum has become a commercial enterprise, which sells the past to the visitor as entertainment.

GOLDEN AGES

Heritage is a billion-Euro business. In a recent novel by the British author Julian Barnes, *England, England*, which centres on the creation of a replica theme park of England located on the Isle of Man, one of the protagonists declares:

> We – England…is - are - a nation of great age, great history, great accumulated wisdom. Social and cultural history - stacks of it, reams of it - eminently marketable,

never more so than in the current climate. Shakespeare, Queen Victoria, Industrial Revolution, gardening, that sort of thing. If I may coin, no, copyright a phrase, We are already what others may hope to become…We must sell our past to other nations as their future![14]

Heritage here becomes the marketing of history for external consumption by foreign tourists or by a native population encouraged to consider its 'own' past as a foreign country that is at once reassuringly familiar and entertainingly exotic.[15]

To oppose a tumultuous, heterogeneous present against a homogeneous, stable past is, of course, to fall victim to the myth of a golden age. As Robert Hewison has argued in *The Heritage Industry,* the transformation of the past through the rose-tinted lens of nostalgia is part of a reactionary politics determined to ward off the perils of potentially disruptive change.[16] The promotion of a national heritage in the preservation of sanctioned sites during the nineteenth century, we should also remember, involved the elimination of other local or nonconformist heritages that were deemed dangerous to national unity.[17] As Cosgrove reminds us, there is a close relationship between heritage and the *spolia* or booty carried away by conquering armies. Heritage involves a frequently violent translocation from the 'periphery' to the centre of power.[18]

The historical vision of a stable, ordered past and the fear of the potential chaos of contemporary change have a long history. Many aspects of the national heritages we champion today, while ostensibly of ancient lineage, are in fact of recent provenance, engineered to invest legitimacy and authority in the state.[19] Heritage and nostalgia are closely connected with conservative ideologies.[20] The heritage debate in Britain, which arose in the wake of Margaret Thatcher's Conservative victory and of the National Heritage Act of 1980, focused on the relationship between what critics perceived as the 'museumification' of Britain and the nostalgic evocation of World War II Britain propagated by the government.[21] The promotion of a British 'heritage,' critics argued, was linked to a 'nationalization' of history, in which the state projected an idealized image of order, which was contrasted to the turmoil of the present. In essence, heritage signalled the fictionalization of history. The past was cleansed of internal conflict, sanitized and offered to the public for easy consumption as the 'truth.'

HERITAGE AND THE HYPERREAL

Heritage has been hotly debated in many European countries, not least in post-unified Germany. The reconstruction of Berlin and the shift of political power to the city that followed the collapse of the wall have raised issues about the country's fraught heritage, which has been obliterated from the new urban landscape. As Karen Till has observed, 'memorials dedicated to socialist leaders were torn down, street names celebrating Communist resistance fighters were changed, and many historical buildings were renovated.' This replanning of the landscape took place because such sites had been constructed in the German Democratic Republic to enshrine different 'truths' and were 'perceived as a threat to the legitimacy of a new Germany.'[22]

In the France of President Mitterand's *grands projets*, Pierre Nora undertook the mapping of those topoi linked to France's *patrimonie* in a massive undertaking that culminated with the publication of *Les Lieux de Mémoire*, translated into English as *Realms of Memory*.[23] Nora's compendium explores the creation of historical sites, which aimed to shore up and reaffirm French national identity. Implicit in this self-conscious project of memory creation, Nora suggests, was the threat of the past's eradication.[24] The language debate in France too has increasingly focused on the threat posed to the French language by the gathering forces of Anglo-Saxon economic and cultural hegemony, which are believed to jeopardize the national heritage.

While Nora and his colleagues were surveying France's *lieux de mémoire*, cultural critics such as Jean Baudrillard developed the idea of history's fictionalization in heritage sites. Baudrillard argued that in contemporary society meaning has been replaced with spectacle,[25] where images from the past and the future, from the local and the global, coalesce. In France, visitors do not have to visit the real eleventh-century Bayeux Tapestry, since before they reach the original they can marvel at a life-size replica.[26] Similarly, while visitors are no longer admitted to the real Lascaux Caves, they can nevertheless wander through a replica, which has been constructed 500 metres from the original. The heritage site replaces the original; it has become a fiction, or what Baudrillard calls a 'simulacrum' – a copy that renders the original redundant.[27] Today, Baudrillard argues, the idea of the 'real' has been problematized, and heritage sites belong to the world of the 'hyperreal' – an arena that finds its ultimate expression in Disneyland. Baudrillard's arguments mark a decisive shift away from the elitist notion of 'art' which the sociologist Pierre Bourdieu, writing in the 1960s, perceived as an ideological institution that excluded the mass public.[28]

WHOSE HERITAGE?

What is at stake in this debate about heritage is the idea of authenticity and the ways in which notions of the past are being transformed by a globalized economic and cultural system. There are those who condemn this as a sham and a political diversion away from pressing social issues. In Britain, critics of the heritage 'mania' maintained that commercial and political interests were driving this new leisure culture. In whose name is 'our' heritage being preserved? A major national conference sponsored by the Arts Council in England, as part of its Cultural Diversity Action Plan, and entitled 'Whose Heritage?', argued recently that: 'museums and galleries need to provide more inclusive versions of history and culture through the full spectrum of their work - programming, collecting, training, and so on, in order to draw on the full strengths of society and to reflect it fully.'[29]

The issue of 'whose heritage?' haunts European societies where heritage is defined, 'protected' and marketed in the name of a common 'birthright' imposed upon all and from which it is impossible to opt out. We cannot choose not to have a heritage. And yet, as a survey commissioned by English Heritage in 2000 showed, 88 per cent of the English public today believe that there should be public funding to preserve their heritage, while only 2 per cent maintain that they have no interest in heritage.[30]

Others argue against the 'heritage-baiting' of critics such as Patrick Wright and Hewison, and the connections they seek to make between the heritage industry, national decline and Thatcherite politics. Raphael Samuel maintains that popular enthusiasm for heritage can be traced back to the 1950s and 1960s. Far from being regressive, this interest in the past is, he argues, progressive. The expansion of heritage to accommodate industrial museums and a host of other 'democratic' and 'domestic' pasts reflects a more inclusive vision of collective memories that had been suppressed by a rigid Establishment centred on the monarchy.[31] Critics who lamented the 'museumification' of society, Samuel claimed, were falling victim to the same reductive idea of the past, which they condemned. As Samuel observes: 'The denigration of "heritage", though voiced in the name of radical politics, is pedagogically quite conservative and echoes some of the right-wing jeremiads directed against "new history" in the schools.'[32]

THE LOSS OF HERITAGE AND THE HERITAGE OF LOSS

Heritage is about loss and is part of the 'disappearing world' phenomenon.[33] In order not to lose the real past (such as the Bayeux Tapestry or the Lascaux Caves) we must replace it with a replica or house it in the custody of a museum. In one of his most celebrated pronouncements, the French philologist Ernest Renan observed in 1882 that for a nation to become a nation the population has not only to remember many things, but also to forget many things.[34] According to Renan, a collective amnesia, as much as a collective memory, is central to the process of nation-building. In order to create a single identity, other, competing identities need to be forgotten. Heritage occupies an equivalent liminality between remembering and forgetting. Perhaps for this very reason it has been crucial to that process of political, cultural, and territorial inclusion and exclusion which we call nationalism.

It may seem perverse in the introduction to a volume on heritage to suggest that heritage – a concept linked in most people's minds with the preservation and celebration of the past – is equally linked to loss and disinheritance. Heritages, like folklores, 'are born disappearing.'[35] Most debates about heritage are framed by the threat of their imminent extinction. Whatever that heritage may be – a language, a landscape, a political culture – if we do not act now, something will be lost for ever. The prospect of loss haunts heritage.[36] Indeed, heritage might be thought of as the preservation of a potential loss. We value things only if they are threatened or have gone. In case we should forget, powerful institutions are there to remind us of our heritage and compel us to forget other histories.

THE ESSAYS

This volume brings together scholars from a broad range of disciplines including international relations, history, comparative literature, geography, art history and museum studies. While the book is characterized by a diversity of approaches, common threads run through each of the 15 chapters. The essays are concerned with historicizing heritage. Many of the contributors explore exemplary moments of heritage-building – from the fourth crusade in the thirteenth century to the twenty-first century – and elaborate on Maurice Halbwachs's critical observation that: 'Depending on its circumstance and point in time, society represents the past to itself in different ways: it modifies its conventions.'[37] All of the essays share Halbwachs's conviction that heritage, as a form of collective memory, is a social construct shaped by the political, social and economic concerns of the present.

The book is divided into four interrelated sections. In Part One, 'Heritage and the Politics of Difference,' the focus is on heritage within the context of a new 'politics of difference,' which emphasizes heterogeneity and multiplicity.[38] The contributors argue here that heritage involves more than the preservation of ancient monuments; it also pertains to the ethical and political structures we continue to inhabit in the twenty-first century – structures that are being increasingly challenged by the new multicultural fabric of European societies. A key concern in all three chapters is on enabling social action and empowering citizens through ethico-political interventions.

James Duncan examines the controversy surrounding the new permanent exhibition on the British Empire at the National Maritime Museum in Greenwich, London. Duncan argues that the exhibition raises important issues about 'the power-inflected nature' of heritage displays and sheds light on the ways in which a colonial past has been incorporated into a singular national heritage. At the same time, he suggests, the exhibition highlights the difficulties involved in representing difference. How is it possible to display Britain's colonial heritage, Duncan enquires, without falling victim to an essentializing discourse of 'otherness' that replicates the very ideology that is being critiqued? In striving to dissipate the notion of grand, imperial narratives, is the museum not reaffirming the impartiality of its own authority? As Annie Coombes has argued, the celebration of hybridity, evident in contemporary curatorial practices, may in fact be part and parcel of those very homogenizing processes from which it attempts to distance itself. As such, the museum is implicated in the disempowerment of the cultures it celebrates.[39]

Although the focus of the book is on Europe, several contributors argue that national European heritages cannot be thought of outside the context of colonization. The problem of representing subaltern histories in post-colonial Europe is the subject of AbdoolKarim Vakil's essay, which examines the complex interrelationship between heritage and national identity in Portugal. Vakil's interest is in tracking changing attitudes to the Islamic past. While the principal emphasis is on Salazarist Portugal, he takes a number of historical moments ranging from the late eighteenth century to the present, and includes discussions of travel accounts, novels and museums, in order to demonstrate how ideas of 'Portugueseness' have been articulated and contested in relation to an oppositional Islamic identity. Vakil argues persuasively that post-colonial Portugal's celebration of its multicultural past and the inclusivist claims of immigrant Muslim ex-colonial minorities to a shared national heritage need to be viewed within the context of 'the recuperative appropriation of colonialist ideologies of hybridity and the deconstructive post-colonial hybridization of heritage.'

As Vakil's essay reminds us, in post-imperial Europe there is a need to make room for other histories, experiences and traditions. This theme is taken up by Stephanos Stephanides, who concludes Part One with an investigation of heritage and multicultural citizenship in contemporary Europe. The focus, in this chapter, is on post-colonial writings from Britain, Spain and France. Stephanides quotes with approval Homi Bhabha's observation: 'Where once we could believe in the comforts and continuities of Tradition, today we must face the responsibilities of cultural Translation.' The hybrid ethnic and cultural composition of European societies, Stephanides argues, raises questions about the constituent elements and limits of national cultures and foregrounds heritage as a site of translation. He concludes by arguing that heritage, as translation, can be both a locus of difference and a place where difference is incorporated, often violently, into the dominant, 'translating' culture.

The European Union (EU) and its institutional networks have been crucial in propagating the idea of a common 'European cultural heritage.' Part Two, 'Heritage and European Identities,' considers heritage explicitly within the context of contemporary European politics. Peter Bugge opens the section by examining many of the contradictory meanings assigned to 'culture' and 'heritage.' He assesses how these terms have been harnessed to 'Europe' as a political project in the twentieth century, and he seeks to chart the different, shifting definitions of a 'European cultural heritage.' Bugge insists that the association of these terms is grounded upon political inclusions and exclusions that are legitimated and naturalized through the projection of a collective European history.

In 'European Identity and the Heritage of National Cultures,' Thomas Risse explores the relationship between a supranational European identity which is promoted by the institutions of the EU, and the specific national cultural and political heritages which this larger, umbrella identity subsumes. Arguing that most discussions have tended to centre on the ways people are obliged to renounce their local heritages in Europe, Risse maintains that this is a misunderstanding of the ways in which collective identities work. He adopts a so-called 'marble-cake' model to demonstrate how people hold multiple identities that are context-dependent. Risse concludes that it is possible to reconcile the political heritages of regional, national, and European identities. The chapter looks at how different nations in the EU – specifically Britain, Germany and France – have incorporated 'Europeanness' into an understanding of their own political heritages.

Nationalism is a cultural process rooted in symbolic practices and the next two chapters consider the importance of heritage within the context of cultural representations of the nation. The contributors show how representations of the past are used both to construct and dismantle identities. Simon Gaunt explores the 'invention' of a modern French identity and in particular examines the pivotal position of the twelfth-century *Chanson de Roland* as a French 'foundational fiction' that grounds French national identity in a heroic struggle. Gaunt's chapter demonstrates the centrality of the medieval past in late-nineteenth and early-twentieth-century constructions of 'Frenchness.' The chapter draws out the underlying connections between literary readings and contemporary political discourse to shed light on nationalism as the promotion of what, following Jacqueline Rose and Slavoj Žižek, he calls 'fantasmic identifications.' Heritage for Gaunt is bound up with the workings of fantasy, a process that enables us to make sense of the world and 'to take up a place in it.'

In the final chapter of Part Two, Thorkild Kjærgaard argues that the museum can become part of a community-building project 'if its aims are made transparent and it openly acknowledges the connections between aesthetics, politics and curatorial policy.' This is one of the few essays in the book that proposes the creation of a heritage site as part of an explicit identity politics. Kjærgaard demonstrates how identity has been negotiated in Schleswig-Holstein, a region divided between Denmark and Germany in 1920 following the Treaty of Versailles, and he examines how local or regional identity and heritage have been consistently suppressed by the ruling nations. In particular, his focus is on the issues surrounding a proposal for the establishment of an Industrial Museum of Schleswig as a conscious effort to promote regional identity. The chapter sheds light on the contested history and negotiation of regional identities and the importance of museums as institutions within contemporary Europe.

Part Three, 'Placing Heritage,' explores heritage's material grounding in geographical space. Each of the four chapters probes the linkages between heritage, politics and place. A key word here is 'landscape.' The contributors show how the meanings of heritage are determined in part by heritage's location in specific places, at the same time as landscape is constructed to naturalize and place particular ideologies. Denis Cosgrove opens the section by elucidating the epistemological relations between history, heritage and geography. He argues firstly that heritage needs to be differentiated from history, and secondly that central to the idea of heritage is its location. Venice, a designated World Heritage Site and 'a focal point in the evolution of Europe's heritage landscape,' serves as Cosgrove's case study. He explores tensions within the meanings of heritage 'between locational stasis and temporal process.' The essay shows how a Venetian heritage was constructed from the appropriated fragments of ancient places and was mobilized 'for social, political and cultural ends' and how, in the nineteenth century, and particularly with John Ruskin's writings, Venice became an exemplary heritage site.

Monumentality is a theme considered by a number of contributors. Karen Lang takes the debates surrounding the 1907 competition for a Bismarck monument, near Bingerbrück on the Rhine, as a case study that sheds light on the promotion and contestation of a German national identity. Lang explores the significance of monumentality in relation to national identity and argues that the controversy sparked off by the 1907 Bingerbrück competition has much to teach us about the internal differences within the ostensible unity of 'Bismarck's symbolic form.'

Joachim Wolschke-Bulmahn, who explores notions of a 'Teutonic' heritage within the context of the search for a unifying national German identity since the eighteenth century, develops Lang's ideas. Conceptions of race, nature and heritage, he contends, became intertwined and found expression in the production of specific 'Teutonic' landscapes, which naturalized Germany's history. Taking their inspiration from ancient Germanic tribes which were construed as living in harmony with nature, Wolschke-Bulmahn demonstrates how landscape architects, during the period of National Socialism, promoted organicist notions of a German identity tied to the German soil. The chapter focuses in detail on three heritage sites, including the Sachsenhain, or 'Grove of the Saxons,' which served as a gathering place for Heinrich Himmler's SS. Wolschke-Bulmahn concludes by arguing that the design of these sites helped transmit 'particular ideas about race, nature and German heritage to their users.'

Wolschke-Bulmahn's article explores the ways German landscape architects recovered and changed the past meanings of landscapes. This is a theme taken up by Stephen Bann, who considers the work of the contemporary French landscape designer Bernard Lassus and argues that specific features of the designed landscape can produce an intensified experience not dissociated from the historical context of the location. In particular, Bann suggests, Lassus's design for the 'Jardin des Retours' in the French town of Rochefort-sur-mer is an attempt to reconfigure the historical associations of Rochefort as an important naval base, occupying an important position in France's maritime heritage. Lassus's gardens embody political and philosophical messages and, as Bann concludes, 'it is part of his intention that the concealed history of a place should emerge at times when we least expect it – even in the unlikely surroundings of a motorway service area.'

How can we break free from a blinkered view of the past and accommodate difference? As Walter Benjamin, whose writings inform many of the chapters in this book, well understood, the crisis of memory precipitated by modernity required new tactics to awaken repressed memories and gain a critical perspective on the present.[40] In 'The Disinheritance of Heritage,' the primary focus is on heritage in relation to power, control and memory. The chapters explore ways in which heritage has been linked to social and political problems surrounding the emergence of the modern citizen, and consider how the idea of a consensual heritage has been manufactured in a manner that often obscures and represses dissenting memories.

In 'The Museum of What You Shall Have Been,' Donald Preziosi examines the history of the museum in relation to the production of knowledge. He shows how museums, like other institutions that emerged in the European Enlightenment, were involved in 'fabricating and factualizing' the world, and were crucial to the promotion of the individual as a subject to be studied, classified and ultimately controlled. Drawing on a number of case studies, the essay traces the implications of the historical devolution of museology for rethinking contemporary heritage industries. It asks us to consider how our changing understanding and experience of the museum is part of a wider debate about new modes of subjectivity and the evolving technologies for their production.

Heritage as a form of 'inheritance' necessarily involves disinheriting recalcitrant elements and imposing authoritarian readings on the past. Alexander Kiossev develops this idea in a chapter that considers the formation of a national literary heritage in totalitarian Bulgaria. A national canon, Kiossev argues, is defined as much by what it leaves out, as by what it incorporates. Beginning with late-nineteenth-century debates about the existence of a Bulgarian heritage, Kiossev demonstrates how the very notion of 'literature' was unstable and fiercely contested, mirroring the uncertain limits of a Bulgarian national identity. The chapter concludes by examining the exclusions and violent suppression of alternative histories that made such a canon possible.

Michael Landzelius expands upon these ideas in an exploration of Sweden's unspoken past. The focus is on the World War II military internment camps where 'anti-social' left-wing 'agitators' were incarcerated as a 'contaminating' presence. Landzelius begins with a critical interrogation of the repressive institutions whose authority was naturalized as the 'law.' The legacy of this denigrating ideology is evident today, he argues, in the collective amnesia that surrounds the issue of the camps. Landzelius concludes by proposing a practical programme for what he calls 'dis[re]membering' the past. This would involve the relocation of Sweden's peripheral or 'abject' histories into the centres of power. Thus, structures invoking traumatic past events such as the experience of the camps would be erected in key sites of power in order to interrogate the politics of heritage from a democratic position. Landzelius's essay is a passionate plea for what might be called a counter-politics of heritage, where silenced heritages of oppression that are buried within an officially sanctioned memory of the past are made to surface and trouble the complacency of our remembering. Landzelius draws on a range of theoretical writings, including Iris Young's ideas about an inclusive participatory framework, where institutional arrangements exist for including the oppressed, suppressed and marginalized. Heritage, he contends, needs to be reformulated within an inclusive, democratic politics.[41]

By way of an epilogue, my essay 'Mourning Heritage: Memory, Trauma and Restitution,' explores changing concepts of 'loss' that lie at the heart of heritage. Beginning with a discussion of war commemorations, I consider how memories of trauma are taking the place of discredited national heritages. My concern is with the increasing demands placed upon national governments to seek forgiveness for the wrongful acts that their nations have committed. I argue that this politics of reconciliation promotes an essentially nineteenth-century con-ceptualization of the nation as a distinct body possessing a reformable moral 'character.' Restitution, I suggest, has become a way of accommodating a diverse, post-colonial and postmodern nation.

Rethinking Heritage: Cultures and Politics in Europe explores the political significance of heritage in the modern world. The book examines how the past has been represented and displayed across media: from museum sites to monuments, political institutions, landscapes, works of literature and films. The contributors consider the assumptions that underpin representations of the past and suggest how heritage functions as a site of power for the production of 'knowledge.' At the same time, each chapter deals with aspects of a contested heritage and with competing understandings of the past. It is precisely such moments of struggle that throw into relief the constructed nature of heritage.[42] The book provides a much-needed interdisciplinary forum for rethinking the politics of heritage and public culture at the beginning of the twenty-first century.

PART I:

HERITAGE AND THE POLITICS OF DIFFERENCE

CHAPTER I

REPRESENTING EMPIRE AT THE NATIONAL MARITIME MUSEUM

JAMES DUNCAN

INTRODUCTION

'The conquest of the earth, which mostly means the taking it away from those who have a different complexion or slightly flatter noses than ourselves, is not a pretty thing when you look at it too much.' It was with this quote from Joseph Conrad[1] that the Wolfson Gallery of Trade and Empire in the National Maritime Museum in Greenwich, England, announced its opening on 11 May 1999. The gallery, opened by the Queen and the Duke of Edinburgh, a trustee of the museum, became embroiled in controversy as it sought to reshape social memory by asking uncomfortable questions about heritage. The new permanent exhibition has indeed proven itself to be an anti-imperial, anti-racist intervention capable of inciting some anger, anxiety and intense interest among the British public.

As an explicit critique of the racist basis of empire and colonial trade relations, it proclaims itself to be 'unflinching' in its intention to reinterpret British heritage critically. Although it may have become a commonplace among academics to view museums as highly politicized sites, most members of the museum-visiting public still expect displays to be celebratory of national identity. The majority of white Britons fail to see museums as politicized or contested sites, because traditionally museums have displayed cultural objects in an anodyne fashion masking the collection practices and underlying political–economic conditions that have allowed, indeed expected, one society to collect, display, interpret and radically recontextualize the cultural productions of another. Furthermore, the white British public has only recently begun to come to terms with the diverse ethnic origin of its fellow citizens, becoming only grudgingly aware that a significant and growing percentage (more than three million members) of the population has ancestors who were among the colonized rather than the colonizers. British heritage as constituted by the growing heritage industry is only gradually acknowledging itself as a contested, ambivalent, and hybrid site with origins spreading out across the globe.

The then British cultural secretary Chris Smith called for 'a more complete version of the truth' and pointed to 'the need to look through more than one pair of eyes.'[2] At a recent conference funded by such state bodies as the Arts Council, the Heritage Lottery Fund and the Museums and Galleries Commission, and attended by the cultural secretary, the prominent black intellectual Stuart Hall was invited to debunk the traditional dominant view that British culture has a homogeneous, essential timelessness. Hall called for 'a radical transformation of social memory' to better reflect 'the British presence and the explosion of cultural diversity and difference which is everywhere our lived daily reality.'[3] The National Maritime Museum, established in 1934, is located in the very heart of the old empire, in Greenwich, on Longitude 0, the prime meridian. Greenwich is the symbolic heart of British imperial naval power. Here one not only finds the Observatory,[4] but also Greenwich Hospital for the relief and support of seamen and their families, built by Sir Christopher Wren. In 1873 it became the Royal Naval College, where officers were trained in naval sciences. In 1998 the Royal Navy left Greenwich and the Old Royal Naval College became the centre-piece of the UNESCO designated Maritime Greenwich World Heritage Site. In the following year, the Gallery of Trade and Empire was opened, a critical endnote to the Royal Navy's presence in Greenwich. It is difficult to imagine a more powerfully symbolic site from which a critique of trade and empire could have been launched.

As James Clifford pointed out, now more than ten years ago, there is an unwritten history of cultural artefacts in museums; a history that interweaves European notions of taxonomic ordering and connoisseurship on the one hand, with that of the unequal power relations between nations and classes on the other.[5] Through their own initiative and in response to progressive critics of museum practices, museums increasingly produce exhibits and catalogues that self-critically highlight the power-inflected nature of collection and display. This has the effect of recontextualizing the history of the object in the museum, redefining such collections from a neutral repository of knowledge about exotic societies to an ambivalent and self-critical reflection on an exploitative and brutal imperial heritage. This imperial project includes among the violent practices perpetrated, the lesser but nonetheless significant epistemic violence of racist representation.

Changing museum practices are attempting to shift the perceived terms of Britain's involvement in imperialism and neo-imperialism. With the appearance of the Trade and Empire Exhibition as well as a new British Empire and Commonwealth Museum at Bristol and a gallery devoted to the prominent role of the British in the Atlantic slave trade at the Merseyside Museum, it will become increasingly difficult for a viewer to gaze upon artefacts and feel unquestioned pride that the British have preserved cultural artefacts for posterity. Now, the history of the British overseas – particularly its basis in a racism that allowed it to justify colonization – and within this broader project, imperial collection practices, have been sharply redefined away from their celebrated roles in advancing civilization and cultural salvage and preservation undermined. British imperial history is increasingly seen in negative terms in which exploitation and plunder are the central focus.

An important corollary of the imperial collection and display debate has been the controversy over of the repatriation of artefacts. So prominent in this debate has been the case of the Elgin Marbles removed from the Parthenon between 1803 and 1812 by Lord Elgin and donated to the British Museum in 1816, that the debate over the assembly of artefacts in imperial capitals has been termed 'Elginism.'[6] As Brian Graham et al. point out, the issue of repatriation of cultural objects to the countries where they were produced is a difficult one both theoretically and practically.[7] Why should national heritage be privileged over international heritage, and why should some cultural objects be returned and not others? For example, should all Vermeers be returned to Holland, all Picassos to Spain, or perhaps to France? And if not, why not?

THE MUSEUM, NATION AND EMPIRE

The first museums were established in Florence, Madrid, Paris and London in the fifteenth and sixteenth centuries. During these centuries of rapid European expansion around the world, a 'culture of curiosity' developed which attempted to reduce the macrocosm to the ordered microcosm of the collection.[8] Between the sixteenth and seventeenth centuries there was a shift in Europe from the encyclopedic collection to collections oriented towards celebrating the newly important nation-state.[9] In 1660 the Royal Society was founded in England, and within ten years a collection had been established whose bounds were set by the limits of the nation. In the eighteenth century, the idea of the national collection developed, with explicitly nationally bounded collections being founded in America, France, Poland, Sweden and Spain. As the idea of the nation became more clearly articulated in the nineteenth century, national museums as creators of distinctive national cultures and histories spread. At the same time Europe began to establish ethnological museums devoted to non-European societies; these helped to define European national senses of civilization and racial consciousness. By the late nineteenth century the national museum had become increasingly integrated into the state apparatus such as the school system and reached a much broader public. Beginning at this time, the museum was also spread to Europe's colonies, marking out the cultural contours of Europe's possessions. By the late twentieth century it was estimated that there were over 35,000 museums around the world.[10] Most museums at the turn of the twenty-first century continue to perform their customary role as legitimators of political units by putting on display narratives of national, regional and local culture and history that foster citizen pride. While there are often tensions within a state, as museums at these various spatial scales vie for the claim to rightfully represent citizens, all have the goal of reinforcing narratives of belonging. There are now, however, other museums and special exhibits in traditional museums that try to destabilize such narratives.

The Gallery of Trade and Empire at the National Maritime Museum has many of the hallmarks of what Sharon Macdonald,[11] following Peter Virgo,[12] identifies as the 'new museology.' It presents multiple perspectives and the voices of the spoken for. And does so in a way that is disruptive of established representational forms, which is to say it is self-reflective, ambivalent and ironic. The net effect of this is to shift the dominant narrative structure from pride to shame. Such a move is, of course, intensely political, for it seeks to reshape social memory and by so doing intervene in what continues to be a racist Britain.

THE GALLERY OF TRADE AND EMPIRE

Upon entering the gallery, the visitor is greeted by two large posters which announce the narrative structure of the exhibit. One has the words 'TRADE, POWER, GREED, EXCHANGE, KNOWLEDGE, COLONISE' printed in large letters across it. The other poster tells us that the British Empire was the largest and most powerful empire of its time and was rooted above all in maritime trade. It goes on to state:

> Many of the objects and pictures you will see in this gallery were originally created to celebrate the power and wealth that came from imperial trade and demonstrate the spread of British civilisation and its values. However, these objects can tell other stories. Although the British Empire was sometimes oppressive, its power was seldom absolute and there was always a two-way traffic in wealth, ideas, goods and people along imperial trade routes. The Gallery doesn't give a chronological history,

but explores some ways maritime trade and empire affected the culture and society of Britain and her colonies. In the process it raises questions about power, racial and national identity and the representation of different cultures.

Thus, it is made perfectly clear to the visitor that what is at stake here is the reconstruction of social memory. It announces its intention to disrupt narrative sequence, tell the old story differently, both by changing the tenor of the tale from celebration to regret, and by interpolating other people's stories into the narrative.

The gallery self-consciously disrupts at a variety of scales including that of the order of the exhibits. The gallery is broadly divided into four sections. Rather than proceeding chronologically from the earliest days of empire to the present, the exhibit tacks between periods. The first section is largely post-colonial with references back to the empire in the twentieth century. Its focus is on the impact of Africans and Asians on Britain. The second section focuses upon the tea trade with China and the slave trade with Africa in the eighteenth and nineteenth centuries. The third section again tacks between the present and the eighteenth century, and focuses upon New Zealand and post-slave trade West Africa. And the fourth section is a film on trade and empire.

At the centre of the first section is a large sculpture of a black man towing a boat entitled 'The Crossing.' The text tells us that this celebrates the arrival of West Indian migrants in the 1950s and 1960s and also the arrival of the art form of carnival. It evokes earlier crossings such as those of slaves and of black sailors on British ships from the seventeenth century onwards. To the left stands an exhibit entitled 'Imperial Travellers,' but rather than referring, as one might expect, to intrepid British explorers, the focus is upon the 'Black and Asian people who came to Britain in the 1950s and 60s and had a great impact on our culture and society.' Next to this is a quote from Edward Said celebrating hybridity: 'No one today is purely one thing. Labels like Indian or woman, or Muslim, or American are no more than starting points.' These themes are illustrated by a series of photographs of carnival in the Caribbean and Britain. Carnival, we are told, 'mock[s] white traditions,' was 'partly a response to racial oppression' and 'celebrates Black culture.'

The exhibit on the right side of the sculpture 'The Crossing' is devoted to representing the role played by Black and Asian seamen on Royal Navy and Merchant Navy ships from the eighteenth century onwards. The text speaks of the importance of these seamen and how many settled in England over the centuries and encountered racial discrimination. While most of these men remain anonymous, the African seaman and slave Olaudah Equiano, who bought his freedom, settled in England, wrote his biography and prospered, is mentioned. His words are to appear elsewhere in the gallery.

This first section of the gallery explicitly seeks to restructure social memory by displacing the emphasis away from the British abroad and towards a celebration of the empire come home to Britain and the role which people of colour played in trade and empire. White Britons are marked in this section: first as the audience, the 'you' to whom the texts on the exhibits refer, and second as a racist presence that enslaved people, inspired carnival as resistance, and denied the role played by people of colour under imperialism. The problematic nature of the underlying notion of an undifferentiated white public will be addressed shortly.

The second section on tea from China and the West African slave trade focuses upon a central exhibit entitled 'The Drawing Room.' Standing at an elegant table is a Jane Austen-like figure taking tea. Off to the side a black arm reaches up from the hold of a slave ship. The text to this striking juxtaposition tells the viewer that elegant eighteenth-century society was supported by slavery, and that as sweetened tea and coffee became increasingly popular, so more and more Africans were enslaved. It goes on to add that the global trade of which these commodities were such an important part came to 'create a self-consciously civilised society [that] eventually came to feel that slavery was incompatible with a civilised society.'

On one side of 'The Drawing Room' is an exhibit on the slave trade consisting of paintings of slaving ships and slave forts on the African coast, maps, slave company charters and logs of slave and anti-slaving ships, all interspersed with quotes from Olaudah Equiano. The exhibit on the other side concerns the East India Company trade with India and China. This shows paintings of opium fields in the interior and factories on the coast of India. Another set of paintings shows tea production in China and the opium wars of the mid-nineteenth century, during which, as the text says, the British 'forced opium into China to solve the balance of payment for tea.'

At the centre of the third section of the gallery is a member of the contemporary All-Black New Zealand rugby team doing the *haka*, a Maori ceremonial war dance that is traditionally performed before matches. The text says this represents a blending of European and Maori traditions, and that some have argued that the *haka* is a European appropriation of Maori tradition and that the team should stop doing it at games. Unfortunately, the text fails to go on to question the nature of traditions themselves and the extent to which all traditions are 'invented,'[13] since many are appropriations from other peoples. The implication of the museum's discussion of the *haka* is a defence of cultural purity in the face of syncretism. The display at one side is entitled 'Colonisation: The White Settlement of New Zealand.' It speaks of the British as the latest settlers of the islands and shows an early-nineteenth-century print of a Maori performing the *haka*.

On the other side of the third section is an exhibit devoted to the British push to control the palm oil trade in West Africa at the end of the nineteenth century. Palm oil was used as a lubricant in British industry and in the manufacture of soap and margarine. The backdrop of the exhibit is a large flag of Nana, the chief of the Isekiri, captured during the naval assault of his capital Ebrohimi in 1894. In front of the flag are a series of objects from this part of West Africa; a wooden statue of a British seaman carved in the Congo in 1882, a Fon stool, an Ijaw statue taken during Rear Admiral Frederick Bedford's expeditionary force against King Koko during the destruction of his capital Little Fishtown (in present-day Nigeria) in 1895, and a Norderfeldt two-pounder machine gun with explosive shells from 1880 used in the attacks against Chief Nana and King Koko. Interspersed with these objects are photographs and accompanying text. The text speaks of the British pushing inland to control the oil trade and the wars that resulted. There are photographs of Lt Walter Cowans and his ship the *Barossa* in the campaigns up the Brass and Benin Rivers, of King Koko of the Brass River, whose control over the oil trade the British usurped, and of King Koko's capital of Little Fishtown after it was raised by Lt Cowans's ship. This is followed by a photograph of King Nana, whose capital was similarly destroyed in 1894, and by a set of photographs of the kingdom of Benin, which resisted trade with the British but was finally provoked and attacked in 1897. One photograph shows the ruler of Benin awaiting execution, another of some of the kingdom's prized 'art' objects. The accompanying text tells viewers that *The Times* of 1898 reported that Lt Cowans sold at auction an execution sword found in the king's compound for £42 and an African mask with *juju* figures for £24.13. The exhibit ends with a photograph of the Ashanti Ewers seized from the royal compound during the campaign and given to the British Museum, and a poster that announces: 'Much art was looted from Africa. Controversy still surrounds ownership of these objects. They made a lasting impression on European painters like Picasso who tried to reproduce "new" forms of African art in their work.'

This exhibit circulates around one minor official, Lt Cowans. It is a story of British banality, the desire to corner the local market for a lubricant. But the result, as the juxtapositions in the exhibit remind us, are far from banal from the point of view of local kingdoms where kings were deposed, capitals destroyed and people machine-gunned. The loot from these expeditions made its way into museums and onto art markets in Europe. As such, the museum as an institution becomes part of this intersection of the banal and the catastrophic.

The final exhibit is a 12-minute film narrated by the Guyanese poet John Agard, who was appointed poet in residence by the BBC education department in 1997, as part of the Windrush season, celebrating the arrival of the first 'immigrants' from the Caribbean. The audience is not told who he is, but he looks and sounds like he might be Indian or possibly West Indian. The tone in which he speaks is ironic and the words are articulated slowly in what sounds like BBC World Service English. But he is explicitly talking back to a white British audience when he continually says 'you.' There is also a weariness to the voice, as if he were exasperated with people who simply fail to understand.

The film is composed of many short clips drawn from commercial films, home movies and documentaries that represent how contemporary British audiences saw the empire. The accompanying text says that cinema became popular as the empire reached its zenith. The clips juxtapose images of British soldiers fighting with Africans and Indians, marching on parade, having elaborate dinner parties and massacring civilians at Amritsar. Another clip is of the 1968 broad farce *Carry on up the Khyber*, set in British India in 1895, which makes the British look pompous, violent and silly. Yet another clip shows natives working, while the voiceover intones, 'it's hard work being a builder of empire.' Agard repeats a refrain over and over throughout the film. 'Why fiddle faddle over right and wrong? When the time has come to invade, let's just attack and call it trade.'

While the first section of the gallery celebrates people of colour and their economic and cultural impact on white British culture, both in the past and present, the other sections document the havoc caused by white British people abroad. The focus on tea, sugar and palm oil serves to illuminate what the late Hannah Arendt has termed the banality of evil.[14] For what these exhibits do is refashion the social memory of trade and empire as a story of banality and violence.

The exhibition is keen at times to blur the boundaries between British whites and people of colour (witness the use of Edward Said's statement about hybridity) in order to reinforce the notion of multicultural Britain past and present. For the most part, however, the exhibition maintains a strategic binary that starkly contrasts essential white violence and greed with the essential goodness of people of colour. It is hard to see how the gallery's political project could be accomplished without this contradiction. And yet the contradiction is troubling, for it fails to address questions of complicity, collaboration and anti-racist dissent among the colonizers. Put slightly differently, the black–white dualism which lies at the heart of the exhibit reproduces the sharp racialized boundaries which lie at the heart of the racist imperialism that the gallery is keen to critique. Such a dualism also posits an undifferentiated white general public, itself an essentialist projection. Increasingly, critics are questioning the very idea of a 'general public.'[15] And while the gallery posits an essential, undifferentiated whiteness as the dominant trope of its exhibits, it is, as I will argue later, very much aware that its visitor base is diverse.

Although seeking to reverse the valences of pride and shame in social memory, I would argue that this exhibition is principally about whiteness. It is about a heritage that is so self-confident of its power that it can be critical of its own past 'self.' This is perhaps made easier by the fact that British colonialism ended long enough ago in India and even parts of Africa that few viewers would have been active participants in what is being condemned.

The exhibits foreground the white British 'self.' For example, the story of the West African oil trade centres on Lt Cowans. The powerful juxtaposition of the woman drinking tea and the slave in the hold is seen from above, from the perspective of the affluent white woman, rather than from below, from the view of the slave. And the viewer watching the film of the 1919 Amritsar massacre stands where the British soldiers are firing rather than where the Indians are dying. From such a site the emotions called forth are those of sympathy rather than terror.

But not all white viewers have been willing to participate in this politics of self-blame. For example, the Gallery of Trade and Empire has been attacked in letters in newspapers and in telephone calls to the director. Critics say it will mislead thousands of tourists, as it systematically omits the good that trade and empire did for both Britain and the colonies. It is clear from the letters that this controversy is not simply about 'history' but about social memory or heritage as a component of identity. Many viewers took the exhibition as a personal affront. Those who argued against the exhibit, and they were in the majority among the letter writers, held the view that museums should not be political. This view, of course, naturalizes the politics of national celebration as non-political. One of the exhibit's opponents compared it to East German propaganda of the 1970s[16] and one to Stalin and Hitler's closely controlled state museums, which engaged in with what he saw as heavy-handed political propaganda.[17] The gallery is represented as totalitarian and (predominantly) leftist. Such attacks are part of a conservative argument that key intellectual institutions such as universities, elements of the media and museums have been captured by a left-wing intelligentsia which use these bases to spread their ideology and obscure the truth about the goodness of the nation. Other letters argue that the Gallery of Trade and Empire is controlled by people who 'insidiously…blazon their prejudices' and 'suppress the good and exalt the bad in our colourful past.'[18] As one irate viewer exclaimed, the gallery 'deprive[s] the British people of any aspect of their history in which they can take justifiable pride…[and] attempt[s] to deprive our children of their national identity.'[19] The links between social memory, national identity and contemporary politics are underlined by this same man. 'Like the mythology of Bloody Sunday…[the gallery] only provides Britain's enemies with another stick with which to beat us.' Another writer continues with this theme: 'One of the reasons why Britain doesn't know what to think about Europe is that there is an influential body at work in society disparaging all we were and most of what we did.'[20] Yet another writer dismisses the exhibit as 'politically correct' for apologizing for what is discreditable in the British Empire. This writer focuses his attention upon what he sees as Britain's others, both those foreigners from outside, and more important, those 'foreigners' within the body politic. This emphasis upon the discreditable, he says, 'is particularly deplorable on two counts.' First, 'the crowds flocking to Greenwich for the Millennium exhibitions will be given the impression that the British see their forebears as brutes and buffoons,' and second, 'contempt and hatred could be inspired in the children of this country's ethnic minorities, for whom this distortion seems to have been designed.'[21]

The director of the museum since 1986, Richard Ormond, responded to these criticisms by arguing that the gallery has an 80 per cent public approval rating. He argues in a reply to his critics in the *Daily Telegraph* and elsewhere that it is the job of the museum to 'take a view' on the question of 'What is National History?' He situates this interest within the context of 'the resurgence of ethnic nationalisms in the post-Cold War world…'[22] He contrasts his view with that of 'critics who would have us play Rule Britannia for the umpteenth time, so its adherents can pretend the past 50 years of maritime post-imperial history have not really happened.'[23] A trustee of the museum joins in this counter-attack, arguing that 'It would be hard to find thinking people who would justify the slave trade… But the curious attempt to purge the National Maritime Museum's symbolic linking of prosperity for a section of eighteenth-century society with the squalor and cruelty of this trade borders on historic denial.'[24] Maya Jaggi puts the point more strongly when she writes, 'Black Britons have a right to see their heritage justly represented.' Institutions like the Gallery of Trade and Empire, participate, she argues, in 'dismantling the lies that we were told, the better to rule swathes of the globe…'[25]

In the following year, the museum decided to respond to the furore by making two changes to the exhibit. The first was to introduce some new exhibits such as the Royal George figurehead, signifying the abolition of slavery in Britain, and to mention other positive aspects of empire. The second was to heighten the sense that the museum is a contact zone between cultures, by encouraging the debate over heritage. As David Spence, the exhibition projects director at the museum, said in a press release, 'in view of the amount of recent debate over the gallery in the media, we thought it would be a good idea to continue the debate directly with our visitors.'[26]

The museum staff appear to wish to manage the debate about heritage so that it stirs public interest but does not discredit the institution. They also appear to be willing to offend a conservative portion of their audience in the hope of attracting a more liberal, perhaps younger, perhaps less white audience. Part of the reason for this may have less to do with the politics of the curatorial staff than with the economics of running a contemporary museum. When Ormond became director, the museum was facing financial problems and sharply falling numbers of visitors. This was in part due to the admission charge that was imposed during the Margaret Thatcher years, and in part due to an ageing audience keen for traditional representations of empire. A new, more radical style of exhibit, it was thought, would attract a new, young audience to the museum and thus ensure the future of the institution.[27]

CONCLUSION

The Gallery of Trade and Empire at the National Maritime Museum constitutes a contested site of remembrance.[28] It self-consciously seeks to intervene in the politics of contemporary British national identities through reshaping collective memory. Museums are important sites of such work, for, as Vera Zolberg tells us, they 'reinforce conceptual categories as to who are to be the included, and who the excluded from the national body.'[29] But such considerations, as she goes on to remind us, often hinge on one's conception of the function of the nation.[30] Is it to assimilate its citizens through the production of a 'unitary construct based on some single "essence" related to Romantic ideas of European literati, or a more cosmopolitan and/or changing one?' The Gallery of Trade and Empire is attempting to move the British public from the former to the latter.

Although it has generated controversy, no one could have failed to receive its principal message. While its style could be considered a bit heavy-handed and simplistic in its dualistic approach, it is undoubtedly more successful as an anti-racist intervention than it would be if it had adopted a more nuanced approach. In contrast, a few years ago the Royal Ontario Museum in Toronto held an anti-racist exhibition in which racist images were presented with ironic commentaries; this attempt failed miserably because too few of the visitors understood the irony and consequently reacted against what they perceived as racism on the part of the exhibition designers.[31] While one can criticize the Maritime Museum for continuing to adopt a white perspective, it nevertheless opens up a space for a more inclusive, de-centred and hybrid heritage through its self-critical attitude. As such, it constitutes what Clifford, drawing on Mary Louise Pratt, has called a 'contact zone' where cultures meet.[32] Such progressive underminings of the precarious integrity of an attempted homogeneous national self open spaces for a more diverse British public to claim its heritage.

We are seeing the dismantling of the conservatives' fantasy image of an essential white British identity set against the 'invasion of the maladjusted immigrants' who represent for these British the embodiment of the imperial past they have yet to come to terms with. Schoolchildren and other British visitors to Greenwich during the year of millennium celebrations saw their heritage not as a closed, harmonious whole, but as full of flaws, incoherent and made up of others come home to redefine the self.

CHAPTER 2

THE CRUSADER HERITAGE: PORTUGAL AND ISLAM FROM COLONIAL TO POST-COLONIAL IDENTITIES

ABDOOLKARIM VAKIL

INTRODUCTION: MONUMENTAL HISTORY

It was no doubt with a sense of irony that José Saramago's publisher opted for Lisbon's Castle of St George as the venue for the launch of his novel *History of the Siege of Lisbon* in 1989. 'To mention castle,' comments the narrator of Saramago's earlier *Journey to Portugal* of 1981, 'is to think of summits and power imposed from above.'[1] How much more so in the case of the Castle of St George which a 1938 government edict, decreeing its restoration in preparation for the eighth-centenary commemorations of the Foundation of the Nation in 1940, labelled 'the very Acropolis of the Nation' and 'perhaps the oldest and most noble element of our patrimony of glory.'[2]

Medieval castles were doubly privileged foci of the Salazarist New State's (1933–74) historical imaginary. Geographical and chronological markers of the historical process of reconquest, castles represented concrete and symbolic markers in the nationalist narrative of a nation forged in war. They were 'living witnesses,' as the language of schoolbooks described them, of the struggle waged by the 'first Portuguese' against the Moors, 'foreign enemies of our fatherland' and 'of our Christian faith.'[3] As mirrors of the nation, castles symbolically rendered and reinforced the regime's historical discourse: static, hierarchical, authoritarian, moralistic and testamentary. History was a moral discourse, a pedagogy of apolitical civic patriotism. Monuments assumed an instrumental role in the education of future generations in 'the religion of Fatherland and

Art.' Correspondingly, 'true patriotic devotion' emerged as the guiding principle in the 'restoration and conservation of national monuments.'[4] The practical translation of this nationalist credo was an interventionist programme of restoration focused on a monument's 'symbolic meaning' rather than its 'documentary value;' on its 'historical value to the detriment of its historicity.'[5]

The Castle of Guimarães, also newly restored for 1940, is paradigmatic of these ideological articulations. Perhaps no image better renders this than that conjured by Salazar himself when, in the speech which officially launched the 1940 commemorations, he evoked 'the millions of Portuguese' communing in an act of patriotic devotion, exaltation and faith, their 'souls genuflecting before this Castle.'[6] Salazar's words were widely echoed in Portuguese propagandist literature. They can be heard, for example, in the didactic narrative of an Adult Literacy Campaign textbook, in which high-school student Zé Manel explains to the young apprentice António why he experienced such emotion as he sang the national anthem and heard the castle's history within its walls. It is only, there, within the monument itself, on the sacred ground of the 'nation's cradle,' that António can for the first time truly understand 'what Portugal means' and the 'extraordinary honour of being Portuguese.'[7]

In Saramago's *Journey to Portugal*, the irreverent 'traveller' stands on that same 'sacred' ground. As he contemplates the Castle of Guimarães, Saramago's protagonist reflects on his own emotional response to the hallowed historic site of countless reverential lessons, but finds it only mirrors his inability to distinguish the stones added in the fourteenth-century rebuilding works from the more recent additions of the 1940s restoration. Finally, repudiating the castle altogether, the traveller communes instead with the sky and rock-hewn ground where he feels the imprint of the anonymous 'common' people, whose history has been silenced by the monument. In effect, Saramago's traveller rejects Salazar's authoritarian nationalist ideology and its mantric recital by the likes of Zé Manel and António.[8]

Saramago himself was to enunciate a more explicitly political critique of identitarian and exclusivist nationalist ideologies in a discussion of Lisbon. Here, he refuses the 'Napoleonic vanities' and hollow rhetoric of the 'eight hundred year' incantations proclaimed from 'castle tops.' Instead, Saramago commemorates Lisbon's hybrid heritage and celebrates the unofficial histories that have played their part in shaping the capital.[9] But it is in the *History of the Siege of Lisbon*, in the voice of Saramago the novelist, that his critique is at its most subtle and engaging. Fifteen years after the revolution that overthrew the New State regime, and half a century after the apotheosis of Salazarist values in the 1940 commemorations, there is perhaps no better measure of the massive shift that has taken place in attitudes to the past, to history and to heritage than

Saramago's imaginative rewriting of the *History of the Siege*. It is to this work that I now turn.

SARAMAGO AND THE REINVENTION OF HERITAGE

The novel centres on a middle-aged proof-reader, Raimundo Silva, who, for reasons he himself does not fully understand, finds himself introducing a deliberate error into a history book he is correcting. In the course of a final routine reading of the text he inserts a crucial word into a sentence, which literally reverses an historical fact. The book in question is a dry, academic *History of the Siege of Lisbon*, which piously retells the familiar story of the recapture of Lisbon from the Moors in 1147. More particularly, Afonso Henriques, the first king of Portugal, requested help from the Northern European crusaders in undertaking the conquest of the prized city of Lisbon, then in the hands of the Muslims. After much deliberation, the crusaders accepted the king's invitation. The proof-reader's decisive intervention, involves the addition of the word 'No' into the key sentence of this episode, changing its meaning completely. Accordingly, the crusaders did not help the Portuguese to conquer Lisbon. As it happens, a new director of the publishing firm, Maria Sara, takes an interest in Raimundo Silva's mischievous and wilfully subversive act. She challenges the proof-reader to follow through the consequences of his intervention in a hypothetical, 'counter-factual' narrative of the siege. Saramago's novel narrates this other imagined 'History of the Siege of Lisbon,' interspersed with the narrative of the proof-reader's own liberation through writing and his developing relationship with Maria Sara.

The alternative history of the siege begins with a *muezzin* in Muslim Lisbon preparing for the call to prayer, and it ends with his death. In fact, despite the imaginative superimposition of Moorish Lisbon onto contemporary Lisbon, and the conflation of past and present throughout the narrative, it is only the voice of the *muezzin* that gives any concrete expression to the Muslim identity of Lisbon. Indeed, the first words articulated in the alternative history, 'Allahu Akbar,' are Arabic and come from the morning call to prayer, which is transcribed in full to the final 'La illaha illa llah.' Correspondingly, the triumph of the Portuguese – and in this alternative history it is the now specifically Portuguese act of national self-volition that Saramago playfully dramatizes – is achieved by the silencing of this other tongue. An allusion to Genesis in the narrative underlines the significance of this linguistic struggle at the heart of the book. The Portuguese are constructing a tower from which to assault the city. Unlike the Tower of Babel, we are told, 'this present one will rise no higher than the battlements on the walls, and as for tongues, Dom Afonso Henriques has no intention of repeating their multiplicity, but of uprooting this one, both in the figurative and allegorical sense as in the literal and bloodily physical sense.'[10] The last words uttered in the narrative are again 'Allahu Akbar,' but this time the call to prayer is left incomplete. At the sound of the call a Christian soldier rushes forth sword in hand and beheads the *muezzin*.[11]

This preoccupation with blurring history and fiction, the written and the oral, memory and power, recurs in Saramago's writing. As the very title, *The History of the Siege of Lisbon*, suggests, the subversion of conventional boundaries forms the very subject of this book. The significance of the victorious siege of Lisbon in Portuguese historical discourses of national identity cannot be over-estimated. Its symbolic import is perhaps best suggested by reference to the nineteenth-century historian Oliveira Martins, who described the conquest of Lisbon solemnly as 'the birth certificate of the Nation.'[12] Indeed, Saramago's narrative gains much of its force from developing a critical and ironic, but often playful, approach to such established narratives.

In Saramago's *The History of the Siege of Lisbon*, the narrator's interjections deride the artifices of nationalist genealogies and totemic symbols. They poke fun at invented traditions and call into question the very concept of a national genesis. Saramago's narrator problematizes a teleological and patrimonial nationalist history. Portugal's ancestral 'founding fathers' are retrospectively displaced and, by the same token, the descendants of the besieged Muslims are metaphorically identified in the novel with the marginalized, disenfranchised population of contemporary Lisbon. History is no longer a linear narration of grand people and great events, but is opened up to include other voices. This strategy of deconstructing a monumental and epic history of the nation recalls an earlier project of Saramago's. His original idea for *Journey to Portugal* was of a series of identically titled books that would each narrate a different journey and as many 'Portugals' as there are routes to travel through it. The indistinct and multiple layers of identically titled *Histories of the Siege of Lisbon* in this book, together with the adoption of a 'polyphonic narrator,' equally destabilize the identities of texts, genres and meaning in this novel.[13]

The proof-reader's symbolic inscription of a 'No' into the historian's *History of the Siege of Lisbon* signals his defiance and liberation. It also proclaims his rejection of the historical discourse which it symbolizes. On the one hand, he calls into question the historian's reliance on the eye-witness account of the event, the so-called 'English Crusader's Letter to Osbern,' and the fetishism of the document that would naively have us, in the quaint expression of one historian of the conquest of Lisbon, seeing through the eyes of the dead.[14] To do so, after all, is to see only from the perspective of the victor.

On the other hand, the dramatic and anachronistic reconstruction of 'period detail' is more suggestive of the recent past than it is of twelfth-century history. Indeed, it recalls in particular the choreography, spectacle and masquerade of the New State's historical recreations as part of the 1947 commemorations of the eighth centenary of the conquest. On that occasion, following an imposed blackout, the castle suddenly burst into light as a simulated battle recalled the capture of the city. At midnight an illuminated cross rose above the castle ramparts, while bells rang out from every church in the city, symbolizing the birth of a new, enlightened era and resurrection out of darkness. As the Portuguese medievalist José Mattoso has observed, the commemorative celebrations of 1947, identifying with the perspective of the conquerors, defined the historical significance of the conquest as 'the inclusion of the city into the domain of Christianity.' The moment of the conquest was made to represent an absolute beginning, the zero point of a new, national history whose reverse was the erasure of the 'barbaric' Islamic past.[15] Indeed, the high point of the 1947 commemorations was the grand historical parade, which staged an imperial fantasy of sixteenth-century Manueline Lisbon complete with elephants and native Guineans, who lent an orientalist tone to the occasion, bedecked as they were in exotic fancy dress. The parade was a ritual re-enactment of the 'civilizing mission' adapted to conform to the regime's own self-image and ideology. Christianity and civilization were conjoined and no less inextricable than Portugal and Catholicism or, for that matter, culture and colonialism.[16] It is precisely this fiction of a grand, totalizing vision of history that the calls of Saramago's *muezzin* threaten to dislodge.

In the course of a discussion of Islam's influence in Guinea, in what is undoubtedly the most comprehensive Portuguese colonial study of that territory, Avelino Teixeira da Mota includes a revealing episode. As he endeavoured to convince a Fula Guinean Muslim of 'the excellencies of the Christian culture of the Whites,' he had met with the distressing reply that '"the whites are always boasting of having a city like Lisbon but after all Lisbon was built by the Arabs."'[17] For Teixeira da Mota this reply was sufficient to reveal the dangerous truth that 'Islamism is a civilization, a culture, and a flag.' More importantly, Teixeira da Mota's admission exposes not only the aporia at the heart of the New State's identitarian reading of the past, but also the prejudices that underpinned the very politics of the 'heritage game' itself.

THE HERITAGE GAME

As elsewhere in Europe, a concern for the preservation and conservation of monuments gained momentum in Portugal during the second quarter of the nineteenth century. This preoccupation with the past arose out of the traumatic experiences of invasion, revolution and civil war, and followed the vicissitudes of the new regime. The expropriation of the monasteries and of the religious orders decreed in the process of juridical and social dismemberment of *ancien regime* structures by the Liberals lent this interest in the preservation of the past a new urgency. Moreover, the forging of a new political culture of popular sovereignty was predicated on a reconfigured national consciousness which hinged and depended, for its authority, on the ability to mobilize a patriotic discourse based on a shared history. Thus, was a national identity constructed as a retrospective legitimation of the nascent liberal state, even while the state was promoted as a reflection of a deep-rooted national culture.

In the making of this new cultural imaginary, the 'rediscovery' of the Middle Ages was central. Different concerns converged to privilege this period: the rediscovery of ancient liberties and medieval 'parliaments,' the Rankean historical focus on the political emergence of the nation and the state, the combination of didactic populism with its predilections for historical novels in the style of Walter Scott, the search for a genuinely national and 'popular' poetry in the collecting of Romanceiros or ballads, the influence of foreign travellers to the Peninsula, and of Romanticism and its cult of the exotic. The combined effect was an unprecedented appreciation of the splendours of Islamic civilization, leading one sympathetic and authoritative critic to speak of a decisive shift from 'arabophobia' to 'arabophilia' in Portuguese literary culture.[18]

In truth, however, as Almeida Garrett's 1826 verse fantasy on the conquest of the Algarve, the very text quoted by the critic in support of his claim, demon-strates, the Romantic generation was only incidentally interested in the Islamic past. It was not specifically the civilization of Islam, much less its religion, that interested the Portuguese Romantics. It was their search for a more national folk culture, with which to assert their autonomy and difference from the Northern European Romantic models, that led them to privilege the distinctly southern Islamic legacy of the Peninsula.[19] Later in the century, when the so-called 'Generation of 1870' racialized the debate over the origins of the nation, it was now the Mozarabs, the Islamically acculturated but Christian peoples of the Peninsula, not the Moors, that focused the dispute over the origins of the nation, the historical specificity of Peninsular medievalism as well as of the philosophy of history. The ambiguities of this distinction are exemplified by the career of Garcia Domingues. After a lifetime as an Arabist dedicated to the study of all aspects of Luso-Arab history, in what came to be his last published interview, Domingues unequivocally asserted the complete absence of Islamic impact on later Portuguese culture, jokingly styling himself an anti-Arab Arabist.[20]

TRIBAL CLAIMS

In the last quarter of the nineteenth century, the earlier Romantic discourse of Portuguese national and civic identity suffered a significant regionalist inflection. On the one hand, the newly emerging disciplines of archaeology and anthropology were recontextualizing the discussions of national particularities within the broader canvas of comparative and universal history. On the other hand, local archaeological discoveries and museological collections, driven by local pressures for political de-centralization and the cultural affirmation of provincial elites were forcing a begrudged recognition of ethnographic difference within the body of the nation. A case in point, is precisely the southern region of the Algarve, whose museum, victim of the tug-of-war between local and national interests, housed an Islamic collection which reflected the region's differential history and identity within the nation.[21] Scholarly and aesthetic orientalism, and the fashion for the Moorish style, hand in hand with the advance in ethnographic collections and oral literature, led to a minor boom in mostly Algarve-centred Islamic-themed writings from the 1890s into the early twentieth century. If Athaide de Oliveira's collections of oral literary traditions on the theme of enchanted Moorish maidens are a good example of this, the paradigmatic case is unquestionably that of António Maria de Oliveira Parreira's historical novel *The Luso-Arabs*, subtitled 'scenes of Muslim life in our country.'

Both authors reveal a deep awareness of Portugal's Islamic past, which they had experienced since childhood as a living presence, and which found expression in the ubiquitous Arabic place names, as well as in popular traditions, local histories and legends.[22] It is this sense of an imposing local presence that one finds half a century later in the work of Garcia Domingues, Portugal's most prolific twentieth-century historian of Luso-Arab history. Thus, an interest in the Moorish past was first and foremost stimulated by the direct experience of an Islamic legacy in Portugal: in place names, in popular traditions and superstitions and conspicuously present in the Portuguese language.

Both authors attempt to reclaim this past. Echoing Athaide de Oliveira, for example, Parreira laments what he calls the black ink-stain that has obliterated five centuries of the peninsula's history. And he denounces this obliteration as a deliberate erasure of the past. In contrast, the whole novel is suffused with a passionate evaluation and celebration of Luso-Arab civilization. A particular aspect of this civilization focused on by the author, is its prolific poetic output, and especially, that attributed to the eleventh-century poet, King Al-Mutamid Ibn Abbad, born in the city of Beja in the Alentejo. Although Parreira identifies with the Christian Mozarabs and not with the Muslim Arabs, the concluding section of the novel returns to and elaborates on the thesis of the Preface, focusing in particular on the figure of Al-Mutamid.

In his description of the poet's death, Parreira recounts an anecdote related in Reinhart Dozy's *History of the Muslims of Spain*. This tells of a Bedouin sheikh who showed hospitality to a traveller from Seville and was rewarded by his guest with a recitation of some poems by Al-Mutamid. The sheikh asks who the author is of this incomparable verse. Upon learning that he is a member of the Bani Lakhm tribe, which is none other than his own, the sheikh immediately exhorts all his kinsmen to celebrate and proudly claim the poetry as a reflection of their glory – theirs, that is, by right of kinship. At this point, Parreira likewise addresses the sons of the Alentejo and the Algarve, and urges them, 'as the Lakhm sheikh urged his tribesmen: "accept the poems of this your cousin."' Thus, like the Bani Lakhm, who, upon learning of the greatness of their kinsman, were quick to claim it as their own, so the Portuguese should 'unearth from under that black ink-stain that covers the history of our land the facts of five centuries' and proudly claim it as an indelible part of Portugal's cultural heritage.[23]

A century later, Adalberto Alves, who had already been responsible for the commemorations of Al-Mutamid organized by the Municipality of Beja in 1985, produced a Portuguese translation of his poetry published by that same local authority. Like Parreira, Alves also closes his introductory biographical sketch of the poet with an account of the Bani Lakhm episode narrated by Dozy.[24] In a more explicit discussion of the Latin root of patrimony as 'that which belongs to the family,' Alves defines the 'Arab-Islamic Heritage in Portugal' as an Arab-Islamic cultural legacy which had became integral to Portugueseness.[25]

Like Parreira, too, Alves urged his compatriots to embrace this 'family' legacy. Indeed, he himself has contributed much to the recovery and celebration of this long period of neglected and repressed history by documenting the legacies of the Arab-Islamic past in Portuguese literature, music and architecture. Moreover, he has complemented this critical activity with a zealous concern to denounce, analyze and correct distorted contemporary images of Islam in the Portuguese media, educational texts and in general culture.[26] In one respect, Alves's translations of the Arabic corpus – of what he calls the Luso-Arab poets – is a contribution to the fundamental redefinition of the Portuguese literary canon. The recovery of the 'forgotten heritage' is often seen as instrumental both to the resolution of what the critic Maria Rosa Menocal calls the 'insurmountable challenge to the narration of European culture and its history' posed by Al-Andalus, and hence also towards the contemporary acceptance of Arabic-Islamic culture as intrinsic rather than alien to the very fabric of European culture.[27]

In another respect, Alves's reclamation of the rightful legacy of an Al-Andalus long denied the Portuguese by 'political and religious intransigence' easily slips into an overcompensating stress on the 'mythic' side or what he himself aptly labels the 'foundational myth-reality' of a Gharb Al-Andalus.[28] Concerned to raise the exemplary status of Al-Andalus as an historical precedent and lesson in tolerance for a world facing anew the challenges of multiculturalism, Alves focuses rather on the mythopoetic value of Al-Andalus, reconceiving the very process of the Islamic invasion of the peninsula as a migratory movement. The Moors are transformed into welcome liberators and their military expansion recast as 'an occupation by the spirit.'[29] Combining a nostalgic discourse of the lost Al-Andalus with the anti-modernist traditionalist critique of Western materialism, Alves's Al-Andalus becomes a utopia, 'a symbol of wisdom, beauty and tolerance.' Where the early-twentieth-century poet-prophet Teixeira de Pascoaes had discovered in the untranslatable word *saudade* and its uniquely Portuguese sentiment the very essence of the distinctiveness of the Portuguese 'soul,' the basis of a regenerative and patriotic *Art of Being Portuguese*, Alves finds *saudade* specifically Portuguese ... and Arabic.[30]

PRODIGAL SONS

In contrast to both the Liberal and Republican civic discourse of national identity, under the Salazarist New State regional folkloric differences were cultivated within a brand of apolitical patriotic nationalism where power was vested exclusively in the centralizing state. The moral discourse of Catholicism lay at the core of this nationalist narrative and seamlessly wove the historical processes of nation formation, consolidation, expansion and empire, with the ideological legitimation of Salazarist regeneration and the apologia of the colonialist civilizing mission. Never was the inexorable logic of this narrative more monumentally and symbolically affirmed than in the triumphant year of the 1940 commemorations of the eighth centenary of the foundation of Portugal.

The celebrations that year of the miraculous interventions of Christ and the Holy Spirit in the triumphant defeat of the Moors at the battles of Ourique and Salado forcefully testify to the Salazarist identitarian construct of Portuguese Catholicism and the absolute otherness of Islam. Yet, like the famous Salazarist maxim 'Portuguese therefore Catholic,' this articulation of nationalist and Catholic rhetoric needs to be understood in its historical and political contexts.

In practice, flying in the face of established opinion, 1940 was perhaps more the exception than the norm. Despite the repeated concerns voiced with regard to the obstacle posed by Islam to the consolidation of Portuguese colonial culture in Mozambique and Guinea since the 1920s, the pragmatic logic of the on-the-ground military situation had Portuguese colonial administrators courting Muslim allies at the service of colonial expansion in Guinea till the mid-1930s.[31] The Catholic hard-line did indeed seem to have become entrenched with the militaristic triumphalism of the 'Historical Exposition of the [colonial] Occupation' in 1937. It even survived the immediate aftermath of the end of World War II sustained by the mobilization against the Afro-Asiatic Bandung front. The convergence of the pragmatic imperatives of a colonial war on three fronts, the winds of change of African decolonization and the no-less-sweeping winds of the Second Vatican Council's theological response to the Muslim faith, however, soon rendered it an embarrassing and repressed memory.

In his influential book *The Orient and the West* (1939), António da Silva Rêgo saw the situation of his day as an imminent clash between a world in which the old antinomy between the West and the East had been redefined in terms of two competing civilizations, locked in mortal combat: Christianity and Islam. Reproducing the classic gamut of clichés, Silva Rêgo defines Islam as an easy, sensual and worldly religion, bloody and militaristic. It was a creed that lacked any intellectual substance and, according to Silva Rêgo, warranted no serious analysis.[32] Throughout the 1940s and 1950s colonial administrators, commentators and analysts vied in issuing urgent warnings about the pending Muslim and Bolshevik threat to Portuguese authority in the colonies. Yet this perception of the colonial Muslim began to change. The strategic importance of the Muslim populations in the struggle against Marxist independence movements was recognized, especially as the wars in the colonies continued. And it is within this context that the attempt to reach out to the Muslim populations forced a redefinition of the old identitarian Salazarist discourse of 'Portugueseness.'

In line with practices pioneered by French and British colonial administrators since the turn of the century, Portugal began to stake out its claim as a protector of Islam. The official financing of the travel of Muslims from the colonies on their pilgrimage to Mecca, a devotional practice that Silva Rêgo had scorned in his book, was its most publicized expression. In Guinea, successive governors supported the construction of new mosques in the colony and addressed the community with official messages on festival occasions. The official commemoration of the birth of Vasco da Gama in Mozambique was marked with a series of conservationist initiatives. This included the well-publicized restoration of the early-twentieth-century Gulamo Mosque on Mozambique Island, and the creation of a small Museum of Islamic Art on the mainland 'because,' as one journalist put it, 'Christianity is not the only national religion within the confines of Portuguese space.'[33]

Bearing in mind the importance of the ideological discourse of the 'Discoveries' in the Salazarist national historical narrative Francisco José Velozo's address to the first congress of the Portuguese communities on the question of the Islamic population of Mozambique, makes particularly interesting reading. The crusade, he argued, had stopped in North Africa. Portugal's expansion along the east coast of Africa and across the Indian Ocean was to be seen in an altogether different light. 'The re-encounter with the Arabized natives and the Arabs,' Velozo maintains, 'to the Portuguese, whose homeland had experienced five centuries of intensive Arabic acculturation, was like a re-encounter with a part of themselves [...] Should anyone doubt this,' Velozo goes on to explain, 'it is because the history of our culture, so strongly influenced by Arabic and Qur'anic culture is still largely unwritten.' To this cultural legacy, therefore, he attributes what he refers to as the 'perfect understanding which has always existed between Muslims and Portuguese Christians.'[34]

But perhaps the most striking expression of the ideological volte-face of the Salazarist identitarian discourse comes in an article entitled 'Portuguese Muslims' published in the lavishly illustrated magazine of the Secretariat for National Propaganda, or Information, as it had by then been renamed. Here the author argues that: 'much as one must keep Catholicism in mind, the Nation neither is nor can be, identified with a religion which is not even that of all Portuguese people [...] How, in an era of ecumenicism,' the author asks rhetorically, 'could it have gone unnoticed that there are some two million Muslims in Portugal?' But perhaps the most radical contradiction of the core values of Salazarist ideology comes in the concluding assertion that 'at this moment, Portugal is one of the nations that with just cause claims that it is wrong to conflate the idea of Christianity and Western Civilization.'[35]

At the same time, capitalizing on this identitarian redefinition of Portugal as a multi-religious and multicultural nation, colonial Muslims in the metropolis obtained the regime's official recognition as an Islamic community. A series of articles by Suleiman Valy Mamede, the President of the Islamic community, were published between 1967 and 1969 in the official bulletin of the General Overseas Agency, the Colonial Office of the Ministry for Overseas Affairs, and further promoted this vision of a Portuguese Islam. Both the general tenor of these articles, that Portuguese Muslims should be considered neither as an ethnic nor cultural minority within Portugal, but merely as Portuguese who professed a different faith, and the author's celebration of the colonial authority's Portuguese translation of the Qur'an as proof of the reality of Portuguese ecumenism, all played directly into the hands of official propaganda.

Portuguese Muslim identities were thus forged in an ambiguous and far-from-innocent strategic collusion.

RETHINKING IDENTITIES, NEGOTIATING BELONGING

On the occasion of the 850th centenary of the conquest of Lisbon, José Mattoso declared that the re-evaluation of the Islamic contribution to the formation of the nation was one of the most urgent tasks facing Portuguese medievalists. In the case of Lisbon, Mattoso added, that meant gaining an understanding of the close ties which had bound the city to the Mediterranean world during the whole of the Medieval period. Mattoso's deliberation closely echoed the plenary speech by Jorge Sampaio, president of the Portuguese Republic, a few months earlier, at the start of the working sessions on 'Arab-Islamic Memories in Portugal.'[36] It was a highly symbolic event that took place in the very bastion of the nation's collective memory, the Torre do Tombo National Archives, on the exact day that 50 years previously the then president had raised the Portuguese flag in the Castle of St George in commemoration of its Christian conquest.

Sampaio gave official expression to two of the themes that have largely defined recent Portuguese discourse on the shifting politics of heritage and identity: firstly, the recognition of an Arab-Islamic legacy as being integral to Portuguese identity, and secondly, the notion that the rediscovery of this particular heritage is owed to an exercise in historical revisionism which is both a fundamental precondition and a symbolic testimony to Portugal's coming of age as a democracy.[37] In November 1998, shortly before President Sampaio gave tangible expression to those words by accepting honorary membership of the Islamic community of Lisbon at the official commemorations of the thirteenth anniversary of its foundation, the president of the Islamic community, recalling the silencing of Saramago's *muezzin* in *The History of the Siege of Lisbon*, celebrated the resumption of the Muslim call to prayer in Lisbon's mosque in affirmation of the Muslim sense of belonging.[38]

HERITAGE AND COMMUNITY

Two museological initiatives, at Loures and Mértola, are illustrative of the complex socio-economic factors that are influencing the reconfiguration of Portugal's heritage. In particular, Loures is a good example of a local community unrecognizably transformed by the social and economic modernization taking place on the outskirts of Lisbon under a left-wing municipal government, which has energetically embraced the new ethnic pluralism of its population and actively promotes multiculturalism as a positive and democratizing factor. Since the 1960s, the local population of Loures has multiplied some sevenfold and become increasingly heterogeneous as a result of internal migrations and, after 1974, of post-colonial immigrant settlement. Muslim communities have a strong presence and as a result of the municipality's policy of community subventions, have established a thriving mosque and some five prayer halls.

In the face of these transformations, the Municipal Museum, which has historically focused on the ethnographic collection and preservation of local 'folk' traditions, has actively sought to reflect the new ethnic diversity of the population. New curatorial trends have converged with progressive policies and led to the promotion of refreshingly innovative exhibitions, such as the 'Through the Streets and Places of Loures' exhibition organized by the museum in 1996.[39] At once a documentary- and artefact-based exhibition, there was also an emphasis on charting the community's changing identity through first-hand testimonials. Thus, the exhibition was explicitly conceived as a form of civic education and empowerment.

Yet, even while 'Through the Streets and Places of Loures' represents an unprecedented step in the integrative redefinition of a Portuguese heritage, perversely, its representation of modern Islam betrays a fundamentally essentialist approach. Seeking to give voice to the communities themselves, the exhibition catalogue includes a number of texts requested from the various 'cultural' associations in their respective 'dialects.' Thus, the Hindu community is represented with texts in Gujerati, Guinean and San Tomense Africans with their respective Creoles. The Islamic community, on the other hand, is represented by texts in Arabic. In reality, however, local Muslims are mostly Indians from Mozambique, for the greater part Gujerati-speaking, and Africans from Guinea. Their 'community' languages, in other words, are Portuguese, Creole and Gujerati; none have Arabic as a spoken language, nor indeed will their reading knowledge of Qur'anic Arabic serve them in the least in understanding texts written in modern Arabic. In short, the Loures case also points to the danger of multiculturalist policies unintentionally promoting traditionalist de-contextualized ideals of 'authenticity,' which are fundamentally misrepresentative of the everyday realities of acculturated ethnic communities. In Loures, the Arabicizing of Islam estranges the community from itself.

The case of Mértola could hardly be more different. Unlike Loures, the 1960s brought Mértola not expansion but collapse and depopulation. The effects of the area's poor agricultural land and the closure of the local copper mines were compounded by the lure of booming industrial urban economies, reducing the population of the region by close to two thirds. With such dire prospects it is not surprising that ethnic minorities are not to be found in the town or in its outlying hamlets, much less a strong Muslim presence. Yet, as we shall see, Mértola's municipal museological initiative has important consequences for the multicultural redefinition of a Portuguese heritage.

When Cláudio Torres, recently returned from political exile after the April Revolution of 1974, visited Mértola at the mayor's invitation in 1978, the town's archaeological project was born. Building on that local partnership, the successful bid for European Community (EC) funding enabled its expansion into a more radically transformative community project. In the best tradition of eco-museology, the archaeological excavation and related museological project became productively and functionally integrated into the life of the community as the core of a more ambitious plan for sustainable economic development.[40] Thus, while the excavation work offers the opportunity for training and the prospect for future employment in archaeology and conservation, the recovery of traditional techniques of artisanship in jewellery, pottery, weaving and gastronomy provide supporting activities to the tourist industry. The principle of integrating artefacts into their sites, with the corollary extension of conservation and restoration to the structures housing them, and the use of the entire urban layout as an exhibition complex, simultaneously renders the town itself, its historical centre and its lived structures, as themselves worthy of interest.[41] The impact of the archaeological project, however, extends well beyond Mértola in significant ways.

Indeed, the Mértola project has been at the centre of what is surely the most thorough and best-publicized reconceptualization of Portugal's Islamic past, which has led to a new historical synthesis. The sizeable collection and uniqueness of the artefacts excavated, and the reconstruction facilitated by the exceptionally well-preserved primitive structures of the medieval quarter of Islamic Mértola, have contributed to this re-evaluation. It was almost entirely on the basis of the Mértola collection that Torres and Santiago Macías curated the groundbreaking 'Islamic Portugal' exhibition at the National Archaeological Museum in Lisbon, the most important such exhibition ever held.[42] The same two authors' contributions, individually or jointly, to a number of diversely conceived exhibitions, events and texts reaching and engaging with different audiences and readerships from diplomats to schoolchildren, further consolidated their influence and reading of the past.[43]

One aspect of this reading, as with the authors' contributions to José Mattoso's monumental and best-selling *History of Portugal*, involves the incorporation of the history of the Gharb Al-Andalus as an important chapter in medieval Portuguese history. As the subsequent illustrated volume on *Islamic Heritage in Portugal* makes more explicit, their aim is to re-establish the Islamic past as a foundational element of Portuguese culture and heritage. Another aspect, however, involves a more radical reinterpretation of the meaning of this heritage. Their shift of focus away from the vicissitudes of power politics and administrative structures privileged by the narrative of triumphant 'Reconquest' onto the level of material culture, reveals a very different story. This is the story of Arabized, Mediterranean customs and practices manifest in the gastronomy, textiles, crafts, fishing, agricultural production and everyday life of southern Portugal which survive to this day.[44] But the correlative spatialization of this temporal continuity, which underpins the entire reconceptualization of the history of the Gharb Al-Andalus and extends to the contemporary population, is precisely its recontextualization in the world of the Mediterranean as an extension of North Africa. At the same time that it ratchets the Islamic past firmly into the national heritage of Portugal, it splits southern Portugal off from the unity of that national history. As Torres himself is quoted as having said in his presentation of the touring exhibition of 'Arab-Islamic Memories in Portugal' to a Brazilian public: 'Genetically the Portuguese population is predominantly Berber and has little to do with the European. It is on the other side of the Mediterranean sea that our past and our history lies.'[45]

But how does this relate practically to the question of Portuguese Muslims? Writing in the catalogue accompanying the National Archaeological Museum's 'Islamic Portugal' exhibition, Eva-Maria von Kemnitz concludes a review of Islamic museum collections in Portugal by referring to the fact that, given the new Muslim communities in the country, the recovery of an Arab-Islamic heritage in Portugal can no longer be regarded as of mere historical interest.[46] As von Kemnitz implies, the claims of Portuguese Muslims upon this heritage as both Portuguese and Islamic are at the core of the negotiation of symbolic capital, civic recognition and cultural belonging. For all that the genealogical claims to an ancestral Arab-Berber legacy by Mozambican-born Indians and Guinean Africans bespeaks of invented tradition, it is an invented tradition with a long established tradition of its own. [47] And one which, inscribed into the very relations between local Muslim communities and the global *Umma*, is at the core of the dynamic of Islamic identity itself.[48] If young Muslims in Portugal have themselves expressed the belief that the incorporation of the Islamic past and the valorization of the Arab-Islamic contribution to Portuguese and European history and culture in school textbooks is an important strategy in Portuguese society's more positive recognition of their status as a religious minority and as Portuguese citizens, community leaders and associations have precisely privileged this aspect in their public relations with the wider society.[49] Whether in terms of its receptivity to excursions organized by the cultural committee of the Muslim Youth Association, or in its enthusiastic participation in the cultural activities organized by the community, Mértola and its team have, in this way too, extended the local effects of its heritage project to a different narrative appropriation of communal empowerment.

THE MOOR WITHIN

Among the facilities offered to Portuguese Muslims making use of the 'Islamic Forum in Portugal' website, is an 'Islamic Web Post Office' service. Here, individualized messages can be sent on multimedia postcards accompanied by a sound clip from a choice of short Qur'anic recitations or the call to prayers. Among the card images on offer are a choice of 16 in the series 'Islamic Heritage of the Iberian Peninsula.'[50] Beside the more famous Andalusian monuments one would expect, the sender may equally choose from a range of photographs depicting the castles of Alcacer do Sal, Silves and Lisbon, the former mosques, now churches, of Mértola and Idanha a Velha, Arabic epigraphic inscriptions from Beja and Moura, or Coimbra's Arco de Almedina. What makes it of particular interest is the fact that, as a note of acknowledgement makes explicit, the photographs are for the most part taken from the iconography of Claudio Torres's and Santiago Macias's 'Gharb Al-Andalus' chapters in José Mattoso's *History of Portugal.* The Portuguese Muslim choosing, in a further twist on Saramago's tale, to append the sound clip of the *muezzin*'s call to prayer onto his or her Castle of St George multimedia greeting card, is simultaneously laying claim to his or her 'Islamic heritage' and negotiating his or her Portuguese Muslim identity.

CHAPTER 3

THE TRANSLATION OF HERITAGE: MULTICULTURALISM IN THE 'NEW' EUROPE

STEPHANOS STEPHANIDES

> The past is a foreign country - they do things differently there.
> *L. P. Hartley, The Go-Between (1953)*

TRANSLATION: BETRAYAL OR SITE OF HERITAGE?

There is a well-known Italian maxim, *traduttore traditore*, which is a play on words linking the practice of translation to notions of betrayal. More often than not, the pun has been interpreted as a comment on the difficulty of fidelity in translation and the related problem of equivalence. Translation, in other words, always involves traducing the original. Thus, critics concerned exclusively with issues of precision and fidelity have frequently evoked the idea of translation as an untrustworthy, albeit necessary, activity. With the cultural turn in translation studies over the last 30 years, however, the maxim can be read in a new light. Perhaps what is more telling about the Italian pun is the way it underscores a link between *traduzione* (traducement) and *tradizione* (tradition). Translation might be infidelity but as such it is also an agent for reshaping tradition. Read in this context, the maxim suggests that the site of translation is tradition or heritage itself.

The problem of translation has long preoccupied European scholars, especially since many European languages and cultures have originated as languages and cultures of translation. The modern consciousness of what it means to 'translate' dates from the Middle Ages. It is worth noting Gianfranco

Folena's observation that in Florentine humanism there was a semantic shift in which *traducere* prevailed over other contending terms such as *transladare* (indicating a leading across rather than moving across), or terms such as 'interpret' and 'transfer.' This shift has remained embedded in the word for translation in modern Romance languages: French *traduire*, Spanish *traducir*, and Portuguese *traduzir*. According to Folena, Leonardo Bruni introduced the use of the word *traducere* in 1400 with reference to a passage from Aulus Gellio, where there is mention of a 'vocabulum graecum traductum in lingua romana.'[1]

What is at stake in this shift is the emphasis on the agency of the translator in literary and cultural innovation. Folena quotes an anti-humanist response to Bruni by Domenico da Prato (c. 1420), who states that the old translators were content to be anonymous, and that they were not motivated by vanity. He disputes the authorship of the translator and declares that whereas the original authors are still alive, their dry *traduttori*, be they bilingual or trilingual, are always dead. This deliberation about translation, authorship, accessibility and authenticity anticipates many of the debates during the Reformation, when the dissolution of a unified religious community in Europe coincided with the spread of 'national' vernaculars and the rise of new printing technologies that facilitated their dissemination.[2]

It is no coincidence that the historical relations between translation and tradition and the authority of the translator have gained renewed impetus in translation and cultural theory during the last two decades. Post-colonialism and globalization, it could be argued, mark a period of momentous change for European heritage and culture not dissimilar to the period of European expansion that followed in the wake of humanism's rise and the Renaissance.

My aim in this chapter is to explore the relations between the practice of translation and the concepts of tradition or heritage within these broad socio-political transformations taking place in Europe. In an increasingly multicultural and polyglot Europe the issue of translation has come to the fore, and my interest is in the way in which 'minority' groups translate the dominant culture and are reciprocally incorporated into that culture through a process of translation. As Homi Bhabha has expressed it: 'Where once we could believe in the comforts and continuities of Tradition, today we must face the responsibilities of cultural Translation.'[3]

While the focus of this chapter is primarily on literary texts produced by 'immigrant' writers, the questions it raises extend well beyond the scope of literary criticism to suggest how identity formation is inseparable from questions of translatability. Thus, I endeavour to adumbrate a general theoretical approach to heritage, drawing on insights yielded from literary studies and anthropology, within which particular case studies might then be considered.

Before turning to look in more detail at a range of post-colonial literary texts, and in particular at Salman Rushdie's writings, my aim is to survey the theoretical ground of translation studies as this has developed over recent years. I begin with a particular emphasis on the writings of Walter Benjamin, who has much to say on the question of translation and whose work in this area hinges, crucially, on concepts related to heritage. Subsequent sections examine ideas of translation within the context of anthropology and ethnography – disciplines which, as we shall see, are founded upon notions of the other's 'translatability.' This process of ethnographic translation often involves the violent incorporation of difference, which is frequently figured as a cannibalistic ritual of ingestion. As we shall see in our discussion of twentieth-century Brazilian *anthropofagia*, however, 'cannibalism' can function as an important trope within post-colonial strategies. Be that as it may, the act of translation involves a familiarization and hence a domestication of the 'foreign.'[4] As James Clifford observes, ethnographic fieldwork 'obliges its practitioners to experience, at a bodily as well as an intellectual level, the vicissitudes of translation.'[5]

As Clifford suggests, there is a close relationship in ethnographic and historical writing between spatial and temporal dimensions. The past is viewed as a 'foreign country' in which, to borrow L. P. Hartley's famous phrase, 'they do things differently.'[6] In summary, then, my aim is to draw upon a range of critical writings in order to show how the theoretical and practical issues raised by translation provide a useful point of departure for exploring the reformulation of 'heritage' in a 'new,' multicultural Europe. As the past is renegotiated and institutionalized in new ways, questions about what past is being preserved and for whom begin to take on a greater significance. Indeed, as I have already indicated, it may well be that translation and heritage have conjoined histories; that in investigating one we are necessarily confronted with the problem of the other. As AbdoolKarim Vakil demonstrates in his discussion of José Saramago's *History of the Siege of Lisbon*, far from remaining a peripheral activity, translation emerges as a key concept for elucidating contemporary heritage debates in contemporary Europe.

TRANSLATION AND WALTER BENJAMIN'S 'AFTERLIFE'

The importance of the ideological and culturally competitive aspects of translation has been analyzed by the so-called 'polysystems' theory of translation introduced by Itamar Even-Zohar and Gideon Toury in the 1970s and 1980s. This explored how translation acts not only on the languages involved, but also on the various semiotic systems that contribute to the construction of cultures and how these relationships are affected by the power relations among unequal cultures. Translation was redefined not as a purely text-bound practice but as a wider socio-political process central to the constitution of culture.[7]

More recently, the work of the cultural critic Walter Benjamin has been rediscovered as an occasion to meditate on the relationship between story/ history and 'translatability,' both within the context of specific texts and of culture as a whole. Benjamin's discussion wrests the concept of translation from the classical paradigm of mimesis and moves towards a concept of kinship between 'self' (target language and culture) and 'other' (source language and culture). According to Benjamin's philosophy of history, the past lays 'claim' to the present, just as the present struggles to accommodate the past. Rendering a 'foreign' language into a 'native' language finds its equivalence in our 'translation' of the past – which is always inalienably unfamiliar – into the present. Thus, in his 'Theses on the Philosophy of History,' Benjamin remarks: 'Like every generation that preceded us, we have been endowed with a weak Messianic power, a power to which the past has a claim. That claim cannot be settled cheaply.'[8]

At the same time, Benjamin suggests that translation 'claims' the source text for present generations and becomes an allegory of the past's resurrection, not its decay. Likewise, for Jacques Derrida, who draws on Benjamin, translation is a moment of growth, inasmuch as the original requires supplementation 'because at the origin it was not there without fault, full, complete, total, identical to itself.'[9] Perhaps Derrida's most significant contribution to the present discussion of translation and tradition is in questioning the stability and unity of an 'origin.' As Simon Gaunt contends elsewhere in this volume, there is never an unsullied 'original' text, but rather, an endless chain of reinterpretations or former translations.

If heritage is most effectively approached as a semiotic system whose claims and meanings are set in motion by cultural and social processes, then it is not merely a way of preserving tradition, but of translating it. The role of memory and forgetting are important here. In 'The Storyteller,' an essay on the Russian writer Nikolai Leskov, Benjamin reflects on the meaning of 'storytelling' and, in particular, on the role of the 'storyteller.' He describes how a story is perpetuated as a memory in the minds of its listeners, who become storytellers in their turn, reshaping earlier versions according to what they have remembered or forgotten. The transmission, or translation, of a story becomes analogous with tradition, which is shaped and reshaped by its inheritors.

While heritage is backward-looking, in that it articulates a desire to preserve tradition, it also gestures toward the future and the community's desire to live on. Benjamin draws a distinction in 'The Storyteller' between what he calls the verifiable, functional 'information' contained within the story, and the poetic, cyclical 'art of storytelling' itself. This distinction helps us to think about heritage as an equivalent of storytelling. In heritage, we may distinguish between the factual 'information' that historical artefacts communicate from the past and the kinds of stories that we make them tell in the present. Benjamin elaborates this idea in more detail in his seminal essay 'The Task of the Translator,' in which he introduces the concept of the 'afterlife' and observes: 'a translation issues from the life of the original - not so much from its life as from its afterlife.'[10]

The impulse to salvage lies at the heart of the process of translation. This is not simply nostalgia for some lost original, but also an attempt to 'salvage a future from the ruins of the past.' As such, it is a gesture toward the 'afterlife.' Benjamin depicts this process in his graphic description of the 'angel of history,' which he evokes with reference to Paul Klee's painting 'Angelus Novus:'

> This is how one pictures the angel of history. His face is turned toward the past. Where we perceive a chain of events, he sees one single catastrophe which keeps piling wreckage upon wreckage and hurls it in front of his feet. The angel would like to stay, awaken the dead, and make whole what has been smashed. But a storm is blowing from Paradise; it has got caught in his wings with such violence that the angel can no longer close them. This storm irresistibly propels him into the future to which his back is turned, while the pile of debris before him grows skyward. This storm is what we call progress.[11]

The 'angel of history' shares a similar mode of being with the translator. Whereas the angel moves towards paradise, the translator attempts to capture the 'pure language' (*reine Sprache*) of an immaculate original. In this biblical vision, however, 'pure language' has been corrupted, and an original purity can never be retrieved.[12] In short, the translator is forever torn between a desire to look back at an original, 'to make whole what has been smashed,' and to acknowledge the exigencies of the present. Translation, as a practice, like heritage, is marked by this tension between an acceptance of loss and a desire for retrieval, between forgetfulness and memory.

In Benjamin's translation theory, translation is a provisional way of coming to terms with what he calls 'the foreignness of languages' in much the same way as heritage seeks to accommodate the unfamiliarity of the past in the present. This idea is articulated in Benjamin's metaphoric description of the language of translation as a garment, which envelopes 'its content like a royal robe with ample folds. For it specifies a more exalted language than its own and thus remains unsuited to its content, overpowering and alien.'[13] Here the language of translation is an imperfect fit of an original. The capacious robe self-consciously draws attention to the insuperable differences and foreignness of the 'other' language, with which it can never be identical. Significantly, Homi Bhabha singles out Benjamin's image in his discussion of hybridity and cultural difference. As Bhabha suggests, Benjamin's metaphor helps us to consider how acts of cultural translation are only possible if the language of translation recognizes its own ambivalence on the 'borderline' of different systems.[14]

ANTHROPOFAGIA: ETHNOGRAPHY, POSTMODERNISM AND CULTURAL TRANSLATABILITY

So far I have sought to highlight critical perspectives on the politics of difference involved in the process of translation. Benjamin's concepts of the 'afterlife' and of 'foreignness,' I have suggested, provide useful conceptual frameworks for elucidating the linkages between the reception of literary works and ideas of inheritance or heritage as they extend from the literary text to culture as a whole. In the remaining pages of this chapter I want to explore in more detail how translation relates to ethnographic practice, before returning to a focused discussion of literary works which deal explicitly with issues of translation, displacement, and heritage.

As Wolfgang Iser has observed in his discussion of tradition and translation, any resuscitation of the past takes place within a context of present needs. Accordingly, the past 'is not just an available entity waiting to be channeled into the present, but is variously invoked according to present exigencies. In other words, current necessities are projected onto the past in order to make it translatable in the present. This mutuality ultimately decides the nature of the past invoked.'

Moreover, it follows that just as 'memory crosses boundaries to a past,' so 'otherness crosses boundaries to an outside.'[15] Clearly, this idea of translation, conceptualized as a crossing of borders, is closely connected to the interpretative procedures of anthropology and of ethnography as a practice, which, like literary translation, is predicated upon the representation of a fundamental 'otherness.' Claude Levi-Strauss, for example, was concerned with the issue of translatability when he stated: 'When we consider some system of belief […] the question which we ask ourselves is indeed, "what does all this mean or signify?" and to answer it, we force ourselves to translate into our language rules originally stated in a different code.'[16]

Ideas of authorship and translation, as these relate to ethnographic fieldwork, have been explored by, among others, Clifford Geertz and James Clifford. Indeed, Clifford speaks of his writings as provisional paths rather than a final fixed and authoritative map, remarking that 'given the historical contingency of translations, there is no single location from which a full comparative account could be produced.'[17]

Just as translation has been used as a metaphor within ethnography, the figurative language literary translators use to describe their work is similar to that used by ethnographers to describe their relationship to the 'field,' providing insights into the nature of the cross-cultural relationship. Susan Bassnett, for example, explores the figurative language that translators use to describe their relationship to the source text. Her observations include references to garments, reflecting light, property and class relations, being faithful or unfaithful. While some translators 'capture' and 'penetrate' the source text, others attempt, like mothers and midwives, to nurture and give new life to the text.[18] Likewise, ethnographers frequently envisage cultures as bodies to explore, map, consume or penetrate.

In recent years, anthropologists and literary translators alike have been interrogating the basis of their own authority and asking: 'Who writes? Who speaks?' and 'What is an author?'[19] As Lawrence Venuti has suggested, there is now an imperative for translators to make their presence felt and 'demystify,' as he puts it, the illusion of invisibility. Venuti argues that the translator's invisibility can be seen as a 'concealment of the multiple hierarchies and exclusions,' in which translation, as a practice, is implicated.[20] In much the same way, post-colonial ethnography, in its anxiety to give a voice to the 'other' and shatter the illusion of its documentary objectivity, has sought to scrutinize its own reductive procedures and reveal the ideological contexts which have shaped its development.

As Clifford reminds us, however, the process of translation is not one-way.[21] On the contrary, translation should be seen as a reciprocal process. Clifford illustrates this reciprocity in a discussion of the complex relationship between surrealism and French ethnographic practice in Africa, which provided a perceptual leap that fed into the artistic avant-garde of Paris in the 1920s.[22] In turn, it is noteworthy that surrealism inspired the Cuban Alejo Carpentier in his aesthetics of magic realism (*lo real maravilloso*). In the celebrated manifesto that introduced the first edition of *The Kingdom of This World*, Carpentier criticizes European surrealism for its empty shock tactics. At the same time, in his attempt to de-centre European realist aesthetics, Carpentier demonstrates a clear affinity with the aims of surrealism.

This idea of mutual translation also underlies the appropriation of cannibalism (*anthropofagia*) in Brazilian *modernismo* in the 1920s and 1930s. Indeed, one of the most significant documents of the movement was the so-called 'Anthropophagic Manifesto,' published by Oswald de Andrade in the *Revista de Anthropofagia*. In this text, Andrade endeavours, as he puts it in the 'Manifesto,' to transform 'the taboo into a totem.'[23] On the one hand, the celebration of cannibalism and of the Tupi tribesman as the original Brazilian, represents an attempt to recover a heritage that has been suppressed by European colonizers as a 'taboo.' In effect, the 'Manifesto' is a celebration of the Brazilian native character as it is expressed in traditional Brazilian folklore and a radical appropriation of the cannibal as the primitive 'specimen' of European anthropology. As Richard Morse has observed, however, for Andrade 'cannibalism recognized both the nutritive property of European culture and a transformative process of appropriation.'[24]

Anthropofagia functioned as an important post-colonial strategy in the creation of a Brazilian national culture; it suggested how Brazil could simultaneously look to its own cannibal past and satisfy its 'primitive' appetite by ingesting the heritage of the colonizers. To that extent, at least, *anthropofagia* marked both a break with the past and an engagement with European modernist forms. In short, Brazilian cannibalism was a regenerative process, and not merely mimicry of a 'foreign' culture – a feeble Brazilian homegrown version of Parisian anthropophagy, expressed in Francis Picabia's *Cannibale Dada*.[25]

Andrade's ideas were to move into the mainstream, displacing ideas of 'purity' in a dynamic model of postmodern carnival and multicultural hybridization. As the Brazilian translator and critic Haroldo de Campos – undoubtedly the most important theorist of this postmodernist version of *anthropofagia* – has remarked: 'In Latin America as well as in Europe, writing will increasingly mean rewriting, digesting, masticating.'[26]

In de Campos's conception of the cannibalistic banquet, culture is a process of constant translation.[27] The cannibal-translator devours the source text in a ritual act that results in the incorporation of the 'other' and engenders the hybrid. De Campos's metaphor of a creative cannibalism extends to his own literary output, which has consciously and playfully 'fed' upon a European literary heritage. Thus, he entitles his translation of Goethe's *Faust*, *God and the Devil in Goethe's Faust*, echoing the title of the renowned Brazilian film by Glauber Rocha, *God and the Devil in the Land of the Sun*.[28] If the cannibal metaphor challenges both traditional hierarchies and the boundaries between source language and target language, it also has strong political implications, suggesting a resistance to any monocultural vision of the future.

THE MIGRANT AS TRANSLATOR IN MULTICULTURAL EUROPE

De Campos's vision of mutual ingestion as an emblem of what he called 'transculturation,' a practice that aims at 'thinking the national in its dialogical relationship with the universal,' has implications for our own analysis of literary heritage in multicultural Europe. According to de Campos, for example, the ingestion of foreign discourses leads to a 'playful and freely associative multiculturalism, an open, multilinguistic hybridization, a carnivalized trans-encyclopedia of the new barabarians…where everything can coexist with everything else.'[29] It is a vision not dissimilar to that articulated by Fredric Jameson when he writes in *Postmodernism, or, the Logic of Late Capitalism* of postmodernism as a force that 'ceaselessly reshuffles the fragments of pre-existent texts, the building blocks of older cultural and social production, in some new and heightened bricolage: metabooks which cannibalize other books, metatexts which collate bits of other texts.'[30]

This theoretical context provides a useful way of exploring concepts of a literary heritage in contemporary Europe, where the process of colonial emigration has been dramatically reversed and where it is no longer possible to consider 'heritage' as a static and monolithic institution. Over the course of the last half-century, the writing of immigrants from former colonies to the European continent has had an increasingly powerful impact on European literature and culture. This is especially, though not exclusively, the situation of literatures written in English and French where many of the most-lauded writers are of Asian, African and Caribbean origin.[31] In the binary of 'strong' and 'weak' cultures that polysystems theory proposes for translation, where is the migrant situated?

While migrants may be a minority in the host culture, they are often perceived by the country of origin as holding a privileged position in the global literary system. For example, the Moroccan immigrant Tahar Ben Jelloun is sometimes accused of catering to French audiences for writing in French; he contends, however (using translation metaphors of fidelity), that he is unfaithful to both his wife and mistress, Arabic and French. In *French Hospitality* he explores the French reception to foreigners by bringing together nostalgia for North African traditions of hospitality with philosophical concepts of hospitality borrowed from the works of Emmanuel Levinas and Derrida.[32]

If the insider–outsider division is problematic as 'self' and 'other' collude in the construction of culture, this is exacerbated in the case of the French Antilles, which are inside Europe politically but outside it geographically. The Antillean writer Edouard Glissant, probably directly influenced by Derrida, demonstrates how deferrals are not merely theoretical issues in the Caribbean, but part of Caribbean language and cultural practices. In *Caribbean Discourse* he points out that in Martinique he has observed more than a dozen Creole translations of a French bumper sticker 'ne roulez pas trop près,' revealing a cultural instinct to constantly defer and differ through translation. He comments that the car owners exhibit an 'inability to settle a common way of writing; subversion of the original meaning; opposition to an order originating elsewhere,'[33] if there is such a place. In the exploration of the inter-space between Creole and French there is no *retour*, only *detour*, and Creole identity is embedded in a '*poetique de relation*' (cross-cultural poetics) rather than in roots.

For the migrant, the boundaries between the home and the foreign have always been blurred. If in translation theory the 'self' is the target or home culture and the source is the 'other' or foreign culture, this easy binary becomes problematic with the migrant translator caught in-between. The writer Salman Rushdie, born in Bombay in 1947, explores many of these ideas in his writings, and particularly the fraught question of 'heritage' in a world characterized by violent displacements. In the title essay of his volume *Imaginary Homelands* (1991),[34] for example, Rushdie's point of departure is the opening sentence of L. P. Hartley's *The Go-Between*: 'The past is a foreign country - they do things differently there.' As he looks at a photograph of his family house in Bombay, taken in 1946, he suggests that Hartley's formulation might be inverted, since the present feels foreign and as he looks at the picture, the past is experienced as a reality. Rushdie elaborates this sensation in his description of an actual visit to the house after an absence of more than half his life and the mental effort involved in trying to piece together shards of memory, like the fragments of ancient pots out of which the past can sometimes, but always provisionally, be reconstructed. Rushdie's metaphor, here, is strikingly similar to Walter Benjamin's image of the amphora as a metaphor for translation, and it was precisely at this moment, he maintains, that his novel *Midnight's Children* (1981) was really born.

While conceding that the past is a country from which we have all migrated, Rushdie suggests that the experience of this uprooting or loss is intensified in the migrant who is distant in space as well as time, out-of-country and even out-of-language. From his inversion of the idea that the past is a foreign country to the idea that the past is home, Rushdie extends the notion of geographical migration to translation and thus reverses the usual paradigm of the English translation tradition where the target language is 'self' (or the domestic tradition) and the source is the 'other.' Though he begins with an inversion of the binary, what eventually becomes evident in Rushdie's writing is that though he may begin with notions of the home and the foreign, 'self' and 'other,' the binary collapses and the diasporic self becomes a hybrid encoded in modes of translation.

In his essay 'Errata,' Rushdie explains and justifies deliberate errors of fact in his personal redefinition of Indian history. His subject, he declares, is not some Proustian search for lost time, but rather his interest is in 'the way in which we remake the past to suit our present purposes, using memory as our tool.'[35] This is a theme to which Rushdie constantly returns. In an interview with Una Chaudhuri he has remarked: 'The texture of the narrative is such that it almost depends upon being an error about history; otherwise it wouldn't be an accurate piece of memory, because that's what narrative is, it's something remembered.'[36]

Although the migrant loses language and home he is not simply transformed by his act, but he also transforms his new world. It is out of this hybridization that newness can emerge.[37] Migrant writers, Rushdie claims in a memorable phrase, are 'translated men,' who (as the etymology of the word 'translated' suggests) have been 'borne across.' For Rushdie, the English language and the migrants' ambiguity towards it, reflect an internal struggle within each of us between the different cultures that make up our composite 'multicultural' heritage and give us our identities.

While calling himself a 'translated man,' Rushdie insists on his agency in the translation. He is not simply 'lost in translation.' In the novel *Shame* (1983), he names one of his characters Omar Khayyam, after the author of the *Rubaiyat* translated by Edward Fitzgerald in 1859 and states: 'I cling to the notion - and use, in evidence, the success of [Fitzgerald Khayyam] - that (in translation) something can also be gained.'[38]

Like Benjamin, Rushdie suggests that any translation is inevitably provisional, since it is an expression of the historian's subjective desires. And in this context, we may recall Benjamin's statement that 'to articulate the past historically does not mean to recognize it "the way it really was"…it means to seize hold of a memory as it flashes up at a moment of danger.'[39] In *Shame* Rushdie explores the historian's engagement with the past, specifically as this relates to the condition of the migrant subject: 'I too like all migrants am a fantasist, I build imaginary countries and try to impose them on the ones that exist. I, too face the problem of history, of what to retain, what to dump, how to hold on to what memory insists on relinquishing, how to deal with change.'[40]

There can surely be no more eloquent exposition of the problems faced by the 'migrant' who is caught on the borderline of different cultures and struggles to create an adaptive system to accommodate them. The migrant remembers the heritage of his lost homeland in an act of imaginative reconstruction, even while he struggles to accommodate the heritage of the 'host' country to which he has been displaced. As we have seen, for Rushdie the construction and reconstruction of heritage are always acts of translation. And because of his marginal position, the migrant is doubly suspect. He wears the foreign robe of translation – a *tradittore* that has overwhelmed a tradition. A voice in *Shame* tells the narrator:

> 'Outsider! Trespasser! You have no right to this subject! Poacher! Pirate! We reject your authority. We know you with your foreign language wrapped around you like a flag: speaking about us in your forked tongue, what can you tell us but lies? To which he replies with more questions: Is history to be considered the property of the

participants solely? In what courts are such claims staked, what commissions map out the territories?'[41]

The critic Sara Suleri has argued in her discussion of *The Satanic Verses* (1989) that the novel is a poetics of relocation for the deracinated subject and that cultural leave-taking and homecoming in the work are mutually inter-changeable. Though Rushdie has been accused of traducing Islam, his blasphemy is not literal. Rather, the novel strives to mediate between the questions 'what historical kind am I?' and 'what kind of idea is Islamic culture?'[42] As such, the book does not replicate a tired binary opposition between Europe and its 'other,' but attempts to bring differences together in a complex process of reciprocal translation. Indeed, the preoccupation with cultural diversity is a major concern in Rushdie's *The Moor's Last Sigh* (1995). In this work, the Moor's beliefs and cultural heritage – indeed, his linguistic identity – come into contact and open conflict with a host of other contending beliefs and heritages, reflected in the novel's different characters. The challenge, Rushdie suggests, lies in creating a cultural system flexible enough to accommodate multiple cultural values and heritages.

CONCLUSION

I have argued in this chapter for translation to be taken as a useful model for elucidating intercultural relations during a period characterized by profound economic, social and political upheavals. The focus has been on the ways in which 'traditional' conceptions of translation, construed as a one-way process wherein a 'foreign' source language is domesticated by the target language, has given way to a realization of translation as a dynamic and ongoing reciprocal process. With developments in critical and cultural theory in the last two decades, ethnography has also become increasingly aware that it is a cross-cultural practice. In a 'new,' multicultural Europe, I have sought to show how writers have been creatively translating between heritages to create new and stimulating works of literature.

I would like to conclude with a brief discussion of Wilson Harris's novel *Jonestown*, a work that explores the linkages between translation and the meta-morphoses of the subject after violent displacement. In *Jonestown*, the protagonist, Francisco, writes a dream-book after experiencing his own death in the Jonestown holocaust. Echoing Benjamin's notion of 'pure language,' the hero seeks release from his suffering in a disconcerting dream where 'unspoken prayer matches hidden texts.' But what are these elusive 'texts' or rather subtexts, which Francisco attempts to uncover? Harris intimates that they are emblems of the hero's fractured self, the sign of difference inscribed within language, the ungraspable and irreducible 'other.' 'Dream-books,' he writes, 'are translations of the untranslatable.'[43] Harris reminds us here that our condition is always in some sense 'split' since, as Montaigne observes in his essay on cannibals, 'there is as much difference between us and ourselves as between us and others.'[44] Translation always involves, to some extent at least, 'a crisis of alterity.'[45] Francisco's dream is one of 'self-knowledge.'[46]

In his dream-book, on his return from the future (his own death), Francisco has a vision of a goddess, whose oracular voice tells him that the act of translation is a 'necessity' and a 'debt,' 'if the past is to yield a kinship with futurity.' As she proclaims:

> I speak as Carnival oracle, Francisco. Not Delphic oracle! Carnival oracle [...] Oracles are steeped in hidden texts that may scarcely be translated. But still translations in your own tongue (let me say), orchestrated fabrics imbued with music - are necessary. Again such translations are the price you must pay, Francisco, to see the Dead alive after knowing them Dead.[47]

Here, Harris reclaims the carnivalesque meaning for the oracle as if to suggest that heritage involves the translation of many partial truths whose masks are spectres of emergent social faces. There is no single, all-encompassing, monolithic heritage. Instead, we return to a past that is always a different place with different ruins that reveal and conceal eclipsed communities piled up in the residues and legacies of former experiences. Spectres are fragmented into multiple actors whose articulation as emergent subjects is specific to historical and cultural conditions. In short, Francisco's dream-book provides an agency for the initiation of a new life after death, which is nothing less than the dream of translation. For Harris, heritage would be, to use his own term, an unfinished genesis of the imagination. His vision, like the one we have been proposing in this chapter, is that heritage is always already cross-cultural. And in the early twenty-first century, as questions of immigration and multiculturalism come to the fore, it is a particularly pertinent insight. Indeed, the movement of meaning that inheres in the performance of translation has intensified in the 'new,' polyvocal and multicultural Europe. Heritage, like culture, can no longer be abstracted from the vagaries of the present and invested with an uncontested authority. On the contrary, heritage is being redefined as a 'contact zone,'[48] a place where different pasts and experiences are negotiated, a site of mutual translation.

PART II:

HERITAGE AND EUROPEAN IDENTITIES

CHAPTER 4

A EUROPEAN CULTURAL HERITAGE? REFLECTIONS ON A CONCEPT AND A PROGRAMME

PETER BUGGE

Europe is in vogue today, as are the concepts of 'culture' and 'heritage.' Conflated into a 'European cultural heritage' this compound is a potent cocktail, with an indisputably positive ring to it. Policy-makers clearly consider that the idea merits a symbolic and a material investment, and both the EU and the Council of Europe have heritage programmes that grant money to protect and promote a grandly envisioned European culture.

But what does this European cultural heritage signify? On consideration the notion is fundamentally paradoxical. One can inherit a dining table or a house, but in what sense is it possible to inherit a 'culture?' Perhaps only in the sense that one is born and brought up within a culture. Moreover, people tend to be selective about what they regard as 'heritage:' some aspects from the past are preserved, while others are discarded. In other words, culture is historically contingent and one generation's understanding of culture is different from another's. Nor does the qualifying adjective 'European' help in elucidating the concept of 'heritage' with which it is yoked. Indeed, the primary focus of this chapter is precisely on the peculiar reification involved in this localization of culture that lies at the heart of heritage as an institution for producing and reproducing identity.

My aim in the pages that follow is to unpack the underlying assumptions behind the conjunction European cultural heritage, and to inquire how and why it figures so prominently on contemporary political agendas. However sceptical one may be about the idea of a European cultural heritage, the interest of institutions like the EU and the Council of Europe suggests that it serves a purpose, and hence deserves closer examination. Thus, while other chapters in this volume focus on particular case studies, my purpose here is to present a broad, comparative survey of heritage within the context of an historically grounded discourse of the 'European.' From this perspective the chapter can be seen as complementary to Thomas Risse's discussion of 'European identity' and national political cultures elsewhere in this volume.

WHAT IS A CULTURAL HERITAGE?

The Oxford English Dictionary (OED) defines heritage expansively as objects of value, traditions, and customs which have been passed down from previous generations. The meaning of heritage, the OED notes, extends to the environment and includes historic buildings, the countryside and generally things of architectural, historical or natural value which are protected and held on trust for the nation. Clearly, then, 'cultural heritage' may be defined in purely material terms. This materialistic approach has been adopted by UNESCO in its Convention Concerning the Protection of the World Cultural and Natural Heritage (1972).[1] The term heritage is similarly employed by the EU Raphael Programme, instigated in 1997 to support European cultural heritage:

> 'Cultural heritage' shall mean movable and immovable heritage (museums and collections, libraries and archives including photographic, cinematographic and sound archives), archaeological and underwater heritage, architectural heritage, assemblages and sites and cultural landscapes (assemblages of cultural and natural objects).[2]

The idea that such objects have a value beyond their utility and constitute a 'heritage' is in itself relatively new. Nevertheless, a selection process must take place, which involves value judgments. As the EU acknowledges, the framework within which such judgments are made changes over time. The Raphael Programme states, for example, that: 'Community action should take into account the changing nature of the definition of heritage and include all types of heritage by encouraging multidisciplinary approaches.'[3]

Until recently, the vast majority of sites designated for protection were churches, castles, statues and the like. Today industrial architecture is also deemed worthy of preservation. Who knows, perhaps at some point in the future inner city slums may even be preserved as monuments expressive of their culture? Or is it only the 'good' and the aesthetically pleasing that need safeguarding as part of our cultural heritage: the Acropolis, say, but not Auschwitz? Should heritage tell the whole, unabridged version of the story? Or should it simply provide an ideal vision to inspire us: a picture-postcard from a glorious past?

Defining cultural heritage in more abstract terms, as a tradition of high culture, makes matters no easier. If a cultural canon is defined along either national, European or Western lines, it leaves itself open to challenge, not just on the grounds of its inclusions and exclusions, but also because of its inevitably partisan, elitist and prescriptive interpretation of culture. The idea of a 'high' culture reflects an exclusive, centralized viewpoint, which is closely bound up with political power. Simply put, the more powerful a nation is, the more seriously its culture is taken.[4] Thus defined, culture becomes a highbrow distillation, infinitely remote from the cultural worlds inhabited by most people. The marginal perspectives of 'low' or popularly emergent culture, youth culture, or women's culture, it could be argued, all threaten this idea of a top-heavy, unitary cultural heritage.

As John Slater observes, social, technological, and economic pressures in the second half of the twentieth century have been crucial in shaping a new kind of commercialized and politicized cultural heritage:

> 'Heritage' is 'culture' institutionalised into 'foundations', 'trusts', 'museums', 'coffee-table books'. It is something we own; it is our heritage. It is often a ragbag of a hygienic and comfortable past…tidily contained within theme parks and carefully mapped heritage walks. Sometimes heritage, confirmed by a manipulated and invented tradition, can have a public and official face in anniversaries, parades and ceremonies. It can have authoritarian overtones…[5]

In Britain, as elsewhere, a veritable heritage industry has sprung up, which presents an idealized version of the past and which serves, in part, 'to mark boundaries and (re)establish community solidarity vis-à-vis growing numbers of outsiders, as well as to earn money.' As Jeremy Boissevain rightly surmises: 'Authentic history, if displayed, would divide, not unite communities.'[6]

As we have seen, the dictionary definition of heritage refers to 'customs,' a concept central to any anthropological definition of culture. From this viewpoint, cultural heritage is a set of values and norms governing a given community: a certain notion of humankind, conventions for regulating public and private behaviour, a certain work ethic and a shared cosmology. In short, as Raymond Williams remarks, this is culture as a 'whole way of life.'

Yet even if we are able to identify aspects of culture that have a long history, for example religion, it would be misleading to construe culture as being in any way fixed. Christianity, it goes without saying, has changed over time. Furthermore, should the appellation 'heritage' be confined to phenomena inscribed with a positive set of associations? Is absolutism less a part of the heritage of political culture in Denmark and France than, say, popular sovereignty? Are despotism and colonialism less a part of the European heritage than democracy or human rights? No matter how it is defined, cultural heritage will always be an ideologically and politically contested arena, a discourse privileging certain expressions and suppressing others.

WHAT DOES 'EUROPEAN' MEAN?

We may choose to define 'European' in geographical terms. Europe's eastern border poses a problem, here, since it bisects Russia and Turkey. The EU sensibly abstains from defining Europe in unequivocal terms, stating simply that the Raphael Programme is also open to 'participation' by the countries of Central and Eastern Europe, Cyprus and Malta and to 'cooperation' with other third countries. For the Council of Europe, the aggregate of member states defines 'Europe.'

Defined in geographical terms, the churches on Moscow's Red Square, the old mosques in the Balkans and the Moorish architecture of Andalusia are all European. But what about the Ancient Greek archaeological sites in Asia Minor? Should they be considered Asiatic or as part of a Turkish or Asian cultural heritage? The traditional answer has been to claim them spiritually for Europe, in spite of their physical 'displacement,' since Ancient Greece has historically been envisioned as the cradle of European culture. Conversely, and with the same degree of arbitrariness, Islamic architecture in southern Spain is held to be European, even though Islam tends to be excluded from the notion of a 'European cultural heritage.'

These cursory examples suffice to demonstrate that the term 'European' is used to signify far more than geography. Rather, 'Europe' embodies a set of values which has evolved over the last two centuries into a grand meta-narrative: a story that traces the long march of a uniquely European or Western civilization from its genesis. According to this mythic schema, after an Oriental prehistory, European civilization began in earnest in Ancient Greece and Rome, finding new vigour in Christianity. After the Middle Ages, it blossomed in the Renaissance and developed through the Enlightenment to reach a crescendo in our modern era.[7]

Examples of this epic trajectory are ubiquitous. Numerous 'world histories' have been structured around it. In recent years eminent academic historians, such as Jacques le Goff, and Norman Davies in his monumental *Europe: A History*, have stressed the crucial importance of Ancient Greece for European civilization. Davies asserts, sweepingly, that 'European history knows no such burst of vital energy until the era of the Renaissance. For Greece, apparently, did not develop slowly and methodically. It blazed.'[8] The Danish philosopher

Johannes Sløk is another who subscribes to this interpretation in his book *The Soul of Europe*.[9] Sløk maintains that Europe, as a cultural and spiritual community, arose when Greek and Roman antiquity came into contact with Christianity. Europe's 'soul,' Sløk contends, is characterized by its dynamic restlessness, a unique scientific rationality and philosophy, as well as a particular view of man centred around the conceptual triad of equality, liberty and the individual. Sløk follows the conventional mythic schema but concludes not with a eulogy, but with an elegy. Contemporary Europe is on a slippery slope of decline and the process needs to be urgently reversed before Europe disappears altogether.

A number of assumptions in Sløk's argument deserve closer attention. Is there, for example, such a clear continuity of values and worldviews linking antiquity to the present day? Did the Ancient Greeks and the Church Fathers consider themselves to be in any way European? And on what grounds can Sløk claim that the 'soul' of Europe is unique and that its constituent elements cannot be found in any other culture?[10]

The idea that Ancient Greece is the cradle of European civilization remains prevalent. Until recently, the authority of Classical culture was perpetuated by its mandatory inclusion in school and university curricula in most European countries. Moreover, the creation of the modern Greek state, which was carved out of the Ottoman Empire in the 1830s largely through the intervention of the so-called 'Great Powers,' serves as a good example of the political importance attached to this Ancient Greek heritage. The foundation of the Greek kingdom, and its integration into Europe, was predicated upon an essential continuity linking the contemporary Greeks to their Classical forebears. Any questioning of this continuity provoked strong opposition from the Greeks even though there is much evidence to suggest that the idea of a seamless continuity is flawed.[11] David Gress insists, for one, that only by questioning these erroneous assumptions can the idea of Western civilization be defended.[12] It is a view shared by the Danish historian Søren Mørch in the first volume of his book *The European House*.[13]

The theory of continuity has often been emphatically rejected, for example, by Oswald Spengler and Arnold Toynbee. In recent years, Martin Bernal has argued that our preconceptions about Ancient Greece as the foundation of Western culture require thorough revision. In his polemical book *Black Athena: The Afroasiatic Roots of Classical Civilization*, published in two volumes between 1987 and 1991, Bernal sets out to demonstrate how indebted Greek civilization was to Semitic and, in particular, Egyptian civilizations, which he controversially characterizes as 'black.' Bernal argues that racist prejudice in the nineteenth century led to the systematic suppression of this fact, and to the construction of an 'Aryan' or 'European' Greek prototype, unsullied by the deleterious influences of a barbaric 'Orient.' Despite the glaring omissions and inaccuracies in Bernal's argument, *Black Athena* nevertheless serves a useful purpose in underscoring the extent to which Europe's avowed heritage has, in fact, been engineered on political grounds over the course of the last two hundred years.[14]

Today, many historians date the making of Europe, to use the title of Robert Bartlett's book on the expansion of Latin Christendom, to the tenth century, where a socio-political and cultural order based on religious unity and political fragmentation appears after the collapse of the Western Roman Empire and of Charlemagne's attempts at its restoration.[15] If one maintains that there were three distinct 'cultural spheres' or 'civilizations' present at that time in geographical Europe – the Byzantine, the Moorish and what I call the 'Latin Catholic' – the latter was probably the one that least expressed continuity with Ancient Greek culture. Knowledge of Greek was minimal, and Greek philosophy and science were to a large extent introduced to Catholic Europe through Moorish Andalusia in the twelfth century. It is significant in this context that the European Parliament (EP) has shown an interest in Moorish culture, and especially in the twelfth-century philosopher, judge and physician Averroës, or ibn-Rushd. In 1998 the EP passed a resolution on Islam and European Averroës Day, stressing that 'European society has multi-cultural, multi-ethnic and multi-religious roots which are vital features of its heritage and its multifaceted identity.' The EP went on to suggest the promulgation of an Averroës Day, which would aim to celebrate intercultural dialogue with 'Islamic countries and non-governmental, democratic representatives of Islamic culture,' who, as immigrants to Europe 'are also increasingly demanding full recognition of their Europeanness and, at the same time, of their national origins and their multi-cultural identity.' In his accompanying report arguing in favour of the motion, Abdelkader Mohamed Ali writes of Averroës that: 'Of all Spaniards, he is the one which has left the deepest imprint on human thought.'[16]

EUROPE AS THE HOME OF CIVILIZATION

But the question remains: when did people begin to call themselves Europeans? And what did they understand by the term?[17] Studies of 'European' as an emergent concept demonstrate that although the names of the continents are of Greek origin there is nothing to indicate that the Greeks of antiquity considered Europe to represent a specific culture. Nor is there evidence that they identified themselves with the concept, something that would, in fact, have made little sense for a people living on both sides of the Aegean.[18]

It was only in the fifteenth century that people began to call themselves Europeans and ascribe special qualities to the continent of Europe. This took place within the cultural sphere of Latin Catholicism. It is only there – and not in Byzantium or in Russia, which proclaimed itself the Third Rome after the fall of Constantinople in 1453 – that 'Europe' or 'European' was used by a population to describe itself.[19] Hitherto Europe had been most commonly referred to as Christendom. The Reformation and the dissolution of the Catholic Church as a unitary force coincided with the discovery of the Americas and a greater awareness of different cultures overseas. As a result, the concept of Europe emerged as a replacement term for the community that could no longer adequately be defined in terms of its religious unity as 'Christendom.'[20]

During the Enlightenment, these experiences were condensed into the concept of 'civilization' – a word that seems to have been coined by Mirabeau the Elder in 1756. The new concept carried a variety of meanings. In Mirabeau's usage, civilization appeared as a universal quality or process by which man moved towards a virtuous, morally just society. Civilization was a potential within man, and by liberating himself from the corrupting influences of the past a person could become 'civilized' and hence create civilization. More commonly, however, the term was employed to describe social phenomena found in Europe as opposed to phenomena found elsewhere. This comparative vantage point involved the appreciation of multiple, contending civilizations in contrast to the idea of a singular, universal civilization.

Civilization, then, was both a state and a process linked to a model of development. The Scottish philosopher Adam Ferguson, co-founder of the Royal Society of Edinburgh, articulated this in his work *An Essay on the History of Civil Society*, dating from 1767, where he portrayed the progression of 'rude' nations towards civil society and civilization. The driving forces of this process were arts (knowledge and skills) and virtue. Ferguson privileged Europe as possessing both, describing America (with its 'wild' peoples) as virtue without arts, and Asia (which incarnated despotism) as arts without virtue. Nonetheless, as a rational being, man was capable of self-criticism.[21] Ultimately, this anthropological notion of self-analysis and a conviction in the potential for progress underlay the revolutions in both America and France and contributed to the formation of those fundamental principles of human rights and democracy, which were turned into universal norms with the UN Declaration after World War II.

It was during the Enlightenment that ideas of 'cultural heritage' were formulated with any precision. This took place alongside the creation of institutions for its protection, such as the British Museum, established in 1753. The 'nationalization' of history and cultural heritage proceeded at a pace with the emergence of modern nationalism and with the advent of the French

Revolution and the Napoleonic Wars. The nineteenth century was the heyday of the national museum. Yet, as the classical façade of the new British Museum buildings designed by Sir Robert Smirke between 1823 and 1847 reminds us, this preoccupation with 'national' culture did not preclude a broader engagement with a European past, and specifically with Ancient Greece. On the contrary, the one drew upon the other.

The nineteenth century was also a golden age for the philosophy of history, a discipline that did much to promote a broad, comparative approach to the study of national culture. Although the interest in Greek and Roman culture and philosophy predated the late eighteenth and nineteenth centuries, it was then that antiquity found its firm place in the grand narrative of an ostensibly European cultural heritage. In particular, Hegel offered a crucial contribution with his thesis on the World Spirit as the creator of history on its march towards human freedom. According to Hegel, the light of civilization was lit in the Orient, but from the moment the Occident inherited the values of Greece and Rome, the Orient disappeared into darkness. History appeared as a European privilege. Other peoples or cultures could only enter this exclusive History if they were touched by Europe.[22]

Only the Europeans had a 'true' history in the sense of a spirited, dynamic past, separating it from and elevating it above cultures locked into a primitive cycle determined by nature. It became a 'pre-judice' in the literal etymological sense of the word: a 'premise' for understanding the world. Europe alone had the philosophy and spirit, which equipped it for progress conceived as a civilizing drive. And this prejudice lives on, a fact evident in Sløk's study:

> Outside Europe we find cultures that are static. Some really are … others do change, but not from within, by virtue of their inner dynamism; the changes are caused by external events or they are enforced by climatic or geographical conditions. In Europe, by contrast, culture is constantly driven forwards by an inner dynamism.[23]

EUROPEAN AMBIGUITIES

Throughout the nineteenth century the contradictions of the term 'civilization' became increasingly conspicuous. The espousal of democracy and progress led to calls for ever-greater individual freedom. At the same time, civilization was construed as a solely European possession, and the inferiority of non-Europeans was increasingly explained with reference to factors found beyond history. This represented a radical break with the anthropology of the Enlightenment. As Ivan Hannaford observes in his discussion of English and German Romanticism before 1815:

In the unfolding of history, some races were advanced and others were retarded. Thus civilization was perceived to advance not through the public debate of speech-gifted men and the reconciliation of differing claims and interests in law but through the genius and character of the Völker naturally and biologically working as an energetic formative force in the blood of races and expressing themselves as Kultur. [24]

In 1824, the German historian Leopold von Ranke declared in his *Geschichten der romanischen und germanischen Völker* that Europe's history had to be understood as a whole, and had been created as a result of interactions between Romance and Germanic peoples. The characteristics of different peoples (*Völker*) thus gave the key to differences in development and it was not long before the superiority of Europeans was being argued on racial grounds. Following Hegel, Ranke not only excluded the 'Orientals,' but also the Slavs, from any part in Europe's development. This is another prejudice that continues to haunt Europe, where the polarity between Western and Eastern Europe is still pronounced but goes unnoticed in 'European' histories that deal exclusively with Western Europe.[25]

In this fusion of racial theory and historical philosophy, the Ancient Greeks were wrenched from any association, racially or culturally, with the 'Orient.' When evidence of 'Oriental' influences was acknowledged, it was deemed to have been radically transformed. As the Danish Assyriologist Mogens Trolle Larsen reminds us, archaeologists reacted with violent protestations at the proposal, put forward in 1850, that the recent Layard Assyrian artefacts be placed under the same roof as the Elgin Marbles in the British Museum. Members of the Royal Academy argued before a parliamentary commission that only Greek and Roman masterpieces could be considered art. By the same token, they warned contemporary artists against seeking inspiration from such 'barbaric' trophies.[26]

Democracy itself was claimed as a European legacy and was thereby monopolized by Europe. Europeans continue to locate their democratic origins in fifth-century Athens and, as Sløk proclaims, view this political legacy as an 'inalienable part of Europe's soul.'[27] It was only in the 1840s and 1850s, however, that the banker George Grote published his voluminous *History of Greece*, which established Athenian democracy as the cradle of European civilization.[28] And it was Grote who identified individual political freedom as the culminating achievement of the Greeks. In 1973, the British historian and classical philologist Moses Finley in his grandly titled book, *The Ancient Economy*, explicitly limited his remit to the Greco-Roman world since the Near East was too different a civilization to allow for even a cursory survey: 'It is almost enough to point out that it is impossible to translate the word "freedom", eleutheria in Greek, libertas in Latin, or "free man" into any ancient Near Eastern language, including Hebrew, or into any Far Eastern language either, for that matter.'[29]

Twentieth-century history and the impact of colonialism, however, serve as salutary reminders that democracy has had no monopoly in Europe. As Edgar Morin remarks in his book *Penser l'Europe*:

> Decolonisation pushed the European nations back to their continent and cleansed Europe of one of its worst sides, whereby it also imperceptibly prepared the cleansing of the concept of Europe itself - namely by removing the tragic ambiguity that made Europe intra muros mean freedom, democracy, and human rights, while it extra muros meant oppression, exploitation, and unfreedom.[30]

Morin's point is a valid one, even though 'remove' is perhaps too strong a word to describe the way in which Europeans have handled the ambiguity of their heritage. After all, decolonization did mean that millions of people from the former colonies came to Europe, settled there and were granted citizenship. Nevertheless, there is little room in standard definitions of the European cultural heritage for these people and their histories.

EUROPEAN CULTURAL HERITAGE TODAY

Since the 1980s and 1990s, political, social and economic upheavals have challenged many of the deep-rooted assumptions that underpin the framework within which identity has traditionally been defined in Western Europe. If a 'European cultural heritage' has functioned as a mechanism for excluding sections of the 'non-European' population, it has also been evoked as an inclusive device. Thus, for Poles, Czechs, Hungarians or Romanians, arguing in favour of a common European heritage, and not least their own nation's share in it, served as a means of challenging their exclusion from 'Europe' proper. Such is the case put forward by Milan Kundera in his well-known article, 'The Tragedy of Central Europe,' with its appeal to save a region which belonged to the West culturally, but which was relegated to the East politically.[31] Even Gorbachev's slogan championing a 'common European home' may be read as an argument for including the Russians as part of Europe. The debate, especially in its 'Central European' versions, however, was not solely about inclusion. The arguments put forward for a 'common history' had less to do with exploding the myth of an inferior 'Eastern Europe' than with pushing the border further eastwards. Thus, the assumptions about Europe and its shadowy other were largely unchallenged and the discourse of 'Europeanization' – even if it was presented as a restoration of historical normalcy – could not but highlight the 'marginality' of those who sought to manifest their European credentials.[32]

One reason for the promotion of a European cultural heritage by the institutions of the EU is that cultural integration is viewed as an important correlative of economic, judicial and political integration. What would Europe, as an economic or political entity, amount to if its populations did not identify themselves as 'Europeans?' It was precisely these concerns about a widespread apathy to the European project and the notorious 'democratic deficit,' which persuaded the EC to adopt the Declaration Concerning European Identity in 1973. This document articulated a crudely functionalist view of identity-building, which was seen not as a prerequisite for, but rather as a by-product of, economic integration. As the declaration stated: 'the European Identity will evolve as a function of the dynamic of the construction of a united Europe.'[33] In the final analysis, however, it was the very absence of such a by-product that prompted the EC to take an interest in the subject and indeed to propose various 'identity policies.'

Relatively few of these identity policies were implemented in the 1970s, but since the early 1980s cultural policies have been put on the EC agenda in earnest. The 1983 Solemn Declaration of EU extended EC co-operation to culture, 'in order to affirm the awareness of a common cultural heritage as an element in the European identity.'[34] Here a European identity was presented as something given, based on an equally given cultural heritage. Drawing on the symbolic order and governmental appurtenances that had underpinned the authority of European nation-states in the nineteenth century, the EC intro-duced a European flag, a European anthem, a European history book, and a European passport. In effect, all the mechanisms that had been mobilized in the formation of national identities were appropriated in the creation of a new supranational 'European' identity.[35]

The success of these policies was limited and in the 1990s the EU retreated somewhat. The Maastricht Treaty's Article 151 (ex Article 128) on culture simply states: 'The Community shall contribute to the flowering of the cultures of the Member States, while respecting their national and regional diversity and at the same time bringing the common cultural heritage to the fore.'

The common European heritage now appears along with national and regional identities as if all three levels harmoniously complemented one another, creating an effortless 'unity in diversity.' Nor is this heritage clearly defined, despite a call for the 'conservation and safeguarding of cultural heritage of European significance;' in other words, the material relics mentioned in the Raphael Programme's definition quoted earlier in this chapter. In fact, one of the express aims of the programme is the exploitation of the heritage sector as a means for generating new jobs and for promoting tourism.

The new Culture 2000 Programme indicates that the EU will fulfil its pledge to invest in European culture, economically in the form of a four-year budget of 167 million Euros, as well as symbolically. The document describes culture as 'an essential element of European integration [which] contributes to the affirmation and vitality of the European model of society and to the Community's influence on the international scene,' and goes on to claim:

> If citizens give their full support to, and participate fully in, European integration, greater emphasis should be placed on their common cultural values and roots as a key element of their identity and their membership of a society founded on freedom, democracy, tolerance and solidarity; a better balance should be achieved between the economic and the cultural aspects of the Community, so that these aspects can complement and sustain each other.[36]

Although it is difficult to disagree with the emphasis on social cohesion, freedom, democracy, tolerance and solidarity expressed in this text, nonetheless, it is hard to see how or why these values can be so readily reified as a common European cultural heritage.[37]

Since its foundation in 1949, the Council of Europe has taken an interest in the 'European dimension of education.' For many years this was primarily defined as an effort to challenge nationalistic stereotypes and promote peace and reconciliation among the peoples of Europe. Since 1989, however, the concept has been interpreted more broadly, and been used in a more direct approach to promote European solidarity and identity through changes in curricula and exchange programmes.[38] The council has also instigated programmes devoted to the European cultural heritage, often in co-operation with the EU, and often with the aim of promoting cultural tourism. The council is, however, even more than the EU inclined to define this heritage in very broad terms, enumerating fundamental ethical, spiritual and religious values, which it considers vital in the process of strengthening the bonds between the peoples and regions within Europe. Thus, the council claims that the campaign 'Europe: A Common Heritage,' launched in 1999, must be linked to a 'deeper awareness of the non material values embodied by the built and material heritage in order to further promote a European culture based on dialogue, democracy and peace.'[39] The relationship drawn here between democracy, dialogue, and a cultural heritage embodied in the built environment, is problematic to say the least. But it is an association reiterated in the literature published by the council, as in a promotional blurb for the book *European Cultural Routes*: 'Cultural routes safeguard and promote the greatest treasure of all bequeathed to us Europeans, namely the set of basic values - such as freedom, human rights, tolerance, interculturalism and yearning for knowledge, beauty and happiness - on which Europe is built.'[40]

The European way, the text affirms, is the right way, since it alone is founded on a fundamental set of democratic values. Moreover, Europeans alone are blessed with a 'yearning for knowledge, beauty and happiness.' These are inherited virtues, we are told, innately present in every European and under threat, since they need safeguarding and promoting. Such affirmations, however, beg the question as to whether the world at large is bereft of all creative and libertarian impulses, and consigned to a state of unfeeling and perpetual bondage.

In short, 'cultural heritage' and 'European' are concepts that must be used cautiously. In the words of John Slater:

> This is not to suggest that we reject the concept of 'civilization' and 'heritage' but merely to wonder whether they are not treacherous historical guides, inconsistent with the unsettling, sceptical, disquieting function of history. If we do use these terms, let us see them first as 'cultures' and 'heritages'. The plurals are crucial. Second, let us see them as hypotheses to be tested, not as values to be transmitted.[41]

A decent life for all Europeans today requires emancipation from, as much as a celebration of, the heritage of the past. We need to be selective in our approach to a 'European cultural heritage,' but this does not mean to say that we can reduce this heritage to the carefully selected portions that we prefer. Heritage must be all-inclusive: the Acropolis as well as Auschwitz and everything in between. And if we choose to emphasize the democratic and pluralistic aspects of this heritage we will also have to take the backgrounds and cultures of the 'new' Europeans seriously as an integral part of it. The idea of human dignity is not a European monopoly, and the fact that human rights as an idea and a programme were first formulated in a European context makes them no more a European property than the Arabic origin of numerals makes them Arabic.

CHAPTER 5

EUROPEAN IDENTITY AND THE HERITAGE OF NATIONAL CULTURES

THOMAS RISSE

INTRODUCTION: WHAT IS EUROPEAN IDENTITY?

As other contributors have argued elsewhere in this volume, the concept of a 'European identity' is exceptionally elusive. Yet, as Peter Bugge contends in his chapter on a common European cultural heritage, consideration of this concept is fundamental in any discussion of heritage, given the fact that national and regional heritage sites are increasingly funded by the EU in the name of a devolved but essentially integrated heritage. Indeed, 'Europe: A Common Heritage' has been adopted as a permanent theme by the Council of Europe, which has also initiated 'European Heritage Days' with the aim of fostering ties between the peoples of Europe.[1] In this chapter I consider the heritage of political cultures in Europe and explore the consequences of 'Europeanization' upon different national identities. Notions of 'identity' and, specifically, of 'identity politics,' have been considered by other contributors, but no attempt has been made to formulate a general theoretical model for understanding identity in relation to the process of 'Europeanization.'

Do people, whether as individuals or as social groups, identify with Europe and with the model of supranational citizenship promoted by the institutions of the EU? If so, how does this impact upon their national, sub-national, gender or other cultural identities? Does possession of a 'European identity' necessarily entail relinquishing a national identity or any other subjective affiliation? In the pages that follow, I argue that pitting a 'European identity' against national or regional identities misses the point, since no identity is exclusive: individuals and social groups hold multiple identities concurrently. Rather, the question ought to be reformulated: how much room is there for 'Europe' in given collective identities? Europe and the European order, I will argue here, resonate in different ways within different political cultures and national heritages.

Heritage is a cultural and political concept inseparable from the history of the nation-state and the emergence of 'national cultures.' As the late Ernest Gellner argued some 20 years ago, cultural identification is crucial to the nation-building process, while nationalism can be defined as the political principle 'which holds that the political and the national unit should be congruent.'[2] The German Supreme Court, in its ruling on the 1991 Maastricht Treaty's proposals to enlarge the EU, underscored the importance of cultural homogeneity as a precondition for political integration. According to the court, the absence of a common culture seriously undermined any further extension of the EU.[3] Thus, an exploration of 'Europeanization' inevitably involves considering the extent to which identification with a homogeneous pan-European culture has meant the erosion of national affiliations. How far have national allegiances weakened, or at least been reconfigured, under the impact of a supranational EU?

THREE MODELS OF COLLECTIVE IDENTITY

After more than 40 years of European integration, relatively little is known about the impact that Europeanization and the gradual emergence of a European polity have had on collective identities. In this chapter I want to distinguish three different ways of conceptualizing a European identity.

First, there is the so-called 'zero-sum model' of collective identity. Here, identification with Europe gradually and increasingly replaces national, sub-national, or other identities relating to territorial spaces. The founding fathers of European integration theory thought, for example, that those political, economic, and social elites who benefited most from European integration, would increasingly identify with Europe and, as a result, overcome their national identities and prejudices.[4] The emerging European polity would gradually command the loyalty of the European people, beginning with the elite.

A glance at the empirical evidence belies this argument. Social groups such as farmers, who arguably benefit most from European integration in economic terms, are not renowned for expressing much affection for Brussels and the EU. Moreover, the theoretical foundations of this concept of collective identification are flawed. It is problematic to assume that individuals have some apportioned space available for identifying with collectivities and that the more one identifies with Europe, the less one can feel loyalty for one's nation-state, region, or locality. Such a 'zero-sum' view of collective identities is, to say the least, dubious.

Social psychologists and sociologists have demonstrated that individuals can have multiple identities, which are invoked depending on the specific social context.[5] On a basic level, social identities describe and categorize an individual's membership of a social group, including emotional, affective and evaluative components. Groups of individuals perceive that they have something in common, and it is on the basis of this shared set of values that they form an 'imagined community.'[6] On another level, this commonality is accentuated by a sense of difference with regard to other communities. As Benedict Anderson articulates it: 'No nation imagines itself coterminous with mankind.'[7] Individuals tend to view the group with which they identify in a more positive light than the 'outsiders.' Furthermore, in Europe, national identities are closely bound up with the 'imagined community' of the nation-state and are, therefore, closely linked to ideas about sovereignty and statehood.[8] National identities often contain visions of political and social orders. Finally, as we have seen, individuals hold multiple identities, which are context-bound.[9] This context-specific nature of national identities also means that different components of the national identity in question are activated depending on the policy area.

Such an understanding of collective identities leads us to consider a second useful theoretical model for elucidating identity. This could be termed the 'layer-cake' model, since it envisages people and social groups holding multiple identities that are tiered as in the layers of a sponge cake. According to this model, the social context within which any interaction takes place determines the particular identity that is invoked. Thus, the *lederhosen*-wearing Bavarian German European who feels strongly Bavarian when he visits 'Prussian' Berlin, might feel passionately German when berating the inefficiency of Italian air-traffic control when he is stranded at Bologna Airport. Moreover, when this Bavarian German visits a saloon in the American Midwest, he might feel a spontaneous kinship with some Italians or French who also happen to be having a drink. As they carp about the poor beer and wine, the German, Italian and Frenchman become conscious of their common 'Europeanness' and shared European heritage. This notion of a multiple identification process has become widespread in studies devoted to researching the question of European identities. Most scholars no longer consider that European and national identities constitute either/or propositions. Even the annual Euro-barometer polls have accepted the 'layer-cake' concept of multiple identities.

Finally, there is a third paradigm of collective identities that might be called the 'marble-cake' model. This concedes that people hold multiple identities, which are invoked in a context-dependent way. However, in this formulation, identities are not construed as being layered in such an orderly way as the example of the Bavarian German European suggested. Rather, the 'marble-cake' model suggests that different identities are enmeshed and flow into each other in complex, reciprocal ways, and that there are no clearly defined boundaries between, say, one's 'Germanness' and one's 'Europeanness.' In fact, it might be impossible to describe what it means to be German (or Italian, for that matter, or Greek) without also talking about Europe and 'Europeanness.' A nation's history and cultural heritage might be so intertwined with European history and cultural heritage that it becomes difficult, nigh impossible, to disentangle the two. And the same might be true for entrenched regional identities, from Sicily to the Rhineland.

Two conclusions follow from this dynamic conceptualization of identity. Firstly, there might be much more 'Europeanness' enshrined in national cultures and heritages and, hence, a much stronger collective European identity than is usually assumed. The identification process might encompass a much longer and probably also more contested history than the 40 years generally ascribed to European integration. Secondly, it becomes unclear whether Greeks, Italians, French or Germans mean the same thing when they allude to their 'Europeanness.' The French notion of *mission civilisatrice*, for example, might translate into a European civilizing mission, but the Germans would undoubtedly feel uncomfortable when confronted with such a grand interpretation of Europeanness. In general, too, Northern Europeans might not identify with the way that the Greeks connect their Europeanness directly to their ancient history, even though we all love to visit Delphi.

In sum, then, the 'marble-cake' model maintains, on the one hand, that there is much more 'Europeanness' intertwined in national, regional, and other collective identities than is typically acknowledged. On the other hand, it contends that the significance of 'Europe' differs profoundly according to the various national, sub-national and other contexts in which it is invoked. Thus, the question of European identity can be reformulated. How far do the meanings invested in 'Europe' diverge? To what extent do they overlap? Is it possible to speak about a common 'Europeanness,' despite the fact that any understanding of what it means to be European will be grounded in particular national historical and cultural contexts? To furnish an example: Athenians might relate their understanding of European democracy back to Ancient Greece. For Germans, of course, this is not an option. Nonetheless, 'Europeanness' also encompasses democracy and liberal values for them, but in their particular understanding, Europe means overcoming one's own fraught history, with its belligerent nationalism and militarism. Finally, in the French collective understanding nationalism has a positive connotation and is linked with the

Enlightenment and republicanism. Furthermore, French 'Europeanness' also embraces liberal values, which constitute the Europeanized version of Enlightenment and republicanism.

EUROPE AND THE EVOLUTION OF NATIONAL IDENTITIES IN BRITAIN, GERMANY AND FRANCE

In the final sections of this chapter, my aim is to employ the 'marble-cake' model of collective identities to explore how 'Europeanization' has influenced national identities in the UK, Germany and France over the last 50 years.[10] The focus is on a 'European' discourse as it has been articulated by the governing elites within the three countries in question during the postwar period. I argue that five distinct identity constructions relating to the nation-state were available and promoted by transnational political groups in debates about Europe during the 1950s. As we shall see, these identity constructions were premised on two broad assumptions involving the ways that Europe related to given national identities, and on visions of a future European political and economic order. The degree to which these identity constructions were represented in the political discourses in the three countries varied considerably. Different identity constructions carried the day and became consensual in each of the three countries.

In the British case, notions of 'Britishness' have been largely constructed in opposition to 'Europe' and have remained so since the 1950s. The prevailing British national identity continues to perceive Europe as the (friendly) 'other.' A distinctive British national identity is perceived as being incompatible with federalist or supranational visions of European political order, a fact that explains why British governments, be they Conservative or Labour, have been consistently reluctant to support a furthering of European integration.

In contrast, a (West) German national identity was thoroughly reconstructed during the 1950s. After the catastrophe of Nazi Germany and World War II, the propagation of a 'European Germany' was seen as a way overcoming the legacy of the German nationalist past. By 1960, this new German national identity had become consensual and has remained so ever since. A 'European' German national identity survived both the end of the Cold War and German unification and explains why German political elites – whether Christian Democrats or Social Democrats – have supported further steps toward European integration.

While Britain and Germany evince continuity, at least since the late 1950s, there have been substantial changes in the French collective identity. In contrast to Germany, a distinct nationalist vision of French identity carried the day in the late 1950s. President Charles de Gaulle's establishment of the Fifth Republic in

1958 combined a history of French centralization enshrined in Enlightenment principles and republican doctrine, with a vision of *grandeur* and *indépendence*. De Gaulle's successors discovered, however, that these visions of France were increasingly at odds with the reality of European integration. As a result, the political elites, beginning with the centre-left during the 1980s and continuing on the centre-right, incorporated 'Europe' into the French collective identity by adopting a vision of Europe as the French nation-state writ large.

EUROPE AS BRITAIN'S 'OTHER'

Probably the most remarkable feature of British attitudes toward European integration is their stability and lack of change.[11] The fundamental orientations toward the EC have remained essentially the same since the end of World War II and have survived the vicissitudes of British policy toward the EC and the EU. More than 20 years after entry into the EC, Britain is still regarded as 'of, rather than in,' Europe. Britain remains the 'awkward partner' who is 'semi-detached' from Europe.[12] This general attitude has not changed since the 1950s when Winston Churchill proclaimed:

> Where do we stand? We are not members of the European Defence Community, nor do we intend to be merged in a Federal European system. We feel we have a special relation to both. This can be expressed by prepositions, by the preposition 'with' but not 'of' - we are with them, but not of them. We have our own Commonwealth and Empire.[13]

British attitudes towards the European project reflect collectively held beliefs about British, particularly English identity, since 'Britishness' has been identified with 'Englishness' throughout most of the post-World War II era. Among the five ideal identity constructions presented above, a nationalist identity clearly prevailed within British political discourse. There is still a feeling of 'them' versus 'us' between Britain and the continent. 'Europe' continues to be envisaged as an encroaching outsider and perceived in oppositional terms as 'the other.'

The social construction of 'Englishness,' as the core of British national identity, comprises the meanings attached to institutions, historical memory and symbols. Each of these components is hard to reconcile with a vision of European political order going beyond intergovernmentalism.[14] It is not surprising that parts of British national identity are often viewed as potentially threatened by European integration. Institutions such as parliament and the crown form important elements of a collective national identity that centres on a particular understanding of national sovereignty. The crown symbolizes 'external sovereignty' in terms of independence from Rome and the Pope, as well as from the European continent. Parliamentary or 'internal' sovereignty represents an important constitutional principle relating to a 700-year-old parliamentary tradition and hard-fought victories over the monarchy. English sovereignty is thus directly linked to myths about a continuous history of liberal and democratic evolution and 'free-born Englishmen.'

British objections against transferring sovereignty to European supranational institutions are usually justified on grounds that they lack democratic, that is to say parliamentary, accountability. Identity-related understandings of parliamentary sovereignty, moreover, are linked to the prevailing visions of a European order comprising independent nation-states. This is demonstrated by the following quotations from 1950 and from the 1990s:

> It does not, however, seem to us – as at present advised – either necessary or appropriate…to invest a supra-national authority of independent persons with powers for overriding Governmental and Parliamentary decisions in the participating countries […] Certainly this Parliament has always exercised the greatest caution as to agreeing to any removal from its own democratic control of any important element of our economic power or policy.[15]
>
> *Labour Chancellor of the Exchequer Sir Stafford Cripps, 1950*

> But - and it is a crucial but - we shall never accept the approach of those who want to see the EC as a means of removing our ability to govern ourselves as an independent nation. The British Parliament had endured for 700 years and had been a beacon of hope to the peoples of Europe in their darkest days.[16]
>
> *Conservative Prime Minister Margaret Thatcher, 1990*

> It is clear now that the Community will remain a union of sovereign national states. That is what its peoples want: to take decisions through their own Parliaments. That protects the way of life, the cultural differences, the national traditions…It is for nations to build Europe, not for Europe to attempt to supersede nations.[17]
>
> *Conservative Prime Minister John Major, 1993*

Here, political independence is recast as an essential cultural difference. Indeed, John Major's appreciation of a Europe comprised of sovereign national states rests upon his evocation of an essentially static and hierarchical, Home Counties Britain, a vision culled from the likes of George Orwell's wartime description of England as a domestic and rural community. At the same time, the threat of European integration became intertwined with the spectre of a corrosive dilution of British identity. It was precisely the need to protect this hard-won identity, enshrined in objects like the red telephone box, which prompted the passionate espousal of a national heritage as part of an authoritarian social policy. [18]

Yet what is of particular interest here is the extent to which Conservative views in the 1980s and 1990s chime with those of the 1950s. There has been a remarkable continuity in British attitudes toward the EU and related identity constructions from the 1950s and indeed even earlier. The quotations above also demonstrate that national identities supersede ideological orientations among the two major parties. In sum, British national identity seems hardly affected by European integration, and 'Europe' is still largely construed as the (albeit friendly) 'other.'

THE PAST AS EUROPEAN GERMANY'S 'OTHER'

While Britain is a case of strong incompatibility between Europe and the nation-state, Europe resonates well with a contemporary German national identity. The German case is one of thorough and profound reconstruction following the catastrophe of World War II.[19] Thomas Mann's dictum that 'we do not want a German Europe, but a European Germany' soon became the mantra of the postwar (West) German elites.[20] Since the 1950s, a fundamental consensus has emerged among the political elites and has been shared by public opinion that European integration is in Germany's vital interest.[21]

After 1945, the newly founded Christian Democratic Party (CDU) immediately embraced European unification as the alternative to the nationalism of the past. As Ernst Haas puts it, 'in leading circles of the CDU, the triptych of self-conscious anti-Nazism, Christian values, and dedication to European unity as a means of redemption for past German sins has played a crucial ideological role.'[22] Christianity, democracy and – later on – social market economy became the three pillars on which a collective European identity was to be based. It was sharply distinguished from both the German nationalist and militarist past and – during the late 1940s and early 1950s – from Soviet Communism and Marxism. In other words, Germany's own past as well as Communism constituted the 'others' in this identity construction.

But throughout the early 1950s, there was no consensus about German national identity among the political elite. The Social Democratic Party (SPD) was the main opposition to Konrad Adenauer's policies at the time. In the inter-war period, the SPD had been the first major German party to espouse the concept of a 'United States of Europe' in its 1925 Heidelberg Programme. When the party was forced into exile during the Nazi period, the leadership fully embraced the notion of a democratic European federation, which would almost naturally become a Socialist order. As in the case of the CDU: 'the "European idea" was primarily invoked as a spiritual value in the first years of the emigration…What Europe would be like after Hitler was a second-order question, though it was taken as self-evident that it would be socialist. In this period Europe was seen as an antithesis to Nazi Germany.'[23]

Consequently, when the SPD was refounded in 1946, its first programme supported the 'United States of Europe, a democratic and socialist federation of European states. [The German Social Democracy] aspires to a Socialist Germany in a Socialist Europe.'[24] Thus, Europe, Germany, democracy and socialism were perceived as synonymous.

The SPD's first postwar leader, Kurt Schumacher, a survivor of the Nazi concentration camps, strongly promoted a 'Europe as a third force' concept for the new German national identity. He argued vigorously against the politics of Western integration, since it foreclosed the prospects of rapid reunification of the two Germanies.[25] Schumacher denounced the Council of Europe and the European Coal and Steel Community (ECSC) as 'un-European,' as 'mini-Europe' (*Kleinsteuropa*), as conservative-clericalist and capitalist. At the same time, the SPD went to great pains to argue that it did not oppose European integration as such, just this particular version.

Following two major election defeats in 1953 and 1957 the SPD changed course. There had always been internal opposition to Schumacher's policies. These party elites supported the identity construction of a modern European Germany as part of the Western community of liberal and democratic states. By the late 1950s this group took over the party leadership. The German Social Democrats thoroughly reformed their domestic and foreign policy programme. With regard to the latter, they revisited the 1925 Heidelberg Programme and became staunch supporters of European integration. The changes culminated in the 1959 Godesberg Programme.[26]

The SPD's *volte face* can be partly explained by perceived strategic concerns. The party needed to attract new voters who apparently supported Adenauer's policies, while Schumacher's opposition did not pay off. The party's new ideological orientation resulted from a change in the leadership, which brought the Europeanist and Atlanticist faction into power. The political goals and collective identity of the new party leaders account for the content and substance of the change.

From the 1960s, a federalist consensus ('United States of Europe') prevailed among the German political elites comprising the main parties from the centre-right to the centre-left. This consensus outlasted the changes in government from the CDU to the SPD in 1969, from the SPD to the CDU in 1982, and the recent change toward a coalition between the SPD and the Green Party in 1998. Even more significant, German unification did not result in a reconsideration of German European policies. With the unexpected end of the East–West conflict and regained German sovereignty, a broad range of foreign policy opportunities emerged creating a situation in which the German elites might have redefined their national interests. But Germany did not reconsider its fundamental foreign policy orientations, since Germany's commitment to European integration had long outlived the context in which it had originally emerged.[27] In the aftermath of unification, the German government accelerated rather than slowed down its support for further progress towards deeper European integration. German backing for a single currency and for European political union was perfectly in line with long-standing attitudes toward integration and the country's 'European' identity.

This German federalist consensus went hand in hand with a peculiar identity construction in the aftermath of World War II. The German notion of what constitutes the 'other,' the non-European, can be related to European and German nationalist history. German nationalism came to be viewed as authoritarian, militaristic and anti-Semitic. The country's nationalist and militarist past constituted the 'other' in the process of 'post-national' identity formation whereby Europeanness replaces traditional notions of nation-state identity. All federal governments from Adenauer onwards were determined to render the European unification process irreversible because they were convinced that the concept of a unified Europe was the most effective assurance against the resurgence of nationalism and the recurrence of conflict. Nowadays, a 'good German' equals a 'good European' supporting a united Europe. 'Europe' accordingly stands for a stable and peaceful order, which marks a fundamental departure from the continent's bloody past, for democracy and human rights (in contrast to European – and German – autocratic history), as well as for a social market economy including the welfare state.[28]

Thus, in contrast to postwar concepts of identity in the UK, the German case is one of comprehensive transformation. German Europeanness as a particular identity construction was contested throughout the 1950s, but thereafter became consensual, partly because it suited the perceived strategic interests of political elites. The European integration process did not create this identity. Rather, it reinforced and stabilized it by demonstrating that Germany could prosper economically and regain political clout in Europe through a policy of embedding itself within European institutions. German Euro-patriotism deeply affected elite perceptions of the country's national interests and attitudes toward European integration. This Euro-patriotism remained stable despite various challenges, which might otherwise have led to changes in instrumental interests.

EUROPEANIZATION AND THE TRANSFORMATION OF FRENCH EXCEPTIONALISM

In contrast to both Britain and Germany, attitudes towards Europe shared by the French political elites underwent considerable changes over time.[29] Policy-makers of the Third Republic (1870–1940) such as Aristide Briand and Eduard Herriot were among the first to embrace a federalist vision of 'les Etats Unis d'Europe' during the inter-war period.[30] However, their visions did not become consensual within their own parties until after World War II.

During the 1950s and in conjunction with the first efforts towards European integration, a national debate took place that revolved around the question of a French identity, as well as the basic political orientations in the postwar era. World War II and the German occupation were traumatic experiences, as a result of which French national identity became deeply problematic and contested. French containment of Germany, as the most significant French 'other,' became a priority. Champions of European integration argued in favour of a 'binding' strategy, of creating supranational institutions in order to curb German power once and for all, while opponents favoured traditional balance-of-power strategies to tackle the German problem:

> The only means to disinfect the German people from Nazism and to democratize it is to surround Germany in a democratic Europe. [31]

> There is no Europe without Germany and there is no solution for the German problem without Europe. [32]

These policy prescriptions correlated with the national identity constructions prevailing in the respective parties at the time. There was no agreement among the French political elites about European integration as a solution for the German problem. The defeat of the treaty on the European Defence Community in the French National Assembly in 1954 revealed the deep divisions among the political elites.

The next 'critical juncture' for French national identity was the war in Algeria and the ongoing crisis of the Fourth Republic. When the Fifth Republic came into being in 1958, its founding father, President de Gaulle, reconstructed French national identity and managed to reunite a deeply divided nation around a common vision of France's role in the world: 'When one is the Atlantic cape of the continent, when one has planted one's flag in all parts of the world, when one spreads the ideas, and when one opens oneself to the environment, in short, when one is France, one cannot escape the grand movements on the ground.' [33]

De Gaulle's identity construction drew upon and endorsed historical myths of Frenchness, which were combined in a unique way. As the leader of the French *résistance* during World War II, he overcame the trauma of the Vichy regime and promoted an understanding of the French nation-state, which combined a specific meaning of sovereignty with the values of Enlightenment and democracy.[34] The notion of sovereignty – understood as national independence from outside interference together with a sense of uniqueness (*grandeur*) – was used to build a bridge between post-revolutionary republican France and the pre-revolutionary monarchy. The concept of the French *état-nation* linked the identity of the nation with democracy and the identity of French society with the republic. Finally, de Gaulle reintroduced the notion of French exceptionalism and uniqueness in terms of a civilizing mission for the world (*mission civilisatrice*) destined to spread the universal values of Enlightenment and of the French Revolution. None of these identity constructions were particularly new, but de Gaulle combined them in a novel way and managed to use them effectively to legitimize the political institutions of the Fifth Republic.

Of course, these understandings were hard to reconcile with federalist visions of a European order. Rather, 'l'Europe des nations' became the rallying cry of de Gaulle's presidency. The specific Gaullist identity construction only remained consensual among the political elites for a decade after de Gaulle's resignation. Beginning in the late 1970s, Europeanization gradually transformed French identity among the elites, a transformation that was fuelled by two major political events: the failure of President Mitterand's economic policies in the early 1980s and the end of the Cold War in the late 1980s.[35]

When Mitterand and the Socialist Party came to power in 1981, they initially embarked upon a project of creating democratic socialism in France based on leftist Keynesianism. This project failed disastrously when the capital market crash hit the French economy, which in turn led to a severe loss of electoral support for Mitterand's policies. In 1983 Mitterand had practically no choice other than changing course dramatically if he wanted to remain in power.[36] This political change led to a deep crisis within the Socialist Party, which then gradually abandoned the socialist project and moved toward ideas once derisively labelled 'Social Democratic.' In changing direction, the party followed Mitterand's core conviction in the EC.[37]

The Socialist Party's shift of emphasis towards Europe involved a concerted effort to reconfigure French national identity. Moreover, the increasing importance of Europe in French identity politics coincided with a renewed interest in France's own past and heritage. This was manifest in the 1980s in ostentatious museum exhibitions and festivals, culminating in the lavish bicentennial celebrations of the French Revolution of 1789. Such commemorative events should perhaps be viewed not as the promotion of an immutable French identity, but as a reappraisal of Frenchness within the context of an ongoing process of Europeanization.[38]

The French Socialists emphasized a common European historical and cultural heritage. They argued increasingly that France's future was to be found in Europe and championed the cause of a 'European France.' The peculiar historical and cultural legacies of France were transferred from the 'first nation-state' in Europe to the continent as a whole, since all European states were products of France's Enlightenment, republicanism and democratic heritage. As such, France had engendered Europe. This identity construction mobilized traditional understandings of Frenchness and the French nation-state and extended them to Europe. In contrast to British identity constructions where Europe is still projected as the 'other,' this understanding incorporates Europe into France's own collective identity along with French ideas about sovereignty and political order. French identity is transformed but only to the degree that ideas about Europe can be embedded into and resonate with previous visions of the state. This change more or less corresponds to the 'marble-cake' model of collective identity discussed above.

A similar shift took place on the French right, where visions of a European order became inextricably bound up with the search for a French identity. One legacy of de Gaulle's political visions, the Rassemblement pour la République (RPR), provides a striking example of the political reconfigurations in late-twentieth-century France. The end of the Cold War was a decisive moment and a challenge to deep-rooted assumptions about France's role in Europe. The fall of the Berlin Wall, the unification of Germany and the construction of a post-Cold War European security order left France – *la grande nation* – largely on the sidelines. French diplomatic efforts failed miserably. As a result, substantial sections of the political elite became aware of the overblown ambitions of *grandeur* and *indépendence*. The way out was Europe.[39] The political debates surrounding the referendum on the Maastricht Treaties in 1992 represented identity-related discourses about the new role of France in Europe and the world after the end of the Cold War. As in the 1950s, fear of German power dominated the debates. Supporters of Maastricht and the European Monetary Union, particularly on the French right, argued in favour of a 'binding' strategy, while opponents supported a return to traditional balance of power politics. This time, supporters of European integration prevailed in all major parties.

In sum, the majority of the French political elite gradually incorporated Europe into notions of French distinctiveness and began to equate the French state with a new European order. However, a minority continues to uphold Gaullist concepts of French *grandeur* and *indépendence*. Of the three countries considered in this chapter, France is the only one where the discourse on national identity among a political elite has been significantly reworked over the last two decades.

CONCLUSION

The cases that I have presented in this chapter demonstrate that national identities are stubborn and are subject only to gradual change. In the case of the UK, Britishness is still defined in contrast to Europeanness and 'Europe' is categorized as the 'other' against which a national identity is defined. Almost two decades of EC/EU membership do not seem to have made much difference. In contrast, German national identity was thoroughly reconstructed after World War II. Once German Europeanness became consensual among the political elites in the early 1960s, this national identity remained stable. German Europeanness preceded, rather than followed, progress towards European integration. Conversely, European integration was a decisive factor in the transformation of a Gaullist vision of French national identity. Since the 1980s, the French elites from the centre-right to the centre-left have identified with a European rather than a strictly French distinctiveness.

How can these different developments be explained? As I argued in the introduction, and in line with the 'marble-cake' model of collective identities, new ideas about political order and identity constructions have to resonate with given notions embedded in collective national identities. Classic British notions of political order, for example, emphasize parliamentary democracy and sovereignty, which is why only intergovernmental versions of European political order resonate with internal and external sovereignty. In the French case, state-centred republicanism (the duty to promote values such as fraternity, freedom, equality and human rights – in short, 'civilization') constitutes a continuous element in the French discourse about political order. Therefore, any European idea which resonates with French exceptionalism and which does not violate the state-centred concept of republicanism can legitimately be promoted in France, including a European rather than solely French exceptionalism. The situation was similar in Germany. German concepts of a social market economy, democracy and political federalism were central elements in the discourse of German exiled elites during the War and among the entire political class in the postwar years. Ideas about European political order, which resonated with these concepts, were therefore considered legitimate in the German political debate. In addition, militarism and Nazism had thoroughly discredited a nationalist notion of Germany. Europe provided an alternative identity construction and, thus, a way out.

But how can we explain changes in collective identities pertaining to Europe, as experienced in Germany in the late 1950s and in France from the early 1980s? Perceived situations of crisis, or 'critical junctures,' together with strategic interests, appear to explain these transformations. In the Federal Republic of Germany, the SPD reached its critical juncture in the mid-to-late

1950s, when members of the party leadership realized that Schumacher's vision of 'Europe as a third force' was no longer a viable option given the realities of the ECSC, the Treaty of Rome and two consecutive federal election defeats. At the same time, the modern Western concept of European identity resonated well with the domestic programme of the party reformers who supported liberal democracy, market economy, and the welfare state while giving up more far-reaching Socialist visions. The desire to gain political power facilitated the ideological change of the SPD programme and their thorough reconstruction of German nation-state identity.

In the French case, it was only a matter of time before the French Gaullist national identity would become incompatible with the Europeanization process and the overall French support for it. While German Europeanness and European integration went hand in hand, the gap between a French nationalist identity and the reality of European integration widened over time. When President Mitterand's economic policies collided with the European Monetary System in 1982 and 1983, he was forced to choose between Europe and his French socialist goals. Mitterand readily opted for Europe to remain in power, but then set in motion a process, which the German SPD had experienced 25 years earlier: the parallel social democratization and adjustment to Europe in the French socialists' national identity. By the end of the decade, Frenchness and Euro-peanness had been reconciled among the French centre-left. The French Gaullists underwent a similar process after the end of the Cold War when they gradually realized that French exceptionalism and its *mission civilisatrice* could only be preserved within a European identity construction. Thus, French Europeanness became consensual among a majority of the political elites from the centre-right to the centre-left during the early 1990s.

In short, more than 40 years of European integration have had different effects on the national identities in the three countries considered. Supranationalism remains largely incompatible with deeply entrenched notions of Britishness and British sovereignty. In contrast, the emergence of a European polity reinforced and strengthened the German postwar 'Europeanness.' Finally, Europeanization gradually contributed to the reorientation of French national identity, so that Frenchness and Europeanness are no longer incompatible.

Given the manifest differences in the way that 'Europe' is perceived and has shaped national identities, we need to be cautious about defining an all-encompassing, monolithic 'European heritage.' As I have sought to demonstrate in this chapter, 'Europe' is configured differently in different national contexts and the legacy of national political heritages remains strong. Today, with a new wave of immigration, deepening European integration and the impact of globalization, the relationship between state, economy and society is changing.

Yet even as these transformations are giving rise to a new political, social and cultural environment, deep-rooted assumptions about identity persist into the twenty-first century. What is required, I have argued here, is a flexible and dynamic model for elucidating identity and its historical grounding at a moment of profound upheaval.

CHAPTER 6

THE *CHANSON DE ROLAND* AND THE INVENTION OF FRANCE

SIMON GAUNT

L'héritage n'est jamais un *donné*, c'est toujours une tâche. Elle reste devant nous, aussi incontestablement que, avant même de le vouloir ou de le refuser, nous sommes des héritiers, et des héritiers endeuillés, comme tous les héritiers.

Jacques Derrida, Spectres de Marx *(1993)*[1]

Il n'y a pas de fidélité possible pour quelqu'un qui ne pourrait pas être infidèle. C'est à partir de l'infidélité possible qu'on se rend à l'héritage, qu'on l'assume, qu'on reprend et qu'on contresigne l'héritage pour le faire aller ailleurs, pour le faire respirer autrement. Si l'héritage consiste simplement à entretenir des choses mortes, des archives à reproduire ce qui fut, ce n'est pas ce qu'on peut appeler un héritage. On ne peut pas souhaiter un héritier ou une héritière qui n'invente pas l'héritage, qui ne porte pas ailleurs, dans la fidélité. Une fidélité infidèle.

Jacques Derrida, Sur Parole *(1999)*[2]

INTRODUCTION: THE FANTASY OF HERITAGE

The notion of heritage entails a complex relationship between past, present and future: the present owes it to the future to preserve the past, but the attempt to preserve the irreducibly irrecuperable leads to transformation and betrayal. In Jacques Derrida's *Spectres de Marx*, heritage is sucked into his discussion of haunting: as he argues, haunting is as much a radical commitment to the future as to the past in that the 'spectre' (as in *Hamlet*) returns from the past to shape the future. Haunting in turn becomes bound up with identity: our heritage becomes part of us, it determines who we are, it distinguishes us from those with a different heritage. But of course heritage itself is an ideological construct involving the telling of a story that is inevitably grounded in selective – even creative – accounts of the past, exclusions and myth-making. I see nothing ethically questionable in this infidelity; on the other hand I do see an ethical imperative to subject the storytelling process to scrutiny.

A crucial element in the construction of modern European national identities since the nineteenth century has been the task of claiming and shaping a national literature as the nation's cultural heritage: consider F. R. Leavis's account of the English 'great tradition,' or Gustave Lanson's elaboration of literary history as a discipline in France. Part of the storytelling and myth-making this involves entails the identification of the 'first' truly English, French, Spanish or Italian writer or text in the Middle Ages: thus the textual monuments that are Chaucer, the *Chanson de Roland*, the *Poema del mío Cid*, Dante. And I use the word 'monument' advisedly here, in that if others underline the importance of material culture to heritage, I should like to suggest that texts are nonetheless a more widely disseminated, ubiquitous and transportable form of heritage. What I wish to offer in this chapter is a case study of the *Chanson de Roland* and its position in French literary history to illustrate how a text from the past is installed as inaugural in a nation's heritage, and the ideological work that is done by this.

However, in the psychoanalytic theoretical framework I adopt here, 'fantasy' is a crucial supplement to the notion of ideology. Fantasy, from this perspective, should not be understood as private and grounded in make-believe; it should be understood rather as the fictions we share to make sense of the world and take up a place in it. If, as Jacqueline Rose suggests following Freud, fantasy is what enables group identifications, then it ceases to be opposed to reality, it becomes rather that which makes social organization possible, or, to use her formulation, 'its psychic glue.'[3]

Texts, like films, are fantasies in which we indulge collectively. And as Slavoj Žižek suggests, they often have the effect of simultaneously underscoring the fantasmic nature of the fantasy and sustaining it.[4] For Lacan, fantasy is a screen (*écran*) and, as with so many of his theoretical terms, he dwells upon its dual function: the screen is a surface onto which representations may be projected, but also a device for screening off that which lies behind. And of course what lies behind the *écran* in Lacanian theory is the 'real,' the void or abyss from which the illusions propagated in the symbolic and imaginary orders protect us. Representations, in other words, screen us from something that we are in every sense incapable of seeing. To quote Žižek: 'The fantasy which underlies the public ideological text as its non-acknowledged obscene support simultaneously serves as a screen against the direct intrusion of the real.'[5] This remark comes in the middle of a discussion of ethnic cleansing in the Balkans. He notes that it is not at all a gratuitous coincidence that Radovan Karadzic is a poet and he asks: 'What voices does a racist hear when he indulges in beating Jews, Arabs, Mexicans, Bosnians…?'[6] His question recalls another asked by Jacqueline Rose, again in the context of a meditation on the relationship between fantasy and national identity: 'When and why do men obey?'[7] The point is perhaps obvious: the 'non-acknowledged obscene support' of a 'public ideological text' such as a poem shot through with nationalistic jingoism is violence. But the further point to make about this is that both are symptoms of psychosis. The psychotic, for Lacan, 'is inhabited, possessed by language;'[8] the paranoid is particularly prone to delusional fantasies, which are, in essence, protective mechanisms. This is why Rose suggests that 'fantasy…can…surface as fierce blockading protectiveness, walls up all around our inner and outer, psychic and historical, selves' and appeals to Freud's notion of fantasies as 'protective fictions,'[9] a notion to which I will return at the end of my discussion of the *Roland* and its uses in the modern period.

THE *CHANSON DE ROLAND*: AN INAUGURAL TEXT

The importance of the *Chanson de Roland* in French literary history is hard to exaggerate. As one of the most widely taught Old French texts, both in France and abroad, its uncontested position at and as the beginning of French literature, is ensured. As the poem's most recent editor observes, mention of the *Chanson de Roland* is enough to provoke a 'deluge' of superlatives: 'the first great monument of French literature, the earliest and the richest of French epic poems, or indeed the best known work of the French Middle Ages, the finest of national epics…it is an emblematic text, a text that offers an origin.'[10]

The *Roland* narrates the story of the battle of Roncevaux. It is set in the eighth century, but composed in the late eleventh or very early twelfth. Charlemagne is withdrawing from Spain after seven years of campaigning against the Saracens. Following a squabble between his nephew, Roland, and Roland's step-father Ganelon, Charlemagne agrees to leave Roland, his companion Oliver and his 12 peers, along with 20,000 men, in the rearguard to protect the army as it crosses the Pyrenees. But in order to take his revenge on Roland, Ganelon betrays his compatriots and the rearguard is massacred, but only after heroic resistance. When he realizes that attack is inevitable, Oliver urges Roland to blow his horn (the olifant) to summon Charlemagne's army back to help: Roland refuses, for to do so would bring shame. But later in the battle, Roland tells Oliver that he will sound his horn, even though they are beyond help, so that Charlemagne might return to avenge them: this time Oliver urges Roland not to blow the horn since to ask for help now would be shameful. But Roland ignores Oliver, sounds the olifant and dies heroically facing the enemy. Charlemagne returns, duly defeats the Saracens, and presides over Ganelon's suitably gory punishment.

The first wave of nineteenth-century scholarship on the *Roland* regards the *épopée nationale* as an oral tradition reflecting a national spirit. It was believed that stories of Carolingian heroism, originally composed by the perpetrators of the great deeds themselves, or by eye-witnesses, were handed down from generation to generation and transformed into songs that became the record of a nation's cultural heritage. The prime exponent of this view, Gaston Paris, famously gave a well-attended, fervently patriotic lecture on the Roland during the siege of Paris in 1870.[11] Paris's ideas dominated the reception of the *Roland* at the end of the century – a period of rampant medievalism in France. In 1880 the *Roland* became a prescribed text in *seconde*, a typical exam question for the *bac* being: 'En quel sens la *Chanson de Roland* a-t-elle pu être appelée nationale?'[12]

The underlying romanticism of Paris's approach was, however, questioned by his star pupil, Joseph Bédier, and it is on the importance of his work on the *Roland* to French literary history in the twentieth century that I wish now to focus. Bédier was born in Paris in 1864 but was taken to the Ile de la Réunion where his family had lived for several generations just months later. He did not return to Paris until he was 18, when he won a scholarship to Louis-le-Grand, he entered the ENS (École Normale Supérieure) in 1883 and became an *agrégé* at the age of 22. When Paris died, Bédier succeeded him as Professor of medieval literature at the Collège de France and there he remained, except for the war years, until he was forced into retirement in 1936.[13]

Bédier was a brilliant man whose work is still well worth reading. He is probably the one single French medievalist to date who has left the most indelible mark on the field, and on French literary studies generally, and in 1920 he was elected to the Académie Française. *Les Légendes épiques*, his magisterial study of French epic poetry – the *chansons de geste* – is a systematic demolition of Paris's account of the *épopée nationale*.[14] Bédier had become increasingly troubled by the fact that he found no evidence for the existence of antecedents of the *chansons de geste*. He was puzzled by their historical inaccuracies and by their palpably written nature. For Bédier, they were written texts, composed by clerks as propaganda for and about the main medieval pilgrim routes: for example, the *Roland* celebrates the significance of Roncevaux, one of the main staging-posts on the route to Santiago. *Les Légendes épiques* was and is controversial. But Bédier's work set the agenda for subsequent research on the *chansons de geste* in that the main issue in the field remains to some extent the tension between the positions of the so-called *traditionnalistes* and the pro-Bédier faction, the so-called *individualistes*.[15]

Despite his rejection of the sort of nationalist reading of the *Roland* proposed by Paris, Bédier's *individualiste* approach turns out to be even more nationalist than Paris's. Bédier was a rabid nationalist, and therefore passionately anti-German. There was, of course, nothing unusual in this. But Bédier's nationalist fervour and germanophobia nonetheless raised eyebrows at the time, and at his own request he was seconded to the Ministère de la Guerre in 1914, where he wrote two widely disseminated and controversial pamphlets on German war crimes and a lengthy history of the French military's engagement in the war, called *L'Effort français*.[16]

Writers about Bédier apologize for this aspect of his career, but nonetheless argue that his scholarly rigour was such that his politics did not impact upon his scholarship.[17] There can be no doubt, however, that Bédier's nationalism does underscore his scholarly work. Thus, to give but one example, in his 1921 Romanes lecture at Oxford, entitled *Roland à Roncevaux*, he greets his audience with a lengthy patriotic elegy.[18] He then explores the significance of the date 1100 for France, failing to mention that 'France' at this point was pathetically weak (scarcely extending beyond the present day Ile-de-France) and that the French king, Philip I, was on the point of excommunication:

> There can, in my view, be no more influential date in French history … in spite of the diversity of its dialects and regional accents, France at the time of the first crusades was also capable of constituting that fine thing, a literary language and a national literary tradition that were original enough from the outset for us to recognize the distinctive characteristics – good and bad – of its creative genius, which were nonetheless humane enough to inspire other civilized nations – not least England.[19]

This claim of French homogeneity *dès l'origine* is of course grounded in the *Roland*. The greatness of the poem, Bédier goes on, comes from *une idée*, namely that God had chosen the French. Soon he is making explicit analogies between the Great War and the *Roland*, appropriating the symbolism of the poppy and the term *champ de gloire* to talk about the text.[20] He concludes, after citing Pascal on *les choses divines* and Corneille on duty, by affirming that the divinest of things is to do one's duty and die for one's county, just like Roland, and his latter-day followers in the Great War.[21] This is typical of Bédier's writing throughout his long career. Furthermore, the references to Pascal and Corneille are typical, chiming well with Bédier's thesis about the *Roland* in his *Les Légendes épiques*, which is that the text is the first – and an appropriately spectacular – manifestation of the French great tradition whose main characteristics would be a classical sense of proportion and restraint, a cult of reason, a willingness to sacrifice the self for duty, particularly for one's nation.[22]

If Bédier's literary criticism partakes of the discourse of nationalist propaganda and contemporary politics, what of his writing about the war? We find, unsurprisingly, that he portrays French troops in a similar light to the thousands of *françeis* who shed their blood for Roland and French officers as latter-day Rolands:

> Question at random one of our veterans about his most vivid impressions of the war. He will not fail to recall, as if it were a naive but touching popular icon, an image of an exemplary officer, whose name he will often have forgotten: this captain, with his sabre raised, cries 'Onwards' to his men!... Thus were our military men... and because they saw them being so brave in battle and so firm but fair in retreat, our soldiers became utterly devoted to them... through them our soldiers formed a link to our ancestors... because of them they discovered, intact and faithfully preserved, their own heritage, namely the warrior virtues of their race.[23]

The echoes not only of the *Roland*, but more particularly of the way Bédier talks about it, are unmistakable here: the bonding between officers and men, the officer who only knows one strategy regardless of the circumstances (attack), the link between the soldiers of today and *les ancêtres*, and above all the love of self-sacrifice are common features of Bédier's writing about the *Roland* and about the war.

Bédier's heroic vision leads him to treat trench warfare with disdain in his book on the Great War. His dismissal of trench warfare tellingly occupies a four-line footnote in a 323-page book, thereby passing over the experience of real French soldiers with astounding alacrity.[24] Whereas Paris had stressed the community of Frenchmen in his account of the *Roland*, Bédier singled out the exceptional Frenchman, standing heroically apart from his men. Collective action becomes but an aesthetic backdrop for the exceptional individual. Thus, when enumerating the number of dead in a 1917 battle in a manner highly reminiscent of the hyperbole of the *Roland*, while also noting that 1200 tonnes of explosive had been used in a single day, Bédier concludes chillingly: 'Ces chiffres monstrueux sont pleins de beauté.'[25]

Now his rhetoric here needs to be seen in context. He belonged to a committee of leading academics that produced a series called *Etudes et documents sur la guerre*. It was chaired by Ernest Lavisse, and its members included Bergson, Durkheim, Lanson and Seignebos, respectively the leading French philosopher, sociologist, literary historian and historian of the period. In 1915 this committee produced a series of nine pamphlets.[26] All these pamphlets follow a familiar pattern: they start out with a statement about the famed neutrality *scientifique* of French academics, give an 'objective' account of the causes of the war, or the issue of Belgian neutrality (to take a few examples), to conclude (to quote Durkheim's snappy phrase) 'C'est donc elle la grande coupable,' meaning of course Germany.[27]

It is interesting, perhaps, to speculate whether Bédier's colonial childhood and adolescence in the Réunion contributed to his strident nationalism. There he followed the same school curriculum as a Parisian schoolboy, and as a 14-year-old his prize for being the best student in literature at the Lycée St-Denis de la Réunion was – what else? – *La Chanson de Roland*.[28] Bédier's early encounters with Frenchness and France are thus of necessity purely discursive, purely fantasmic. All the same, I am less interested in putting him on the couch than in exploring his impact on French literary history and constructions of national identity.

Bédier's association with the other members of the committee that produced the *Etudes et documents sur la guerre* was very close before, during and after the war – particularly with Lanson, the founding father of French literary history. In the early stages of Bédier's career, French *universitaires* were struggling to emulate the German university system. The success of Lanson's move to establish modern French literature as a worthy subject lay in his application to post-medieval texts of what was called 'philology' as practised by French medievalists.[29] His closest medievalist associate was Bédier.[30] For Lanson, literary history was unequivocally a political enterprise: 'nous ne travaillons pas seulement pour l'érudition, ni pour l'humanité; nous travaillons pour nos patries,' he wrote, the purpose being to 'réaliser l'unité nationale' though literary history.[31] Lanson offered an historical account of French literature that led to the replacement of rhetoric in the school curriculum with literary history. But if Lanson was the author of the greater part of this history, Bédier wrote the first chapter. And their narrative has a profound impact on French political fantasies of national identity from the nineteenth century onwards.

The *Roland* was taken as a starting point for a notion of *patrie* that combined the sacred and the patriotic, a notion that was to be imparted to all young Frenchmen. Nowhere is this myth-making more striking than in the writing of the chair of the committee responsible for the *Etudes et documents sur la guerre*: Ernest Lavisse. This eminent historian had a monopoly on the writing of history textbooks in the late nineteenth century, producing manuals that were still in use throughout much of the twentieth. He puts his views on the function of *l'éducation nationale* forcefully:

> To tell the truth, if the school boy does not bear away our nation's glorious past imprinted on his memory, if he does not know that our ancestors fought for noble causes on all their battlefields…if he does not become a citizen imbued with duty and a soldier who loves his rifle, the schoolteacher has been wasting his time. You, children of the people, take note that you learn history in order to learn to love your country. The Gauls, your ancestors, were brave men. The Franks, your ancestors, were brave men. The French, your ancestors, were brave men.[32]

At its inception, French literary studies and the heritage it sought to impart cohered around a narrative with a barely concealed ideological agenda. The coherence of this narrative rested on the positioning of certain texts as foundational in an aesthetic and ideological account of Frenchness that informs the nation's identity. And the most significant of these texts is the *Roland*, which was studied by French *enfants du peuple* as evidence of the valiance of their ancestors, the Franks. In the modern period, the *Roland* becomes a formative text in French national identity and the parallels between Lavisse's writing and Bédier's are instructive. But the symbiotic relationship between literary and other discourses emerges perhaps most alarmingly in the new French military code published in 1913, and in use throughout the Great War: 'L'armée française, revenue à ses traditions, n'admet plus dans la conduite des opérations, d'autre loi que l'offensive.' Moreover, 'Les batailles sont surtout des luttes morales.'[33] The author or authors of this text would have studied the *Roland* in *seconde* and in *terminale*. They seem to have learned their lessons well.

THE RECOGNITION OF HEROISM

But how justified is this francocentric view of the *Roland*? Let us now look at the text itself. Roland chooses knowingly to die. As Oliver points out, if he had blown his horn when first asked to do so, the lives of the men in the rearguard, including the 12 peers, would have been saved. Why then does he act as he does? Roland seems to act for the benefit of absent observers. In the first instance, he performs for Charlemagne, as we see when he admonishes Oliver for urging him to blow his horn: he acts, or so he claims, for Charlemagne's glory. The point is immediately reinforced by Archbishop Turpin, always ready to give God's stamp of approval to Roland's bellicose urges: 'Archbishop Turpin is to the other side: he spurs his horse, climbed to the brow of a hill and calls to the French to give them a sermon: "My lords, barons, Charles left us here. We must indeed be willing to die for our king. Help sustain Christianity!"' (1124–29).[34]

But it is not enough to die for one's king, as Turpin subsequently makes clear: the king must know it. Turpin's prophetic description of Charlemagne and the returning French army dismounting to weep over the bodies of his beloved 12 peers is one of the most moving and engaging passages of this extraordinary poem (1737–52). Summoning Charlemagne back serves no useful purpose for the living. It ensures rather their well-being after death. But what interests Roland here? His main concern seems in fact to be that his reputation as a fearless warrior be recognized, that it be enshrined in a text like the *Roland* itself. Twice Roland refers to his textual future, refusing to act (as he sees it) in a cowardly manner, first so as not to belie his *geste* (or legend) and secondly so as to ensure that no *male chançun* (bad song) is ever sung about him:

> Thus says the count: 'I will not; may God confound me if I belie the *geste*.' (787–88)[35]

> [Roland to Oliver]: 'I will strike with Durendal my sword, and you companion, strike with Halteclere. We have borne them in so many countries and fought to the end so many battles. Bad songs should not be sung about them.' (1462–66)[36]

Roland's actions anticipate a textual future beyond death, one might say the gaze of absent observers, but no one scrutinizes his actions more closely than he does himself as he tries to ensure he gets his destiny right.

In psychoanalytic terms, Roland's desire to die is intersubjective, since he seems to derive pleasure from doing what he thinks others want of him.[37] What he craves is recognition from absent others, who through their absence occupy the position of the Lacanian Other in Roland's fantasmic account of his actions. His audience therefore exists first and foremost in his own mind's eye, which suggests that he himself is the main observer of his actions, which become thereby the object of what Žižek calls his own impossible gaze, impossible since he will not be there to see what he has achieved.[38]

We should note the perversity of this. According to Lacan's definition of perversion, the subject becomes the object of the Other's *jouissance*,[39] which is what happens here. But this leads Roland to behave in a manner diametrically opposed to what we expect from a good military leader, which is that he put his men first.[40] For to behave otherwise would be to belie his *geste*, to provoke vile songs.

Roland's death is then a fantasy in the psychoanalytic sense of a narrative that binds people together, what Rose calls 'psychic glue:' the fantasy is his own, but also the listeners' or readers'. That the poem invites us to identify with the narrative voice that glorifies Roland is beyond doubt. If the characters refer repeatedly to 'our' Frenchmen, to Charlemagne as 'our' emperor, so too does the narrator, as in the very first line: 'Carles li reis, nostre emperere magnes.' The poem posits a 'we,' to which listeners and readers belong, a 'we' that is indistinct from the 'we' used by the characters. It constructs its future listeners and readers as the recipients of the heritage it creates. Roland's fantasy, in other words, is to be shared by the future listeners he anticipates for the *geste* to which he hopes to be faithful. We, as readers of this text now, are potentially at least interpellated by it, part of its intersubjectivity.

It is, of course, significant in relation to the text's success in the modern period that this fantasy involves the construction and defence of territorial borders that only exist by virtue of their defence and to this day the significance of Roncevaux as a site delimiting France is marked by a monument, bearing witness to the fact that the content of the legend may be considered as heritage. Roland's litany of his conquests as he dies addressing his sword Durendal ensures a site where his heroism is recognized and remembered (which we might call France), a grounding for his identity as a chivalric hero. This contributes to the idea that the carnage is meaningful rather than meaningless, but disturbingly raises the possibility of an antecedent groundless, de-territorialized subject. Modern scholars (including Bédier) are therefore not entirely wrong to read the *Roland* as proposing, for the first time, a certain model of French heroism, but it is nonetheless clear that reducing the text to this when the main focus of attention is a crisis in the hero's subjectivity and a desperate, selfish bid for recognition and immortality, is extremely limiting.

CONCLUSION: PROTECTIVE FICTIONS

What lies behind the aesthetic screen of Roland's death? The lyricism and rhetoric deflect our attention from the fact that Roland's brains are supposed, quite literally, to be hanging out, that he is on a battlefield strewn with mutilated bodies. The clear-cut distinction between Saracens and Christians, between right and wrong, is repeatedly and heavily marked in the *Roland*, most famously in the much-quoted line 'Paien unt tort e chrestïens unt dreit' (1015). This is the obscene support of Roland's heroism. What is screened off and not allowed to intrude, however is the real of the carnage that is produced, but then aestheticized into acceptability.

When Žižek writes that 'fantasy is the very screen that separates desire from drive: it tells the story which allows the subject to (mis)perceive the void around which drive circulates as the primordial loss constitutive of desire,'[41] his words are apposite for the *Roland*, whose hero works hard to justify his irrational death drive, thereby legitimizing his death as desire. Formless drive is given coherence as desire. Roland's wish to guarantee the outcome of his own preordained story suggests that he wanted to die all along to ensure the survival of his legend. The circular fictional loop of the *Roland*'s myth-making is apparent in his attempt to invest his sword Durendal, the symbol of his heroic deeds, with precisely the right yet excessive amount of meaning: the song itself testifies to the fulfilment of Roland's desire.

According to traditional literary history, what the *Roland* teaches us is that there can be no greater good than to die for France, which is why it is such a fitting inauguration for 'French literature.' Though expressed in different terms, recent *Roland* criticism clings to the premises that lie behind this view. Peter Haidu, for example, sees in the poem the first articulation of statehood, sovereignty and subjection, so that the *Roland* is no longer simply foundational for modern French national identity, but for the very idea of modern European national identities.[42] But such a reading begs a number of historical questions, as well as the questions of textual interpretation I have already raised.

First, one might ask exactly what is meant by 'douce France' and the *francs* that inhabit it in the *Roland*? The French monarchy in the twelfth century controlled only the area around Paris, so the expanded vision of France that Roland offers is fantasmic, playing upon inaccurate folk memories. The *Roland* offers us little in the way of historical document and much in the way of a twelfth-century fantasy of origins, to which modern readers respond enthusiastically. Furthermore, the text elides the sense of 'Franks' and *français*, even though the former seems to have been a generic term used by all kinds of Germanic peoples about their men. Similarly, to imply that Charlemagne is *français* is probably knowingly controversial, since both the German emperor and the French king seem actively to have sought to claim him as antecedent.

A second set of questions is begged by the text of the Oxford version itself. The manuscript is English and the poem is recorded in an Anglo-Norman dialect, the French spoken by the English ruling classes. Of course it is entirely possible that the Oxford *Roland* represents an Anglo-Norman version of a 'French' poem (whatever we understand by French in the twelfth century), but it is still a little careless of the French to have apparently lost the top copy of *le premier grand monument de la littérature française*.[43] The idea that the *Roland* is a manifestation of coherence and homogeneity in the French literary tradition *dès l'origine* is then quite fanciful, indeed fantasmic. It would seem that at the time of its earliest dissemination, the French were singularly incapable of recognizing *le premier grand monument de la littérature française*, which makes its status in modern literary history all the more remarkable.

Le premier grand monument de la littérature française turns out then not to be particularly French and not to be particularly monumental either. What I am trying to show here is obvious: the present appropriates the past and uses it to justify its own preoccupations and preconceptions. Thus the *Roland* is claimed as an antecedent as much to shape present and future identities of Frenchmen as to preserve the past. As I have tried to show, this appropriation of the *Roland* is in part justified, but in part a misreading, a perfect example of Derrida's faithful infidelity towards heritage.

If the *Chanson de Roland* is part of France's heritage, this is less because it is a real starting point for French national consciousness and identity than because it was monumentalized in the modern period. Many comparable texts continue to languish in obscurity, but they are not part of France's 'heritage' in the same way because they have not been subjected to the same process of myth-making.

I suggested that what lies behind the screen of the fantasy articulated in the *Roland* itself is the 'real' of violence; what may lie behind the screen of the rather different fantasies articulated in modern receptions of the *Roland* and in their broader reverberations in French culture may be the unpalatable truth that French national identity has no ontological necessity. It is thus a protective fiction, a fantasy built on other fantasies to produce an edifice with all the solidity of a house of cards.

CHAPTER 7

CONTESTED HERITAGE AND IDENTITY POLITICS: THE INDUSTRIAL MUSEUM OF SCHLESWIG

THORKILD KJÆRGAARD

INTRODUCTION: HERITAGE AND COMMUNITY-BUILDING

Elsewhere in this book, Denis Cosgrove explores how the Venetians transformed their capital into a particular kind of heritage site, where the serene republic's imperial *spolia* were appropriated to construct a Venetian identity. This chapter deals with the opposite case. It looks at how a particular region in Europe was systematically deprived of any possibility of constructing its own identity through the destabilization and destruction of its cultural heritage.

Beginning with an historical outline of Schleswig-Holstein and its relationship to the neighbouring states of Denmark and Prussia (Germany), the chapter goes on to examine some of the ways in which the development of a local identity was suppressed during the eighteenth and nineteenth centuries. This is a suppression that continues today, I maintain, as evidenced in the curatorial practices of certain Danish museums. By way of a conclusion, the chapter considers the proposal for an Industrial Museum of Schleswig and explores the issues at stake for the survival of a regional heritage.

The emphasis in what follows is thus on exploring 'heritage' as a contested site.[1] What concerns me, in particular, is the crucial role of heritage in the construction and reproduction of identities. There is a copious literature arguing for the imperative to expose the museum's 'unspoken aims and policies,'[2] but there have been relatively few positive proposals for the creation of museums as part of an explicit identity politics. In this chapter, I put forward such a proposal and argue that while unspeakable acts have been committed in the name of nation-states (in this case Denmark and Germany), nationalism and regionalism as interrelated forms of cultural identification can function as important integrating ideologies and provide a crucial 'self-identity.' As Anthony Smith remarks: 'It is through a shared, unique culture that we are enabled to know "who we are" in the contemporary world.'[3] To this extent, at least, my suggestion of establishing an Industrial Museum of Schleswig stands in stark contrast to the 'democratic thought experiment' proposed at the end of this volume by Michael Landzelius. The institutionalization of historical consciousness and the legitimating function of museums, I argue, can become part of a community-building project[4] if its aims are made transparent and it openly acknowledges the connections between aesthetics, politics and curatorial policy.

CONTESTED HISTORIES: SCHLESWIG AND HOLSTEIN

The region in question, some 25,000 square kilometres in size, lies at the bottom of the Jutland peninsula, formerly known as the Duchies of Schleswig and Holstein. This is an area confined on two flanks by sea: to the east the Baltic, to the west the North Sea. To the south, Holstein stretched as far as the city of Hamburg and the River Elbe. The River Kongeå defined the northern border of Schleswig, some 80 kilometres north of the present border between Denmark and Germany. The border between the two approximately equal-sized duchies, which for centuries were closely connected but never united, ran from east to west, along the River Ejder.

This geographical locale has long had a distinct identity, separate from that of its two bordering nations. The region has traditionally been bilingual, and even trilingual. In the south, in Holstein and the southern part of Schleswig, German is spoken, in the north, Danish is the common language, while in the west Frisian, a language related to Dutch, can sometimes be heard. The two dominant languages, however, remain Danish and German. While Danish was and still is widely spoken, German continues to be almost universally understood.

The territory's linguistic composition is a reflection of its cultural diversity, which is a mix of Danish and German, with Dutch elements along the west coast. Schleswig-Holstein's geographical proximity to the Netherlands and the channel region, including Flanders and England, has inevitably impacted upon its development. The region has an impressive intellectual and artistic history, and in the seventeenth century produced many acclaimed scholars, painters and musicians. In the eighteenth century it was strongly influenced by Enlightenment ideas, while subsequently Schleswig-Holstein was open to the influences of the French Revolution and receptive to the democratic tenets of the nineteenth century.

Historically, the two duchies have also had an advanced and prosperous economy in comparison to their neighbouring countries. That this was so, however, is not surprising, given that the nearby channel region had been an economic hub since the late sixteenth century. Agriculture was advanced, but above all Schleswig-Holstein was the workshop of the north and a forerunner of early industrial development. Copper, paper and textile mills, as well as road and waterway construction, were developed very early on. A canal connecting the Baltic with the Ejder, which flows into the North Sea, was completed in 1780. The canal, which more or less defines the border between Schleswig and Holstein, remains an impressive technical feat. Later, steam power, steam ships and railways were rapidly introduced and established a pioneering communications network.[5]

Given this background and the region's numerous resources, one would reasonably assume that Schleswig-Holstein might have developed independent cultural and political institutions, together with an impetus for nation-building, or at the very least a movement for regional autonomy – and indeed, so it has. But this momentum was systematically suppressed by the vigorous nation-building processes of its dominant neighbours Denmark and the German states – above all Prussia, which from 1870 was reborn as the German Empire.

The subjugation of Schleswig-Holstein and the thwarting of any effort to create an independent identity is demonstrated in numerous overt and covert interventions by the neighbouring powers. A few examples will serve to illustrate how both Denmark and Prussia manifestly undermined local efforts to build independent cultural, social and political institutions that might other-wise have nurtured and promoted a strong regional or even national identity. If a cultural heritage is systematically destroyed, it follows logically that the formation of any enduring, deep-rooted identity is effectively curtailed.

Events in the seventeenth century, a period of early nation-building in Europe, provide a good example. Under the protection of Sweden, which competed with Denmark for the political hegemony of Northern Europe, the Duke of Gottorp, based in the city of Schleswig (which owed formal allegiance to Denmark) acquired increasing influence and opportunities for political aggrandizement during the 1620s and 1630s. In 1658 Denmark, following its defeat by Sweden, was compelled to recognize the Duke's full independence. The newly autonomous Gottorp Court was small but highly competent and ambitious. It became a 'cultural court' of a type familiar elsewhere in Europe, particularly in Italy. Numerous artists, architects, scientists and writers were attracted to the city of Schleswig, enticed by favourable economic prospects and a climate of intellectual activity. In particular, the Castle of Gottorp became the epicentre of a cultural ferment on an even par with some of the greatest cultural centres of Europe, making important contributions in the fields of art, history, architecture, geography and the natural sciences. The castle was rebuilt and adorned with one of Europe's most elaborate baroque gardens.[6] Along with the development of what in the nineteenth century might well have become specific Schleswigian or perhaps Schleswig-Holsteinian national symbols, the Gottorp dukes contributed much to the development of governmental and other social institutions, as well as to the economy of the region. New towns were founded, and an independent postal service established. Meanwhile, early industrial development took place with the creation of brickyards, copper mills and textile factories. These initiatives were boosted by a significant influx of Dutch and French immigrants, some of them refugees from religious persecution, who were invited to settle in Schleswig. At the same time agriculture was modernized, and the Gottorp government sought to attract international trade, exploiting its favourable geographical position between the Baltic and the North Sea.

The sophisticated and prestigious Gottorp Court, which rapidly gained a European reputation, was the target of a hostile Danish foreign policy, which was bent on its destruction. The moment came in 1721 after the Great Nordic War. Following decades of setbacks, Denmark was restored as a leading power in Northern Europe. Sweden could no longer protect Gottorp. The Duchy of Schleswig, together with the possessions of the Duke of Gottorp, was incorporated into the kingdom of Denmark. The symbolic apparatus which had developed during Gottorp's independence was dismantled, and the system of government destroyed. Nothing tangible remained: paintings, furniture, silver and tapestries were transferred to Copenhagen, where they remain to this day in the museums of the Danish capital and its environs. The majestic park around Gottorp Castle was laid waste, a huge sculpture of Neptune, symbolizing a land between the waters, was wrecked and submerged in the garden lake, from which it was recently recovered. Every effort was made by Denmark to eradicate Gottorp from history. This annihilation of Gottorp in 1721 is, to my knowledge at least, one of the most radical and brutal examples of the elimination of any cultural heritage in early modern Europe. To find an equivalent example one might turn to the total destruction by the Red Army of Königsberg (today Kaliningrad), the epicentre of Prussian culture, in 1945.

For the rest of the eighteenth century Denmark attempted, not without a certain degree of success, to annex Schleswig and Holstein culturally through what might be described as a policy of intensive identity engineering. Numerous books, including school textbooks, were sponsored by the government in Copenhagen to prove that the two duchies shared a common cultural and historical identity with Denmark and that, as a consequence, integration was natural, even inevitable. For a while these efforts appeared successful. Schleswig and Holstein became ever more closely connected to the Danish kingdom; a vast, homogeneous state-system that then encompassed Norway, as well as Iceland, Greenland and a number of minor colonies in America, Asia and Africa.[7]

The Duke of Gottorp had long gone, and all that remained in his place were local princes, who were tolerated as long as they remained powerless and loyal to the Danish crown. Danish success, however, was to prove only temporary, and during the nineteenth century Danish hegemony was challenged. Nationalistic ideas, which had spread throughout Europe after the French Revolution, gained a strong foothold in Schleswig and Holstein. Nationalism provided the population with a unifying ideology and it was mobilized with a religious zeal. The region's independence and its golden age in the seventeenth and early eighteenth centuries were remembered. This memory became a spur to the reinvention of an independent Schleswig-Holsteinian state.

As throughout Europe, 1848 was a decisive year. The Schleswig-Holsteinians declared themselves independent. The brother of the Duke of Augustenborg, a minor local prince, spurred on by the prospect of becoming the leader of Schleswig-Holstein, agreed to head the revolt. After three years of civil war, however, Denmark succeeded in crushing the insurrection. The Augustenborgs were sent into exile and their ducal stronghold in the town of Augustenborg, which had, like the Gottorp Court of the seventeenth century, been a significant cultural court, was confiscated.[8] Ultimately the castle was turned into a lunatic asylum by the Danish state. As it had done 130 years earlier, Denmark endeavoured to eradicate the independent culture of the region by undermining a major site of cultural heritage and an important symbol of regional identity. In 1721 it had been the palace of the Gottorp dukes, now, in 1850, it was the seat of the Augustenborg family.

There were other forces apart from Denmark working to undermine any movement towards the creation of a separate identity for Schleswig and Holstein. In the nineteenth century Prussia began to interfere in the region's internal affairs. Between 1848 and 1850 Denmark had been instrumental in crushing regional autonomy, but soon afterwards Prussia assumed a dominant presence. In 1864 Bismarck's Prussia declared war against Denmark, and after a short, bloody war Schleswig-Holstein was annexed by Prussia. This was in accordance with the wishes of many Schleswig-Holsteinians, who were exasperated by Denmark and held out hopes that Prussia might offer them greater freedom. They were sorely disappointed, however, when they realized that Prussia was no more inclined than its predecessor to accept Schleswigian or Holsteinian independence. Prussia transformed Schleswig-Holstein into a highly controlled province ruled directly from Berlin.

The incorporation of the region by Bismarck's centralized state, and the suppression of any attempt at developing an independent cultural identity, is clearly demonstrated by the events surrounding the fate of what was, undoubtedly, the region's most prized collection of archaeological artefacts, which had been amassed over two decades since the civil war of 1848–50. Flensburg, the biggest of the Schleswigian towns, housed the Flensburg Collection, which contained many valuable objects, such as the so-called 'Nydam Boat' from the second or third century. In the same way that Denmark had unscrupulously ransacked the region's cultural heritage in the past, appropriating potent symbols of local identity, now Prussia was to do the same. The Flensburg Collection, removed by the Prussians in 1864, was destined never to return. The magnificent archaeological trophies were transported to Kiel and Berlin and the collection dispersed.[9]

At the Conference of Versailles after World War I, it was decided that the Schleswig-Holstein question should be resolved through a referendum. The people of the region would be given the opportunity to choose between Denmark and Germany, a schema which was in accordance with President Wilson's ideas of national self-determination along the lines of language affiliation. The choice presented, however, was premised on a gross simplification of the region's history. The delegates at Versailles ignored any possibility of there being a third way: the kind of compact represented by the Swiss Federation; a bilingual or even trilingual Schleswig-Holsteinian state or, as seemed more likely in 1920, a Schleswigian state in a loose confederation with Denmark or Germany, or an autonomous region under the protection of the League of Nations. An independence movement that might have been mobilized to fight its cause – including the farmer Cornelius Petersen's Schleswigian 'home rule movement,' which became a regular threat to the Danish state in the 1920s – was effectively bypassed. After the referendum, which took place in early 1920, the old Duchy of Schleswig was divided. As predicted, the northern, Danish-speaking part, voted for Denmark, while the southern, German-speaking part voted for Germany. Holstein remained German without a referendum.[10]

The division of Schleswig and the ensuing incorporation of the northern part into Denmark and rest to Germany was considered to be the final and just solution to a long-standing problem. In the following years Denmark and Germany both eagerly supervised the newly acquired provinces. Separatist movements were feared, and when they occasionally appeared, they were ruthlessly suppressed. In north Schleswig, the part that went to Denmark, great efforts were made to extirpate any remaining trace of Schleswigian independence. The newly acquired lands, which had never formed part of the kingdom of Denmark, were reorganized according to Danish administrative practices.[11] As far as culture is concerned, the region's museums were systematically appropriated by Denmark, in much the same ways as the Estonian, Latvian and

Lithuanian museums were recast as Soviet after their incorporation into the Soviet Union in 1945. A new history for a newly imagined country, which would be 'forever Danish,' was invented: Sønderjylland (Southern Jutland).

TELLING SILENCES: DISPLAYING THE PAST

A good example of Denmark's manipulation of regional history after the 1920 referendum is provided by the Museum of Sønderborg Castle, in the town of Sønderborg, where the director of the day, Jens Raben, translated the original protocols of the contents of the museum from German into Danish, and subsequently burned the old protocols. Thereafter, Sønderborg Castle has been a quintessential symbol of Danish identity. When one strolls through the museum today, one is presented with an exhibition of Denmark's seamless history that stretches from the Middle Ages to the present day. At no point is the visitor made aware of the region's contested past or, for that matter, of the fact that the historical tableaux might obscure a more complex picture of the area's fraught history. Had it not been for the systematic suppression of regional independence by the Danes and Germans, Sønderborg Castle might well have found itself at the centre of an independent Schleswigian or Schleswig-Holsteinian state. The ancestors of the local people are glibly dismissed as 'enemies;' the insurgents of 1848 being enemies of the Danish state. Every trace of 'otherness' has been suppressed, in a political act of amnesia, to the extent that captions accompanying the exhibition are in Danish and English, rather than in the two languages of the region, Danish and German. No acknowledgement is made of the bilingual character of the town of Sønderborg, despite the fact that the offices of the German-language newspaper of the area lie only 500 metres away. We are a long way here from the kind of self-reflexive, politicizing strategies discussed by James Duncan in his chapter on the Maritime Museum in Greenwich.

Much the same situation can be seen on the German side, although perhaps not to the same degree. Under the Weimar Republic, any attempt at expressing a local identity was forcefully opposed, as it was to an even greater extent under Hitler's Third Reich. Since the creation of the German Federal Republic in 1949, German policy in relation to the area has been less prohibitive, and has even encouraged the celebration of local differences. Thus, in contrast to the Danish situation, the information provided for visitors at the Schleswig-Holsteinisches Landesmuseum at Gottorp is both in German and Danish, an implicit acknowledgement of the region's individual and bilingual character.

In much Danish propaganda and, to some degree in German propaganda, the 1920 division of Schleswig is referred to as the 'reunification,' a peaceful resolution of a potentially explosive Danish–German issue. From the perspective of the local population of Schleswig, however, the division of Schleswig was experienced as a traumatic split of ethnic groups, which had peacefully coexisted since medieval times. Furthermore, the division of the old Duchy of Schleswig had a detrimental economic effect, dividing a formerly prosperous region and imposing the added burden of cross-border taxations. A once economically and culturally thriving region has been transformed into a moderately successful but hopelessly marginalized area at the southern periphery of Denmark and the northern periphery of Germany.

CONCLUSION: A POSITIVE INTERVENTION

Notwithstanding this almost total eradication of local history, some efforts are being made to preserve and bolster a regional identity and to celebrate the area's heterogeneous heritage, both artistic and industrial. A brief but splendid effort was the 1997 exhibition Gottorf im Glanz des Barocks.[12] However, a more enduring manifestation of the region's contested heritage would be achieved by the implementation of a recent initiative aimed at establishing an Industrial Museum of Schleswig. The museum would serve a dual purpose: it would both celebrate Schleswig's heritage and commemorate the industrial revolution in Northern Europe more generally. The proposal is to establish an independent museum to showcase the highlights of the region's industrial history. To this extent, it would function as an explicit community-building project, with overt and acknowledged political ends. The museum would openly seek to legitimate a cultural heterogeneity that has been disavowed for centuries. While the vast bulk of academic literature on heritage and museum studies has been devoted to critiquing the legitimating function of museums, I would argue here against the grain that museums can perform crucial functions in laying the cultural ground for inclusive and energized politics.

An ideal joint location for the museum would be two impressive industrial monuments in the area: Kupfermühle in Wasserschleben, Germany, and Cathrinesminde in Broager, Denmark. The former is a large copper mill founded in the middle of the seventeenth century, an important centre of early industrial development, currently owned by a local museum association. The latter is a former brickyard founded at the beginning of the eighteenth century, which is currently part of the Museum of Sønderborg Castle. These two industrial plants lie only a few kilometres away from one another and are both situated in the heart of the region, close to Flensborg Fjord. They constitute an axis surrounded by a number of satellites, ranging from harbours, to agro-industrial sites, timber yards, canals and textile factories.

A museum of this kind would create a broad and varied picture of the rise of industry in the region over past centuries. It would provide a heritage site, which could, in due course, serve as a much-needed focal point for the reinvention of a Schleswigian identity and contribute to the empowerment of a population that has been culturally and economically marginalized. Democracy as a political system requires such an open politicization of culture and the nurturing of a communal identity for its effective operation, a fact readily acknowledged by the EU. An Industrial Museum of Schleswig would support and promote regionalism and regional ideas in Europe, one of the central pillars of the European idea as it is embodied in EU policy. Indeed, it is to be hoped that the EU will support the project so that the former Duchy of Schleswig may at last celebrate an economic and cultural heritage that has been suppressed for so long.

PART III:

PLACING HERITAGE

CHAPTER 8

HERITAGE AND HISTORY: A VENETIAN GEOGRAPHY LESSON

DENIS COSGROVE

The wide-ranging debate over the politics of heritage joined in recent years signals history's sometimes unwilling theoretical engagement with post-structuralism and postmodernism and its practical engagement with the realities of a post-colonial, polyvocal and globalized world. Heritage, one might say, signifies the decolonization of the past. Today's hybrid cultures and flexible or multiple identities, constructed and transformed more and more through acts of consumption, release new politics of self-registration and performance. Little wonder that the museum has become an open and contested space.[1]

The genealogy of the museum itself tracks the cultural evolution of modernity through nationalism and imperialism: from the Baroque *Wünder-kammer* where humanist collectors sought to create order and identity from disconnected but fabulous fragments arriving from conquered 'new' worlds, through the great 'national' institutions of late-eighteenth-century London and early-nineteenth-century Paris and Berlin, where imperial states competed as global cultural cosmopoli, to the 'folk' museums which naturalized more demotic, ethnically founded nation-states of the early twentieth century. Today, as singular, nation-based and territorially circumscribed identities fragment and individuals adopt multiple and mobile senses of self, the role of the museum as a place for fixing and legitimizing diverse and localized social identities increases and intensifies, despite criticism and deconstruction of the museum as an institution. In the UK, for example, over 75 per cent of the 1450 museums currently open were founded after 1970; 838 have opened since 1960 compared with only 215 during the entire nineteenth century.[2] Unsurprisingly, as James

Duncan argues elsewhere in the present volume, there is a simultaneous collapse in agreement over the artefacts and narratives appropriate for display by museums, over their rights to possess and give voice to the past.

Arguably, all this is an example of how 'geography' – locational aspects of the displayed past and of those who bear witness to it – has increased in significance, as 'history' – the documented and agreed narrative of the past – has declined. It is this relation, of geography and history that I shall explore in this chapter. To do so, I shall use the example of Venice, an officially designated World Heritage Site,[3] formerly one of the Europe's most historically enduring polities and, in the view of John Ruskin, a founding figure in heritage conservation, a city located geographically at the meeting point of Europe's three great cultural streams: Classical paganism, Christianity and Islam.[4] Before turning to Venice specifically, however, I want to consider the epistemological relations between history, heritage and geography a little more fully.

HISTORY, HERITAGE, AND GEOGRAPHY

History as we understand it today – a formalized, scholarly discipline – is essentially a text- and language-based study whose origins lie in Renaissance humanists' attempts to overcome what they took as the myth and fancy of medieval chronicles and establish a more objective record of the past. The historian places faith primarily in the written record, the archive of written sources, whose genesis may be properly authenticated, dated and con-textualized, originally by philological, today by more varied and scientific, techniques. The more continuous and objective the record, the more historically 'reliable' the account based on it should be. And the account of historical truth itself takes the form of text or narrative which, in turn, is judged in large measure by faithfulness to 'the record.' Documentation matters even more than the disinterestedness of the historian, for the rhetorical dimension of historical writing has always commanded a degree of respect – although when historians stray too far into imaginative or literary composition they risk critical attack, as the career of the historian Simon Schama attests.[5]

Heritage is not history. People do not write, read or relate heritage. Heritage is, rather, curated and conserved, possessed and performed. Heritage is arte-factual more than textual; it is realized in material objects such as works of art or craft, tools and buildings, sites, special places and even whole landscapes, or else it is performed in speech or dress, in ritual, ceremony, dance or song. A manuscript may be a vital source to the historian because of the written infor-mation it records of the past. As heritage, its material existence, measured by age, connections to other items and above all by its capacity to connect past to present interest, is what gives it significance. As David Lowenthal has insisted, because the totality of the past can never be preserved, heritage is inevitably fragmentary: a disconnected element of a formerly encompassing life.[6] While the historian seeks to connect what is also a fragmentary record into either causal explanation or narrative description, the fragmentary nature of heritage is essential to its definition; its connections are determined above all by their contribution to the formation and maintenance of identity in the present. Heritage is received from the past by an individual or group; it is the past's gift to the self-ascription and integrity of that individual or group today. Thus, the test of heritage is its authenticity: through it the present 'touches' the past. What Walter Benjamin recognized as the defining feature of an artwork in an age of mechanical reproduction is true also of an item of heritage: its 'aura,' its capacity to offer a direct, unmediated link to an original maker, determines its value.[7] This, together with the artefactual and performative nature of heritage, means that heritage is inevitably and specifically 'located.' Location and human identity – 'place' – determine the meaning and significance of heritage. This becomes immediately apparent when an item of heritage is translocated, hence the argument over the return of museum items transferred from their originating place and people.

And, arguably, heritage is always in some respect translocated. Consciousness of something as 'heritage' implies its actual or potential removal, either by temporal hiatus or, more politically fraught, by a conquering invader. Conventionally, in battle and warfare, *spolia* were the most precious objects of the conquered, items whose removal and display by the conqueror bore material witness to the changed relations of victory and subordination between the parties; hence the desire by the conquered to reverse the process and recapture the aura of its heritage. The modern usage of 'spoil' as both noun and verb conveys exactly the social relation involved in the politics of heritage. Place and time of origin constitute the vital elements of aura and authenticity, which constitute heritage. Heritage is thus bound to its geography, and landscapes have a special significance within heritage debates. The case of Venice offers a powerful example of the social processes and meanings involved in the geography of heritage.

VENICE AND THE LANDSCAPE OF HERITAGE

Venice is a focal point in the evolution of Europe's heritage landscape, since the city's material landscape was the object first of conscious heritage construction by Venetians and subsequently of veneration by others. The city has been a principal destination for cultural tourists from across Europe since the seventeenth century, and thus the location for some of the earliest debates over the meanings and value of heritage. The great sites of Venice that today attract a ceaseless stream of visitors and an equally continuous flow of anxious debate over their protection were themselves constituted from fragments and references of an earlier past, from the *spolia* of Venetian conquest and the invented traditions of Venetian cultural history. Thirteenth-century Venetians built a civic landscape from the looting of Byzantium, fifteenth-century Venetian humanists and artists created the modern graphic vocabulary of the *locus amoenus*, landscape of an imagined past, imperial Venice in the sixteenth century defined lagunar space as *terra sancta nostra* – sanctified place and community – by combining elements of natural landscape with a highly imaginative past. When the Venetian Republic was itself defeated and despoiled by Napoleonic France, Venice emerged as a principal *lieu de mémoire* in the age of Romantic nationalism. Through the poetic writings of Northern Europeans, Venice's stones helped shape the principles of heritage for a modern world. The continuous reworking of the past as heritage within the Venetian lagoon, which I summarize here, serves at once to exemplify and to complicate the ways in which a landscape is mobilized as heritage for social, political and cultural ends.

VENICE AND BYZANTIUM

Historians date the height of Venetian prosperity and political power to the century following the fall of Constantinople to the Ottomans in 1453. These were the years of 'imperial Venice,' when the city dominated trade in the Eastern Mediterranean as the principal European organizing centre for the overland spice and silk from Asia, competed as a major actor in the geopolitics of the continent, and constructed much of the architectural landscape visible today along the Grand Canal and in the Piazza di San Marco. Reading the texts of Venice's first historians, such as Contarini, Sanuto and Bembo, who wrote at this time, or the rhetoric of its public buildings, Venice's cultural debt is first to Greece (although not to Athens) and then to Rome.[8] St Mark's body, buried in the basilica named for the evangelist and the heart of its civic landscape, had supposedly been 'translated' from Alexandria; his church and the Doge's Palace for which it serves as chapel gesture east to Byzantium. Rome provided the imperial vocabulary for the later state offices, library, mint and loggetta, which define the borders of the piazza and piazzetta. The relations between these two cultural sources determine the visible landscape of Venetian heritage.

Standing among the pigeons in St Mark's Piazza today and looking towards the church at its head, prime objects of the tourist gaze are the four gilded horses prancing above its arched portals. Most tourists know from guidebooks that these bronze sculptures date from the ancient world. Brought to Venice in 1204, they were removed to Paris by Napoleon and returned after the fall of his empire. But the horses visible from the square today are merely copies, substitutes for the regilded originals now protected in a special room above the church. This example of fragment, mobility and deceptive appearance typifies Venetian heritage. Less familiar to the tourist is the fact that the bronze horses, together with the winged lion that rides atop his column at the edge of the lagoon, are merely the most eye-catching elements of a landscape of Byzantium scattered through the public spaces of Venice. The fourth crusade, proclaimed by Pope Innocent III in 1198, but diverted from its Holy Land destination under the leadership of the Venetian Doge, Enrico Dandolo, attacked and pillaged Constantine's imperial capital in 1204, systematically looting its antiquities, relics and treasures. As the art historian Patricia Fortini Brown points out, in the looting, Byzantium bronzes were especially vulnerable to destruction; vast numbers were melted down for their monetary value, much of the resulting coinage ending up in the treasury of St Mark.[9] The horses and lion, together with the four porphyry tetrarchs placed adjacent to the basilica, were the only large items to be taken whole to Venice, most of the loot arrived as fragments. Over the succeeding two centuries, a fatally weakened Byzantium, battling Ottoman power, sold and pawned much of the remainder of its moveable treasure, mainly to wealthy Venice, to finance the declining empire's military defence.

For the Venetians, Byzantine *spolia* provided materials for the *renovatio imperii christiani*, the supposed renewal of the city as a bulwark of Christendom in the face of a resurgent Islam. The idea was based on the fabrication of a past for the basilica, in which the tale of the translation of the evangelist's body played a key role. *Renovatio* was achieved through the politics of heritage: by working late-antique and Byzantine elements into the decoration of the most public building in the city, the basilica. These elements included both actual fragments and decorations taken from the Greek city, and imitations 'ranging from obvious copies to totally convincing fakes.'[10] By the mid-thirteenth century:

> …no Venetian walking in the centre of his city could fail to be aware of Byzantium. It was like a museum of Byzantine artefacts and souvenirs. The Piazza had been paved with red bricks set in a herringbone pattern. Dominating the façade of St Marks were the four gilded bronze horses, the first and grandest of the secular trophies brought from Constantinople… Quantities of marble of different colours and columns, especially of porphyry, imported from Constantinople added to the` grandeur of the reconstructed church. Such was their influence on Venetian art and

taste at the time that it is now difficult to tell which of the column capitals came from Constantinople and which were local work.[11]

The haul of material treasure taken from Byzantium was not merely material, it included sacred relics whose role in the renewal was as significant as the architectural appearance of the city. St Mark's reliquary was enriched by a phial of Christ's blood, an arm of St George and a part of John the Baptist's head, among other items of sacred heritage.

The fate of Byzantine *spolia* within medieval Venice indicates something of the enduring nature and uses of heritage. While undoubtedly much of the wealth looted went into private pockets – melted down for coinage, reset for personal jewellery or sold on for immediate gain – the conscious transfer to Venice of key items such as antique statues, architectural fragments and holy relics, and their placement within public spaces, were regarded as principled acts of civic responsibility. Identity as a worthy citizen of the republic was reinforced by contribution to *renovatio*. Half of the 600 columns on the basilica are of Byzantine origin, together with many of the facing slabs that decorate its walls, donations of soldiers and merchants. These, together with the monumental bronze and stone statuary, proclaimed to citizens and visitors in the most public location that Venice was successor to Byzantium, heir to its sacred and secular aura. Material fragments of an imperial Christian past are woven into a landscape that reworks as it revalidates the Venetian past within a rhetoric of continuity.

Fortini Brown has examined this thirteenth-century *renovatio*, which included the reshaping of the open areas of the piazza and piazzetta into an articulated civic space based on the ancient imperial forum, in terms of a distinctive Venetian sense of the past. This, she suggests, arose from the embarrassing fact that Venice, unlike every other Italian medieval city-state, had no Roman lineage upon which to base either its Christian or humanist claims to foundation and identity. Venice was thus obliged to invent a past, and in this the discontinuity and fragmentation of objects, as well as their very materiality, took on a particular significance. The Venetian sense of the past brought together two concepts of time inherited from antiquity. Firstly *kairos* in the sense of time as opportunity or propitious moment, and secondly *chronos*, time as eternal and continuous. This helps us understand the combination of actual *spolia*, fake antiquities and relics in Venetian heritage. Historical continuity (*chronos*) was represented by authentic fragments from Rome's eastern successor and would later be invented by chroniclers (suggesting for example that the original Rialto predated Romulus and Remus). *Kairos*, the propitious or opportune moment, was suggested by the miraculous survival of a fragment and its incorporation into the physical landscape, by the miraculous event such as St Mark's trans-lation, or the survival and recovery of a holy relic. In all of this, the historical veracity of an element in documented time was less important than its material existence in the present moment, thus the forging of so many 'antiques' was not a matter of deception so much as of demonstration. As Fortini Brown puts it:

> ...the special quality of the *renovatio* of the thirteenth century was of a *venezianità* grounded in what might be called an 'aesthetic of diversity.' It rested upon two major principles: accumulation, or aggregation, and incorporation. Tangible works that can be seen and touched - buildings, spolia, mosaics, sculpture, artifacts - were more powerful than texts in creating a civic identity of a reassuring historical density, for they were unmediated testimony: unprovable, thus unchallengeable.[12]

In this construction of a civic identity, two elements are worth noting particularly: the significance of 'autopsy,' seeing for oneself or touching the evidence of the past, and creating coherence out of its inevitably fragmentary nature. In both of these, geography and landscape played a critical role, and these would be enhanced within the specific evolution of Venetian humanism.

HERITAGE LANDSCAPE

A more financially productive gain by Venice from the weakened Byzantium was various islands and enclaves in the eastern Mediterranean. Principal among these was Crete, purchased for 1000 marks in August 1204. The Venetians would hold the island until 1669. Crete not only became one of the republic's most financially rewarding and agriculturally productive colonies, but it also served as a geographical heritage, suggesting to Venetian humanists possession of a direct connection to the Classical past. Among humanists and artists, Crete became imagined as a *locus amoenus* or place of imagined harmony between nature and human life. The significance within the Venetian Renaissance of Byzantine scholars such as Manuel Chrysoloras and others who relocated from Constantinople to Venice following the Greek tragedy of 1453, is well documented. Chrysoloras's scholarship emphasized the material survival of antiquity in the form of monuments and ruins rather than the textual record favoured by Petrarch, and the Greek's work was a foundation for archaeology. This approach to the Classical past held understandable appeal to less bookish artists, architects and travellers.

Among the last, Cristoforo Buondelmonti has a particular significance. In 1414, armed with Ptolemy's newly translated *Geography*, he undertook a journey through the Aegean in search of Greek texts, the most influential of his finds being Horapollo's *Hieroglyphica*, significantly a work that relates to inscriptions on stone. Equally important were the inscriptions Buondelmonti himself transcribed from sarcophagi and tablets. His search took him through the ruins of ancient cities and landscapes and was described in his *Liber insularum archipelago*, or book of islands, the first of a new and particularly Venetian form of geographical treatise. In it, Crete holds a special place as the island of Homer's 'hundred cities' whose combination of topographic beauty, ancient ruins and contemporary fertility rendered it, in Buondelmonti's eyes and descriptions, the paradigm *locus amoenus*. In this pastoral retreat a fecund nature softened the ravages of time in elegiac classical ruins, which in Crete offer an alternative, Greek, location to Pliny's Tyrennhean coast.[13] This landscape heritage would become a central trope of Venetian villa art of the succeeding century.

Locus amoenus depends precisely on the fusion of the natural world and past human presence, the ghosts of place. Activating *genius loci* in the design of landscape gives evidence of *chronos* in the mythic sense captured by the Latin phrase *in illo tempore* ('once upon a time') and of mythic geography too ('in a country far away'). Such activation was the task of Venetian artists and writers through the sixteenth century: from Giovanni Bellini and Giorgione to Titian and Veronese, from the *Hypnerotomachia Poliphili* and Sanazzaro's *Arcadia* to Bembo's *Asolani* and Gallo's villa writings. But *kairos* too plays its role here, for it was the fortunate conjuncture of space and time – their possession of sea and land empires – that allowed Venetians the opportunity to recreate *locus amoenus* in their own landscape. The tangible, witnessed presence of the Classical heritage of landscape would be actualized both within their own insular and lagunar space – *terra sancta nostra* – and on the *terra firma* to which their financial and cultural investments were increasingly directed in the sixteenth century.

The role of fifteenth-century painted images illustrating sacred events in the Venetian townscape as 'eye-witness' evidence of their actual historical occurrence has been amply demonstrated by Fortini Brown in an earlier study.[14] That function of the image as 'autopsy' was carried over to the landscape paintings, the *delizie* (mansions) and the villa designs of the following century. In Luigi Cornaro's descriptions of villa life in the gentle hills and reclaimed plains of the Padovano, or in his schemes for perfecting shape of the city within a reclaimed lagoon, as well as in the images of sixteenth-century map-makers from de'Barbari's image of 1500 onwards, we see Venice represented as a perfected realization of the Classical landscape ideal, the presiding genius of lagunar nature realized in the civic perfection of *terra sancta nostra*. The Classical heritage of landscape, naturalizing the republic's constitution, was a key element in the 'myth of Venice' which defined civic identity during the imperial phase of Venetian history.

THE STONES OF VENICE AND A NATIONAL HERITAGE

The Venetian myth of permanence ordained by nature and realized in its inheritance of Classical political virtues was brought to an end in 1794 by Napoleon's armies. Long one of the gaudiest stops on the European grand tour, the city was immediately transformed by English Romantic painters and poets into a symbol of the heritage of liberty extinguished by imperial France. Byron, Wordsworth and Samuel Rogers all found in Venice a *lieu de mémoire* whose passing and continued material presence spoke to contemporary concerns. Thus Byron:

> ...thy lot
> Is shameful to the nations – most of all,
> Albion to thee: the Ocean Queen should not
> Abandon Ocean's children; in the fall
> Of Venice think of thine, despite thy watery wall.[15]

It was precisely this sentiment that John Ruskin would adopt and expand in his three-volume *Stones of Venice* (1851–53).[16] This hugely influential work opens with a dramatic statement of heritage values:

> Since the dominion of men was first asserted over the ocean, three thrones, of mark beyond all others, have been set upon its sands: the thrones of Tyre, Venice and England. Of the First of these great powers only the memory remains; of the Second, the ruin; the Third, which inherits their greatness, if it forget their example, may be led through prouder eminence to less pitied destruction.[17]

On the basis of a forensic examination of the principal public buildings of Venice, which produced fierce criticism of standard nineteenth-century restoration techniques, Ruskin not only developed his thesis of Venice as a moral heritage and lesson for modern Britain, but worked out principles of architectural and landscape conservation that became a foundation for heritage politics throughout the twentieth century. Above all, the chapter entitled 'The Nature of Gothic' in Volume Two, printed as a separate text by William Morris's Kelmscott Press in 1892, articulated Ruskin's belief that the material remains of the past possessed an integrity which demanded their protection as sacred relics, to be revered but not violated by any modern intervention.

This preservationist (as opposed to conservationist) approach to heritage was undoubtedly a response in part to Victorian methods of 'restoration,' but it was also consistent with Ruskin's embrace of Romantic nationalism, which proposed that the character of nations was rooted in their physical geography and that their cultural landscape reflected an enduring, transhistorical national identity. Their landscape was thus their principal heritage. Ruskin had developed this argument in his first published essays on *The Poetry of Architecture*, and in one of the most powerful passages in 'The Nature of Gothic' he takes the reader on a flight over Europe, from Mediterranean shores to polar ice, noting how every aspect of physical landscape, climate, vegetation, fauna and flora change in harmony with the shifting latitude. Finally, Ruskin invites us to observe and rejoice in the ways that the human art and architectural heritage of each region also corresponds in form and spirit to the 'gradation of the zoned iris of the earth;' they are 'the expression by man of his own rest in the statutes of the land that gave him birth.' [18]

This is of course an intensely political construction of cultural heritage. Not only does it use the legacy of architecture and art to fix and naturalize a map of European national identities, it mobilizes Britain's northern, 'Gothic' heritage specifically within a critique of modern urban and industrial society. Ruskin's argument was closely attuned to the nationalist sentiments of European states in the closing years of the nineteenth century and would remain over the first half of the twentieth. His writing was thus hugely influential. The sectionalism and historical incoherence of such heritage claims have been amply deconstructed over recent years. Contradictions are apparent even within Ruskin's own corpus of writings: the cultural and linguistic hybridity which in his view undermined the integrity of Swiss domestic building, when observed in Venice, is taken to underpin the glory of its architecture as the confluence of Classical, Christian and Muslim culture; the Doge's Palace is figured by Ruskin as the 'central building of the world.'

CONCLUSION

The tensions exposed within the meanings of heritage, between locational stasis and temporal process, apparent in both the Venetian landscape treatment of the past and Ruskin's subsequent representation of Venetian landscape, have a general significance. The heritage artefact or performance, preserved and curated, can be treated as a tangible link with past time and as a confirmation of enduring identity in a volatile present. It can be made to bear witness to the past through autopsy: eye-witness evidence. Mapping identity through heritage in this sense fixes its geography and justifies a politics of restitution and 'museumization,' for example demands for the restitution of the *spolia* of European empire today. That feature of Venetian time denoted by *chronos*: enduring, mythic time is evident here. By contrast, the very survival of an object deemed to be heritage, its inevitably fragmentary nature, acts as testimony to change: temporal process and chance, destruction and survival. From this perspective, heritage does not offer autopsy, but rather it opens a space for imagination, for mapping the fragment into a contemporary space made up of many such fragments, authentic or fake, reworked through the creative powers of memory, as the Venetian use of their Greek 'inheritance' reveals. Preserving the heritage fragment inescapably involves its relocation, reconstruction and re-presentation within the different landscape of the present. This permits a more active and dialogical politics of contested, flexible identity. Here is time conceived as *kairos*, opportunity to be seized and shaped for the future. Both perspectives on heritage generate their characteristic geographies: the former characteristically composed of bounded, containing spaces, the latter of connections, nodes and networks. As the Venetian geography lesson demonstrates, these may coexist as well as contradict each other, but the outcome is always a political space.

CHAPTER 9

THE HERITAGE OF THE BISMARCK NATIONAL MONUMENT IN THE WEAVE OF HISTORICITY

KAREN LANG

We know of course that the past consists not of crown jewels that belong in a museum, but of something always affected by the present.

Walter Benjamin (1923)[1]

INTRODUCTION: MONUMENTALITY AND THE NATION

For the art historian Richard Muther, 'The nineteenth century knew only the monument and the monument was everywhere' in Germany.[2] This was especially true at the end of the century, when the unification of the nation by Bismarck in 1871 and the death of the former chancellor in 1898 stimulated an output of monument production in keeping with the pace of industrialization itself. As the countryside became overrun with Bismarck towers, monuments to local and national figures were erected in urban centres and city parks. The new genre of the German national monument was accorded special significance after 1871. Rising above the cacophony of local and individual histories, the national monument proved a useful focus and stimulus for feelings of patriotism and national identity. In order to achieve this emotional effect, political, regional, and religious differences had to be subsumed into a 'national' German style.

Thomas Nipperdey defines the national monument as 'an attempt to make manifest national identity in a visible, lasting, and tangible symbol.'[3] The national monument is comprised of both manifest symbols of nation, and less well-defined notions of national identity (*Nationalbewußtsein*). In the national

124

monument the constellation of abstract ideas comprising *Nationalbewußtsein* must be translated, first of all, into concrete symbols of the nation. Secondly, and even more importantly, if the monument is to fulfil its function, these ideas about the nation must be grasped by the beholder. The aesthetic problem of the national monument is, then, how to channel an abstract notion of national identity so that it will be received in the intended fashion by every beholder.[4]

National monuments, memorial prints, pictures in magazines and souvenir postcards served to symbolize and advertise the nation, thereby creating and disseminating an image of the nation to the widest possible audience.[5] That monuments, in particular, could invoke an emotional response from the viewer made them especially useful instruments with which to foster a sense of national identity. In order to evoke an emotional response, the national monument sought access to 'irrational elements.' Eric Hobsbawm suggests that after the 1870s, 'and almost certainly in connection with the emergence of mass politics, rulers and middle-class observers rediscovered the importance of "irrational" elements in the maintenance of the social fabric and the social order.'[6] The 'irrational elements' of German myths, legends, and symbols were therefore deployed in this period as an appeal to the German citizen who, it was hoped, would emotionally vacate the actual reality of *Gesellschaft*, the contemporary industrial society, and join the community or *Gemeinschaft* of common senti-ment for a shared Teutonic past. A common past was further underscored at this time through the celebration both of previously established rituals and of 'invented traditions.'[7]

Not surprisingly, Bismarck, founder of the Reich, became the most popular subject for the German national monument.[8] Unlike monuments to the Kaisers Wilhelm, the Bismarck monument addressed the citizens of the newly unified nation, the *Volksnation*. A uniquely German form was therefore sought for these monuments, one which would convey a new and particular sense of Germanness (*Deutschtum*) to the 'imagined community' of the nation.[9] In keeping with the tenor of the times, the German national monument had to be monumental in scale. When Arthur Moeller van den Bruck declared in 1916 that 'monu-mentality is a manly art,' he not only referred to a contemporary trend toward colossal dimensions in German architecture and monuments.[10] He also, and more importantly, alluded to the manner in which scale, simplicity of style, unity and mass translated into a monumental effect, which would warn or remind the viewer of the concentrated power of the nation. To be sure, 'the human, all too human, had no place within the confines of such an art.'[11] Just as the Bismarck national monument advertised the nation through the commemoration of the man who had created it, so these monuments addressed the citizen rather than the individual. If monumental character was better conveyed through pure mass and form than through ornament or content, then this presentation was likewise fitting for a national shrine.

The 1907 competition for a Bismarck national monument on the Elisenhöhe, near Bingerbrück on the Rhine, not only reheated debates on how best to represent the man who had unified the German nation. Bridging the first decades of the new century, the Bingerbrück competition likewise revealed the strain of a new nation that, like Janus, looked simultaneously forward and backward and was therefore at odds with itself over its own representation. To be sure, the contentious debates over form and monumentality surrounding the 1907 competition reveal a disunity within national culture.[12] If this interplay of unity and dissent can be said to represent the making and unmaking of a German heritage centred around Bismarck, a 1990 exhibition at the German Historical Museum entitled 'Bismarck – Prussia, Germany, Europe' displayed the past in the service of a unified history of the reunified nation. In this exhibition, Bismarck monuments – including written documents, maps and sculpture – were interwoven with discourses of nationalism so as to create unity through symbolic form. Focusing on the 1907 competition and concluding with the 1990 exhibition, this chapter examines the heritage of the Bismarck national monument in the weave of historicity.

SIEGFRIED CONTRA FAUST: THE 1907 BISMARCK COMPETITION

The monument complex at Bingerbrück, scheduled to be unveiled on the centennial of Bismarck's birth, 1 April 1915, was intended as the definitive commemoration of the Iron Chancellor. This competition represents an unofficial, non-government-sponsored attempt to produce a marker which would nevertheless become a definitive national statement, one that would shape national consciousness, and in so doing, would serve the ends of an 'official' national self-representation. That such a competition could be conceived without government support is not surprising when one considers the power and nationalist orientation of the Bismarck cult at the turn of the century – Bismarck, it seems, would never die.[13] Indeed, the Bingerbrück complex was conceived as ur- and meta-monument at once: in its conception and display, the monument had both to locate and represent the origins of the ruler in the mists of a Germanic past, as well as allude to a deeper unification – the so-called national goal of Germany (*Nationalziel*) – set in train by Bismarck but not possible during his lifetime.[14] Within this very obligation lies the Germanic (*völkisch*) and the monumental, the past, present and future, the need for a new form, and thus the complicated representational node around which this contentious competition turned.

The chosen location for the monument, a hill called the Elisenhöhe overlooking the Rhine, was an area rich in German history and historic monuments. The historic remains of the area date back to the Roman Empire; the concentration of these traces gave this site a particularly 'Germanic' resonance. In an article written during the preliminary stages of the monument competition, the editor of the *Deutsche Bauzeitung* introduces the site to the reader with an evocation of its important remains, including the palace of Karl the Great, the towers of Mainz that 'shimmer in the distance' and thus 'remind one of the battles of the Middle Ages,' as well as the various and highly treasured Burg ruins.[15] In featuring the Rhine, symbolic marker of Germany's western border in the popular imagination, the location also, and more crucially, referenced Germany's chequered relations with France and thus the history of the German nation and its unification.[16] The potential symbolic power of the location was further made manifest when it was pointed out that this location 'must be viewed as an important connecting link between the southern Germanic and the northern Germanic tribes (*Volksstämme*).'[17]

Since this 'monumental landmark' was to be a pilgrimage site 'not for the single individual or for small companies (*Scharen*), but also for continuous festivities to which many thousands from the entire country would come together,' it was stipulated that the monument 'fully masters the festival plaza.'[18] The focal point of the monument, whether directed toward the festival plaza or outward, facing the Rhine, was left up to the individual competitors. It was declared, however, that 'decisive weight' would be placed on a design that could be seen from the Rhine and so have an effect from a distance, as well as an effect from directly below the Elisenhöhe.[19] The visible parts of the substructure were to be of greywacke or quartzite, 'Germanic' materials of the surrounding area. No instructions were given for the form of the monument, but the cost of execution was not to exceed 1.8 million marks.

The competition call, open to all Germans, was published in the middle of September 1909, and in November of the following year 379 entries were registered. On 22 January 1911 the members of the jury visited the site. The jury not only consisted of artists and architects, but also of scholars, gallery directors such as Alfred Lichtwark of the Hamburg Kunsthalle, and, 'as a guarantee that the decision would not be the eccentric judgment of aesthetes,' prominent men from the fields of industry and business, such as Dr Walther Rathenau, a board member of the powerful electrical firm AEG.[20] After a thorough visit of the site, the jurors concluded that 'special value [would] be placed on making sure the monument fitted into the landscape,' and more decisively, that 'any attempt to

9.1. Hermann Bestelmeyer (architect) and Hermann Hahn (sculptor), 'Siegfried Dolmen,' 1911. Competition drawing. Illustration from *Deutsche Kunst und Dekoration* 27/6 (March 1911), p.437.

achieve an effect through excessive proportions [would] not meet with the jury's approval.'[21]

After much deliberation the prizes were announced on 26 January 1911, and a few weeks later the competition entries were exhibited in the Kunstpalast, Düsseldorf.[22] 'Siegfried Dolmen,' the relatively modest design by the sculptor Hermann Hahn of Munich and the architect Hermann Bestelmeyer of Dresden received first prize (figure 9.1). In the Hahn and Bestelmeyer design a circle of four German linden trees lines the inside of the 50-metre-wide granite temple, in the centre of which a 10-metre-high statue of the young Siegfried is reflected in a large basin of water (figure 9.2). A portrait relief of the chancellor is placed on the back wall of the monument, facing the festival plaza. His memorable phrases were to be etched at the top of each of the temple's 18 pillars.

Nothing here is arbitrary: every element of this monument has symbolic meaning in the German context. Along with the oak, the indigenous linden tree was considered a symbol of the German territories. The circular ring of granite was likewise regarded as a primal 'Germanic' form. Finally, Siegfried is none other than the protagonist of the Niebelungen saga. Siegfried, here wrapped in a lion skin and testing the blade of his rather long, upturned sword refers to 'the fateful position of the German people [*Volk*],' which have been 'led by Bismarck to new, greater deeds.'[23]

While Bismarck had been likened to Goethe in the realm of literature, he is here likened to Siegfried in the world of myth. In this genealogical construction the figure of Bismarck takes on the qualities of the hero of the Niebelungen saga, who had created a magical sword with which to kill a threatening, two-headed dragon. As Siegfried, 'Bismarck becomes the latter-day mythical hero who

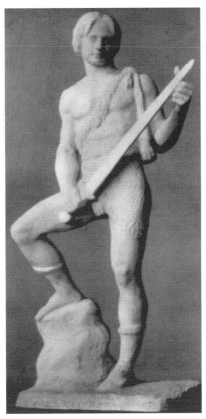

9.2. Hermann Hahn, 'Siegfried,' 1911.
Competition maquette. Illustration
from *Die Plastik* 3 (1911), plate 18.

forged an invincible sword out of the small German states, slayed forever the
two-headed dragon of internal dissension and external threat, and so raised the
hoard of German unity.'[24] With allusions to both myth and history, the
conflation of Bismarck and Siegfried extended the genealogical line of the
chancellor into the earliest days of a Germanic past, and provided mythological
precedents and historical legitimacy for his actions. The use of the linden trees,
the circular dolmen and Siegfried likewise demonstrate how symbolic forms
and mythological figures were becoming highly charged with nationalism at the
turn of the century.

'Siegfried Dolmen' won particular favour by the jury on account of the
'excellent qualities of the design,' and because it was felt that the monument fit
well into the landscape, like 'a crown on the head of a hill.'[25] Further described
by the jury as an 'old Germanic hero monument, a simple stone circle with an
architrave,' the Hahn and Bestelmeyer design seemed to offer an authentic

'Germanic' form, yet one which simultaneously referred to Hellenic precedents. The association of the Germanic with the Hellenic in the form of a German national monument is but a more recent incarnation of the popularity of the Hellenic for the *Bildungsbürgertum*, or educated bourgeoisie. As Eliza May Butler's classic study of 1935, *The Tyranny of Greece over Germany*, demonstrates, the educated elite had been enchanted by the ancient Greeks since the mid-eighteenth century, when Winckelmann began his love affair with Greek sculpture.[26] In an important recent study, Suzanne Marchand focuses on the intellectual climate and cultural institutions which mediated German philhellenism throughout the following century, examining how Grecomania became more deeply woven into the fabric of German intellectual and literary life through classical education in the *Gymnasien*, the development of archaeology as a practice and a field of study and the establishment of museums of ancient artefacts.

In short, German Grecomania was

> …the self-congratulatory obsession of the liberal *Bildungsbürgertum*. [Consequently,] the story of philhellenism's decline is closely bound up…with the waning of the liberal nationalists' ability to impose this taste on the rest of their countrymen and to retain control of philhellenism's institutional manifestations…[By] the turn of the century, philhellenism had become a defensive aesthetic conviction, which the *Bildungsbürgertum* had to renew in order to confront the threat that the wider reading public might desert their Graecophile cause and with it the whole series of institutions which had grown up to tend this passion.[27]

Marchand provides the cultural and intellectual context with which to understand the choice of a 'Hellenic' design for a German national monument, and offers a clue as to why the liberal and highly educated Lichtwark and Rathenau should have advocated such a design. The Hahn and Bestelmeyer entry certainly brought together the 'Germanic' and the 'Hellenic' in a design appealing to their philhellenism. Moreover, this relatively modest design also made a new and 'modern' statement, one which linked modernity with the classical past, thereby providing the nation with an appropriate and venerable history in representational form.

The selection of 'Siegfried Dolmen' created an immediate and loud outcry among artistic circles and the general public.[28] If, for jury members Lichtwark and Rathenau, the less bombastic Siegfried was a welcome change, since it 'captured Bismarck more immediately' than 'all the painfully embarrassing, stylized idols' or 'disgraceful markers (*Schandmäler*) of the current artistic taste,'[29] the majority violently disagreed. Critics and the public, who made their opinions known in letters and in self-styled 'town meetings,' repeated a similar refrain: 'the relation to Bismarck was negligible' and the design demonstrated 'elegance but not strength.'[30] Consider the words of the critic Max Osborn:

A Bismarck monument whose main motif is not strength, but - elegance! It would appear as an Easter egg to the Rhine farers below…No, here a wholly other note must be struck! Not subtle delicacy of taste but sustained strength must here reign. A work that, without cheap '*Volkstümlichkeit*,' will fix itself without hesitation in the memory of the nation as a symbol of the colossal life's work.[31]

What was clearly at issue here was the incommensurability of the Hahn and Bestelmeyer design with the 'essence' of Bismarck and the national profile of militant strength begun under his tenure as chancellor. The young Siegfried was simply not a powerful enough symbol, and as for the quasi-Hellenic 'old Germanic hero monument,' it was neither suitable nor sufficiently monumental. While artistic worth was praised by the jury, the nation wanted monumentality, by which was meant a representation of sheer power with which to reflect the desired profile of the powerful nation, or *Machtstaat*.[32] Only such militant strength could express their version of Bismarck and his 'colossal life's work' in 'a sublime expression of veneration.'[33]

What actually constituted such sublimity was 'Faust,' an entry by Wilhelm Kreis, which had originally received a mere consolation prize from the jury.[34] (figure 9.3) Art critics rallied round this design, plucking it from obscurity and making it the paladin of their cause. Described by the jury as 'a kind of modern Pantheon,' Kreis presents a memorial hall with a monument in the interior, a fully architectural conception which he considered a wholly new design.[35] Kreis's

9.3. Wilhelm Kreis, 'Faust,' 1911. Competition drawing. Illustration from *Deutsche Bauzeitung* 45/21 (15 March 1911), opposite p.172.

plan indicates a memorial hall 60 metres high, or twice as high as the palace in the capital city of Berlin. From his work on the Bismarck towers, Kreis had learned that in the open landscape a 'cubistic mass, as equally wide as tall, produced the greatest and clearest effect.'[36] Following this principle he set his memorial hall on an exceedingly broad and massive foundation that extended in terraces down the Elisenhöhe. Two colossal stone eagles flank the memorial hall at the front, overlooking the Rhine.

A six-metre high statue of Bismarck by Hugo Lederer confronts the viewer on the interior of this 'modern Pantheon' (figure 9.4). In this Egyptian-inspired form, Bismarck is seated on a throne, right hand resting on a globe and clothed in a simple toga and sandals. Lederer's gigantic statue of Bismarck as God and king at once is an expression of sacred and temporal power whose message would surely not be missed. Placing the statue on the interior of the memorial hall, Kreis sought to capture the full attention of the beholder. According to him, this Bismarck 'in the interior of a solemn temple' would 'shake the viewer to his depths,' leaving an 'indelible impression like no monument outside could do.'[37]

In writing about the inspiration for his memorial hall, Kreis provides a laundry list of models 'which offer the correct form by which we can still find

9.4. Wilhelm Kreis, 'Faust,' 1911. Interior view with sculpture of Bismarck by Hugo Lederer. Illustration from *Deutsche Bauzeitung* 45/21 (15 March 1911), p. 177.

the sublime today.' It becomes clear to the reader that what Kreis means by 'correct form' is an appropriately Germanic form at 'one with the landscape,' one that 'united with nobility and beauty, exerts power over us.' Beginning with the acropolis, Kreis moves on in his article to the Castel del Monte, which he praises as a 'German landmark on foreign soil.' The author saves his greatest laudation for the mausoleum of Theodoric in Ravenna, however, informing us that this important building 'has become a pilgrimage site of all German architects.' In a deft sleight of hand, Kreis joins the present with the past: Theodoric 'was a hero somewhat in the manner of Bismarck, and ... this, his building, arising in the culture of the antique and produced from the nature of the strong *Germanen*, can serve us as a model for the expression of every art with which we honor Bismarck.'[38] Kreis thus locates 'Germanic' form in the south, a gesture which may seem forced to the reader of today. Yet it was just these 'southern' forms, most particularly the mausoleum of Theodoric, which provided the kind of massive, architectonic precedent for what were considered essential qualities of German monumental art.

If the Hellenic overtones of 'Siegfried Dolmen' were said to represent a 'false Teutonic style,' then Kreis's design was the epitome of 'a truly Germanic art.'[39] The term 'Germanic art' was variously defined in this period, yet contemporary commentators seemed to agree that central to this conception was 'intensification through opposition,' or 'mastery of the mass.'[40] An ardent supporter of the Kreis design from the outset, Albert Hofmann dedicated a long and lavishly illustrated serial article to the competition in *Deutsche Bauzeitung*. Rather than focusing on the Hahn and Bestelmeyer design, Hofmann presents the reader with its counterpart in the competition entry by the architect Hermann Billing and the sculptor Hans Bühler. Here we are also presented with a circular temple, yet one whose sublimity turns on intimidation. The proportions of the Billing and Bühler monument are indeed staggering, as the relatively microscopic human form next to the left pillar of the entranceway to this shrine makes clear.

On the same page in which this entrance to the Billing and Bühler temple is illustrated, Hofmann implies that if Greece was the seat of the 'Germanic' for the jury, then the monumental architecture of ancient Egypt, Assyria and Rome provide the best illustration of the 'mastery of the mass in the service of a mostly sacral, therefore sublime thought.' It appears that for the editor of *Deutsche Bauzeitung*, and for the supporters of the Kreis and Lederer design in general, monumentality meant not only colossal dimensions, but also forms which would 'shake the viewer to his depths.' For those in favour, Kreis and Lederer presented a 'monumentum *aere perennius*,' a timeless conception that expressed 'the longing of our time in which the work of the Bismarck will find its completion.'[41]

The debate concerning the prize-winning design raged for months. Because the outcry was so great, the artistic committee met at the end of May to decide upon a future course. It was agreed that a selection of approximately 80 entries would be displayed for six weeks, beginning on 1 June, at the Paulinen Schlosschen in Wiesbaden. It was hoped that Kaiser Wilhelm II would visit the exhibition during his stay in Wiesbaden to attend the annual *Festspiel*, thereby lending a seal of monarchical validity to a competition that had become nothing short of a 'tangled labyrinth,'[42] a condition resulting in a decrease in monetary support for the national monument on the part of the German *Volk*. The Kaiser, however, declined on the pretext that he was 'booked' during his stay in Wiesbaden, a gesture which added insult to injury since it was well-known that he did not approve of the jury's selection in the first place.[43]

Since it was repeatedly stressed – in a variety of ways – that this competition was 'first of all an opportunity for the nation, and only secondarily, one for the artistic community,' it was decided that only a second competition could rectify the mistakes of the first. To this end, the 20 prize-winning participants were given the chance to rework their designs, to be delivered by 1 November, with particular instruction to 'bring the figure of Bismarck more into appearance;' in addition, a final caveat was stated: 'the use of an ungermanic (*unvolkstümlichen*) symbol would certainly not help' garner approval by the jury.[44] The decision of the second competition was essentially the same as the first, the only change being an 11–5 vote for the Hahn and Bestelmeyer design.[45] Because the jury had once again failed to give the nation what it wanted, the executive committee convened in early December, deciding unanimously in favour of the execution of the Kreis design, a decision heralded as a 'blessing for German monumental art.'[46]

It is not without coincidence that the decision of the executive committee for a more imposing design fell during the second Moroccan crisis. A time, in other words, when it was felt within Germany that the country was both beset and virtually without allies. This feeling of isolation and impuissance was translated, it seems, into the urge for an overcompensating, monumental profile, as if the nation could erect in stone an advertisement of what it could not sustain in reality. Kreis's second design remained similar to his first, though he did reduce his pantheon from the original 60 to 27 metres, or roughly the height of the Berlin Palace. Despite the decreased dimensions, the reworked plan lost none of its monumental effect or its popularity with the public.

In the new conception, a statue of Hagen and one of Siegfried stood on either side of the entrance to the memorial hall as 'complementary representations' of the 'character of our Germanic tribe (*Volksstammes*).'[47] As if referring to the Great War ahead, a battle relief was placed above the portal. The head of a soldier in 'demonic form, displaying all the passions of battle,'[48] served as a capital on each of the 12 pilasters on the exterior of the temple. On the interior, the seated Bismarck remained along the periphery, 'mahnend und warnend' ('admonishing and warning'), eyes fixed ahead as if gazing into 'our' future.

The bitter dispute over the Bingerbrück competition led some critics to question whether it was possible to erect a national monument at that time. This most recent fiasco seemed only further proof that 'the national spirit of Germany lay in a difficult opposition with itself.' As a result, the country had 'no uncontested national shrine, no uncontested national heroes.'[49] In the face of this lack grew an ever-greater need for the creation of a national rallying point, and Bismarck became the figure around which the nation could rally. For the dissenting members of the jury and the 'nation,' Bismarck was not the young Siegfried with the 'noble head,' a 'youth fit to fight,' yet one 'paired with intellectual power.'[50] Their Bismarck was the man who could declaim in an 1887 speech in the Reichstag, 'We Germans fear God and nothing else in the world.' It was this image of the chancellor, and of the country he had created, that they wanted to see represented in their national monument.

In the words of Walther Rathenau, the majority in 1911 wanted '"their Bismarck," as they aggressively call him, as Colossos, as Memnon, as Buddha, as Zeus incarnate.'[51] Rathenau's words echo those of Aby Warburg, who, in his commentary on the Hamburg Bismarck of 1906, had pointed to just such a 'my Bismarck, our Bismarck' as the lowest level of aesthetic desire.[52] Rathenau's remark, moreover, points to the desire to deify Bismarck and to represent his apotheosis in colossal dimensions. This urge toward monumentality marked the age. Referring to the Bismarck national monument at Bingerbrück, Paul Cassirer ironically describes how the 'wanderer who came up the Elisenhöhe was supposed to step into a shrine, was supposed to be seized by the shudder which the memory of a great dead man produces, was supposed to find a thing that was a symbol of the greatness of Bismarck.'[53]

For Cassirer, the desire for giganticism was the result of the recent and radical changes wrought by technological and industrial advances in Germany. In no other land had the 'external possibilities... so rashly changed,' he writes, 'except perhaps in America.' The '*geistige Kultur* could not keep pace with the external changes,' and so 'because the poets could not comprehend, they ventured on the greatest plans, because the architect could not build a farmhouse, he built colossal cathedrals and palaces.'[54] While Cassirer finds the origins of the urge toward monumentality in the 'external changes' resulting from advances in the technological and industrial spheres, one must also point to the political and social spheres. Social divisions, unrest and political defeat created a monumental unease, which likewise found expression in the colossal. If, according to

Nipperdey, 'monumentality serves the myth making of the nation,'[55] it also served to paper over the divisions in the now 'united' German nation.

In *Der rheinische Bismarck*, Rathenau goes on to make a Nietzschean comparison between the *Unreife*, the immature ones desirous of 'their Bismarck,' with the *Reife*, the mature ones who understand that it is 'not enough to produce a work which pleases the majority in 1911;' that a 'work which merely pleases the masses of the present time will never outlast the ages.'[56] On this score, it seems, Rathenau was wrong. Though the outbreak of World War I in 1914 brought the plans for the Bismarck national monument to a halt, the monument did have a brief afterlife in the Nazi period. The design selected by the Nazis was neither 'Siegfried Dolmen' nor 'Faust,' but a plan by Ernst Petersen originally overlooked by the 1911 jury. Petersen was aided in his work by Wilhelm Kreis and Alfred Fischer, and on 15 February 1933 work began on the monument with 335 men of the so-called voluntary labour service (*Freiwilligen Arbeitsdienstes*).

The new monument complex was divided into two parts: an *Ehrenhof*, or honour court, dedicated to the western regiments who had fought in the Great War, faced the Rhine, slightly below burned an eternal flame; a gigantic sports arena, the 'Platz des Deutschen' ('Plaza of the Germans') intersected the *Ehrenhof* at the back. Between these two parts, an interior court was planned that connected the marching grounds with the parking area. As if echoing the jury of 1911, the layout of this design was especially praised for 'linking the monument most favourably with the surrounding nature.'[57] For the reporter of 1933, the bend where the long axis of the Ehrenhof meets the cross axis of the stadium 'takes on the hardness and strength of all monumentality.'[58] While the Nazis did not select Kreis's 1911 design, they nevertheless commemorated the Iron Chancellor with a colossal form whose monumentality advertised the strength of the *Machtstaat*.

THROUGH THE EYE OF BISMARCK: MONUMENTS FOR A NEW GERMANY

The debates over form and design for the Bingerbrück competition provide a glimpse into German national representation at the turn of the century and into the Nazi era. The disputes over the Hellenic and the monumental reveal a strain toward consensus rather then a coherent image of national culture. While the jury had requested a work of less than colossal dimensions, the majority of the competition entries exhibit staggering proportions. Such monumentality was also favoured by the 'nation.' After his death, Bismarck had likewise grown to mythic proportions in collective memory. Only a colossal form, it seems, could match such a mythomorphosis. As synonymous with the German nation – both present and future – Bismarck's stature could only grow greater, as the nation itself inched closer to the national goal set in train under his tenure as chancellor. According to this logic, the Bismarck national monument had to be monumental.

Just as Bismarck had become synonymous with the German nation for the German citizens, so he himself becomes internalized in the representation of nation that is Kreis's memorial hall. In this design, Lederer's statue of Bismarck is encrypted within the memory of nation, a memory memorialized here with Kreis's 'modern Pantheon.' Symbolically, Bismarck rests within the nation as its own interiorized or ur memory. The viewer, who would have made his or her way up the Elisenhöhe and onto the monument complex, would have been confronted in this instance by a colossal symbol of the German nation. The nation memorialized here has exceeded its founder in strength and succeeded him in time. Bismarck, founder of the German nation, nevertheless remains a part of the story, as he is given symbolic form – even if that form is not as immediately visible as the national pantheon wherein he rests.

Although at times overshadowed by his own accomplishments, Bismarck, the historical figure, would nevertheless remain an integral protagonist of German history. In the inaugural exhibition of the German Historical Museum, founded shortly after the German unification of 1989, we are presented with national culture presided over by the 'eye' of Bismarck. In digitized monumentality, Bismarck's rastered eye announces the exhibition 'Bismarck – Prussia, Germany, and Europe,' held at the Martin-Gropius-Bau, Berlin (25 August–25 November 1990). Noting the purpose behind the exhibition, curator Christoph Stölzl comments in the preface to the catalogue: 'No one has thought of erecting a new monument to Bismarck. "Enlightenment and understanding" of a common past – that is the motto of the German Historical Museum.'[59] Perhaps. Yet Bismarck is memorialized here not only in the turn-of-the-century monuments erected to him, but also in the choreography of the exhibition itself. Indeed, the 'eye' of Bismarck, which serves to advertise the exhibition, is also its central organizing principle.[60] The visitor in the vicinity of the museum would not only have been confronted by the metaphorical gaze of Bismarck, but also, by allegorical extension, the gaze of the nation. As the visitor entered the vestibule of the museum, the torso of a model of a monument by Reinhold Begas directed 'the line of sight to the exhibition.'[61]

Once inside, monuments continued to play a predominant role in the exhibition. In the words of the exhibition designer, Boris Podrecca, the ramp leading up to the final room

...reifies the 'legend' that Bismarck became in his own lifetime as a national cult figure. It takes the viewer through the stations of the monuments erected to him. This change of levels makes the message easier to understand without having to resort to any additional technique and at the same time neutralizes the heroic element by penetrating it optically.[62]

Or does it? On one level, at least, the staging of the exhibition replicates a turn-of-the-century German experience of pilgrimage to the site of the monument (in this case the museum) and of an ascension up to the monument itself (in this instance, the ramp that conveys the viewer to the highest room, which concludes with a bust of Bismarck, who stares down into the exhibition space below).

While attempting a critical presentation of Bismarck's legacy, 'Bismarck – Prussia, Germany, and Europe' unwittingly provided the newly united Germany with its own monument to Bismarck, and to the history of German unification: Bismarck, in other words, as central protagonist in a new German national family romance of nation, culture, politics, and victory.[63] In 'Trafficking in History,' Patrick Wright comments on the consequences of a timeless history versus an active historicity:

Abstracted and redeployed, history seems to be purged of political tension; it becomes a unifying spectacle, the settling of all disputes. Like the guided tour as it proceeds from site to sanctioned site, the national past occurs in a dimension of its own - a dimension in which we appear to remember only in order to forget.[64]

If the weave of historicity can be read in the fault-lines over monumentality and form in the 1907 competition, an uncontested history appears reinvigorated in the 1990 exhibition. Here a Nietzschean monumental history triumphs over the present, the local and the individual. The path to nationhood leads through the eye of Bismarck rather than through the darker corridors of the German past: Bismarck as national culture for a reunited Germany.

CHAPTER 10

'TEUTONIC' LANDSCAPE HERITAGE: THE SEARCH FOR NATIONAL IDENTITY IN EARLY-TWENTIETH-CENTURY GERMAN LANDSCAPE DESIGN

JOACHIM WOLSCHKE-BULMAHN

This chapter explores ideas about a national, 'Teutonic' heritage and considers the impact of these ideas on concepts of landscape design in early-twentieth-century Germany, particularly during the period of National Socialism. My aim in the pages that follow is to elucidate some of the ways in which heritage has been mobilized in Germany to bolster reactionary political ideas. At the same time, I examine how specific ways of seeing the German past have been connected, historically, to particular ideas about landscape design.

The first part of the discussion traces the development of a German nationalist ideology through the nineteenth century and shows how ideological concerns were reflected in early-twentieth-century German landscape design. The second part takes three specific sites as case studies to illustrate the general point: two cemeteries and the Sachsenhain or Grove of the Saxons, a gathering place for Heinrich Himmler's SS.

The two cemeteries, the so-called Ahnenstätten (Places of the Ancestors) were used by the Deutschvolk-Gemeinde (German People's Parish), an organization which had close ties to the Tannenbergbund (Tannenberg League) a group founded by the celebrated World War I general, Erich Ludendorff (1865–1937). The specific historical context of these commemorative projects was the importance attached to the ancestral German land by Nazi ideologues. As Simon Schama has observed, it was Rudolf Darré, the Minister of Agriculture and the man who coined the Nazi slogan 'Blut und Boden' ('Blood and Soil'), 'who pushed for a policy of *Naturschutz* (Protection of Nature) as a state priority.' Moreover, this conservationist drive was intertwined, as we shall see, with a celebration of the ancient Teutonic tribes of Germania, which the Roman historian Tacitus described in the first century AD.[1]

All three sites functioned as places of commemoration and were inscribed with highly symbolic and ideological meanings. But how were these spaces made to manifest their symbolic content? In what follows I attempt to answer this question and explore some of the ways in which design helped to transmit particular ideas about race, nation, nature, German history and German landscapes to their users. It should be noted here that terms such as 'race,' 'people' and 'nation,' were not used in any well-defined way, but were often interchangeable. Personally, I reject the use of the term 'race' and concur with Stephen Jay Gould when he asserts that it represents 'an outmoded approach to the general problem of differentiation within a species.'[2]

GERMAN LANDSCAPE DESIGN: THE SEARCH FOR A NATIONAL IDENTITY

The designs of the three sites in question, the Grove of the Saxons and the cemeteries of Seelenfeld and Hilligenloh, can only be fully understood if they are considered within a specific German historical context: namely, the search by reactionary German groups in the early twentieth century for an 'authentically' Germanic or 'Teutonic' history.

The search for a national identity gained momentum, at least in Europe, during the eighteenth and nineteenth centuries. In Germany this was closely linked to a re-examination and celebration of 'nature.' Particular natural settings, it was argued, reflected a genuinely Germanic character and provided evidence of the nation's uniqueness. George Wilhelm Friedrich Hegel (1770–1831) maintained that a 'people' could claim the status of a 'nation' only if it could establish an indisputable link with the natural environment.[3] Accordingly, a nation was an organic social formation that reflected the deep reciprocal bonds tying people to their homeland. The search for national identity corresponded 'with a very specific aesthetic of nature. The nationalization of history corresponded with a nationalization of nature.'[4]

Evidence of national identity was sought not exclusively in the Middle Ages when nations were formed, but also in prehistoric times. The ancient Germanic tribes stood for 'authentic' Teutonic traditions. The dilution of this original Germanic culture and 'race' were deemed to have taken place in the wake of invasions by so-called 'non-indigenous' populations, beginning with the Romans two thousand years before. As a consequence, German culture had to be restored to an alleged state of original, prehistoric innocence. Ideas about nature and the history of the nation became intertwined in the thinking of people who set out to substantiate the superiority of the Germanic people. Nature and history merged into a seamless continuity, since the Teutonic people were seen as living in harmony with nature.

This ideological preoccupation with the German past was to have a profound impact on garden design. Hegel and other German intellectuals disseminated ideas about an organic unity between the German landscape and German history. Their ideas were further developed in works such as the well-known book *Contributions to an Instructive Garden Art for Incipient Garden Artists and Garden Enthusiasts* by the landscape gardener Friedrich Ludwig von Sckell (1750–1823), which called for the use of 'patriotic species' of trees and shrubs for particular places,[5] 'plantings of "patriotic character,"' 'simplicity,' and 'patriotic pictures.'[6]

Alexander von Humboldt (1769–1859) was also to shape attitudes to natural garden design. In his *Ideas for a Physiognomy of Plants*, published in 1806, Humboldt referred to 'patriotic plant characters'[7] and discussed the formative influence of a country's vegetation on the development of its distinct culture. According to Humboldt, 'the knowledge of the natural character of different regions of the earth (is) most intimately connected with the history of the human race, and with its culture.'[8] Humboldt argued that

> The character of a people, the gloomy or happy mood of mankind [is] mainly dependent on climatic conditions…The poetic work of the Greeks and the harsher singing of the Nordic primitive people owe their peculiar character in large part to the form of plants and animals, to the mountain valleys which surrounded the poet, and to the wind, which blew around him.[9]

Humboldt attached great importance to the outer appearance of plants, their physiognomy, and held that this had a determining impact on the character of a people. Moreover, these ideas were major influences on the landscape architect Willy Lange's (1864–1941) conception of natural garden design, which was based largely on Humboldt's doctrine of plant physiognomy.[10] Lange was arguably the most important promoter of natural garden design in Germany in the early twentieth century.[11]

Around the turn of the eighteenth and nineteenth centuries, the search for national identity among German intellectuals was more or less progressive in character. The yearning for national unification was the principal driving force, not, as in the early twentieth century, the aim for world power. As the critic Jost Hermand has observed in his account of the *Volkish* movement from the period of the Hohenzollern Empire to the Third Reich, intellectuals such as Justus Möser (1720–94)

...envisioned a state in which each individual would feel responsible for the workings of the whole, everyone would feel *volkish*, Germanic, or Teutonic and the fatherland would become the object of universal love - in short, one with which the common 'peasant' and the common 'artisan' could also identify.[12]

Nevertheless, the idea of the 'nation' remained somewhat ambivalent in character. Reservations about or even hostility towards other people were elements of German nationalism from the beginning. Johann Gottlieb Fichte's (1762–1814) *Speeches to the German Nation*, for example, presented the Germans as a people 'whose natural disposition toward freedom dates back to prehistoric times, when they had been a pure and untainted race, a time before the influence of foreigners and the introduction of class divisions. The goal of the coming wars of liberation, as Fichte saw it, would be to recover this natural inclination.'[13]

The ambiguity expressed by Fichte, of a German nation which is intrinsically freedom-loving, but which has been 'tainted' and ultimately corrupted by foreign influences, was subsequently to develop into a full-blown reactionary programme. After the failed revolution of 1848 and with the establishment of the German Reich in 1871, the nationalization of all spheres of life in Germany became even more pronounced and often violently reactionary in character. German superiority was affirmed, and the glories of Teutonic history were progressively contrasted with the impoverished and degenerate cultural traditions of other people.

At the turn of the nineteenth and twentieth centuries, this Teutonic heritage was being mobilized with some urgency to justify the German Reich's bid for world domination. Particular attention was paid, with regard to a Germanic heritage, to the specific relationship of the German people to nature. One should mention, in this context, the importance of the art historian Josef Strzygowski (1862–1941), the writer Willy Pastor (1867–1933) and the landscape architect Lange. Pastor was a particularly influential figure. In numerous publications, such as his book *From Germanic Prehistoric Times*, published in 1907, he champions the history of the ancient Germanic tribes and endeavours to correct the fallacy, as he sees it, 'of the often defamed "barbaric" early history of Germania.'[14] Like many of his lesser-known contemporaries, Pastor's publications were intended to demonstrate the exceptionally high cultural level attained by prehistoric Germanic tribes. For Pastor there was no doubt that 'as well as the decisive waves of people, the decisive waves of culture came from the North.'[15] He was a passionate proponent of what he grandly labelled the 'doctrine of the Nordic origin of any culture.'[16]

At the same time, Strzygowski protested that the high level of Nordic art and the specific relation of the Nordic people to nature and landscape had been shamefully neglected in the field of art history.[17] Yet it was difficult for intellectuals such as Pastor, Strzygowski and Lange to substantiate such assertions of the Nordic superiority. The Germans had clearly produced no examples of architecture or art on a par with the Greeks and the Romans. One solution to this predicament was to appropriate the cultural achievements of other peoples as part of the German heritage.[18] With this in mind, Pastor stated in a 1904 publication, for example, that the Ancient Greek temples were evidence of an essential 'Germanic spirit.' And he concluded: 'This simple gabled building, this straight-forward and simple art, that is not at all Roman in character, that is totally Germanic in spirit.'[19] Similarly, Heinrich Friedrich Wiepking-Jürgensmann (1891–1973), one of the leading Nazi landscape architects, writing in 1937 on the Germanic megalithic tombs on the island of Rügen, drew attention to their harmonious integration into the landscape: 'When I reached the top of the tomb I suddenly knew: it is the same spirit that has built the Greek masterpieces on the Mediterranean Sea! A longing was fulfilled!'[20]

Another way of attempting to establish Germanic cultural superiority was not to stress cultural achievements, but to refer to a unique Germanic relationship with nature. Pastor ascribed the harmony enjoyed by the Germanic tribes with nature to environmental changes during the glacial period, which separated out the Germans and their rugged primeval forests from the rest of the world. According to Pastor: 'This was the last great separation. The last, and the most important. Now, finally, the planet succeeded in creating the Germanic people, a race that would prove capable physically and spiritually of guiding the destiny of the human race.'[21]

Such deterministic ideas of 'Germanness' and the triumphalist view of Germany's role in facilitating man's 'rebirth' are also reflected in Lange's publications on garden design. Lange and Pastor were friends, and they frequently referred to each other in their publications.[22] Lange was Professor of Garden Design in Berlin and one of the most significant garden theorists in early-twentieth-century Germany, who claimed that the German nature garden was the highest form of garden art and proof that Germany would be a cultural inspiration for humankind in the field of garden art.[23] 'History,' Lange remarked prophetically, 'will call this new stage of garden style, which is firmly based on its precursors, the stage of the German garden style. Germany has chosen to lend its name to this style in the history of gardens and to become once again "an improver of the world." '[24] Lange's espousal of the nature garden as the culminating form in garden design was probably taken from art historians and theorists such as Alois Riegl (1858–1905), who promoted the idea that the use of geometrical styles in architecture and other art forms was a sign of a low level of cultural development.[25]

The difficulty of establishing the cultural superiority of the Germanic tribes on the basis of their architectural and artistic works, as we have seen, led conservative intellectuals to argue that the harmonious relationship between nature and the Germanic people was a sign of their exceptional character. From this perspective, the outstanding character of Nordic culture was reflected, not in the transformation of nature into cultural artefacts, but rather in the adaptation of culture to nature, in its harmonious interdependence. Cultural history was idealized as natural history, as indicated in the title of Pastor's book, *The Earth in the Time of Man* (1904), which bore the subtitle 'Attempt at a natural scientific history of culture.' Pastor argued that nature, the German primeval forest, 'had contributed the most to creating the specific race, which is today the most important element of our planet.'[26]

The clearings made by the early Germanic tribes for their settlements in the primeval forests were invested with considerable ideological significance. Thus, Pastor published a collection of essays indicatively entitled *Clearings*, and in a chapter of *The Earth in the Time of Man*, entitled 'Lichtungen,' he quotes at some length from Tacitus's description 'of the first clearings in the Germanic primeval forests.'[27] In all probability, the identically titled volume *Clearings* by the American landscape architect Jens Jensen, who had close contact with German colleagues, was borrowed from Pastor.[28]

Pastor glorified the Germanic appreciation of landscape, as this was embodied in sacred places and monuments. 'The works seem to grow out of landscape pictures,' he observed, before concluding:

> Let us imagine a massive dolmen, then it is the same as if our view would wander over a plain to the open Nordic grey sea. The *Rundlinge* and *Bautasteine* fit excellently in the picture of rough coasted landscapes with steep cliffs, rocky coasts, defiant erratic blocks; so well that their formation becomes something self-evident with regard to natural history.[29]

The idea that these Germanic sacred sites existed in harmony with nature was undoubtedly reinforced by the fact that they were made out of natural materials, whose original form had been only slightly modified in the process of construction. Moreover, the stone blocks had been brought to Central Europe during the glacial period. The tombs and monuments appeared to merge into the surrounding environment, and it was therefore easy to interpret them as expressions of an exceptional Germanic affinity with the landscape.[30] As Pastor observed, 'Any excellent architecture grows organically out of very specific landscape images.'[31] Referring specifically to the design of these megalithic tombs, Pastor declared: 'They become covered with earth, mounds arch above them, and the majestic curve of the mounds reflects again the monumental character of this whole culture.'[32]

NATIONAL SOCIALISM: REBUILDING GERMANIA

With the coming to power of the National Socialists in 1933, the search for national identity in a Germanic nature reached a new dimension. This was especially so in the field of landscape design. Although even before 1933 landscape architects had published numerous works with titles such as *The German Garden*, there were many different ways in which a 'German' garden might be defined, ranging from formal to informal designs. During the period of National Socialism, however, natural design was clearly considered to be the most decisive characteristic of German landscape design, as can be seen in Hans Hasler's 1939 book *German Garden Art*, which developed many of Lange's ideas about the nature garden.[33]

Ideas about the German people's innate relationship with nature had a particular impact on early-twentieth-century landscape design in Germany, and led to the development of sophisticated concepts of natural gardens. This is reflected most clearly in the work of Lange and Alwin Seifert (1890–1972). One of the assumptions underlying their concepts of natural landscape design was that the German people were closely bound to nature and therefore required appropriately designed cultural environments, including gardens and landscapes.

The designs of ancient pagan Germanic graves, gathering places and council rings, such as the use of boulders and their situation in the landscape, were studied with particular interest. Natural design was praised as truly 'Teutonic,' while formal design was maligned as being on a lower cultural level and characteristic of so-called degenerate 'southern Alpine races.' As Jensen expressed it in an article published in the proceedings of the International Horticultural Congress held in Berlin in 1938: 'The Nordic, or if you please, the Germanic mind, is not imbued with formalism of any kind. To him it is an affected thing. It does not speak the truth as the truth should be told by an intellectual people. To him it is foreign.'[34] This statement echoes Lange's remarks about the assumed relationship between natural garden design and the Nordic people, and formal design and the Mediterranean people, made some 10 years previously.[35]

Wiepking-Jürgensmann, one of the most influential landscape architects in twentieth-century Germany, was a particularly outspoken proponent of racist ideas about landscape design in National Socialist Germany, and held the chair in landscape design at the College of Agriculture in Berlin between 1934 and 1945. After World War II he was appointed Professor of Landscape Architecture at the University of Hanover. Wiepking-Jürgensmann was convinced that, in contrast to other peoples, the Germanic people possessed from the very beginning an inherent feeling for the landscape. He sought to prove this by investigating the locations of their burial places in the landscape. German art for him was 'not conceivable without the cult of death and veneration of ancestors,'[36] and

Wiepking-Jürgensmann interpreted the numerous grave mounds of the ancient Germanic tribes as proof that: 'they represent the greatest human achievement that is passed down to us from the time of our ancestors ... The grave mounds of those times are masterpieces of landscape design, documents that require our love and our utmost veneration.'[37]

The ideas expressed here by Wiepking-Jürgensmann and reiterated by many others during the same period had a considerable impact on landscape design. The study of prehistoric German landscapes became an important part of Wiepking-Jürgensmann's curriculum and several of his students wrote their postgraduate dissertations on related topics. One such student was Werner Lendholt (1912–80), who later became Wiepking-Jürgensmann's successor at the University of Hanover. In 1937 Wiepking-Jürgensmann introduced Lendholt's work to a wider-reading public in the pages of the magazine *Gartenkunst*, the most influential landscape architecture magazine in Germany at that time:

> Mr Lendholt had the task of proving on the basis of the large-scale map of Hohenzieritz, that our ancestors already had possessed a highly developed sense of landscape beauty during the Bronze Age, and that they were already landscape designers. The task Mr. Lendholt has set himself is part of the investigation of the entire Ur-Germanic space as they relate to these aspects. His work has produced wonderful confirmations. We now know that we possess an ancient culture, and we know that the Germanic idea of Midgart does not belong to the world of myths.[38]

In short, the brief account which I have given of a self-conscious and deeply political drive to locate Germanic culture in a landscape engineered to recall the rugged terrains of primeval Germania, serves as useful context for reading the design of the Grove of the Saxons and the Places of the Ancestors at Hilligenloh and Seelenfeld.

THE DESIGN IDEOLOGY OF THE SACHSENHAIN AND THE HILLIGENLOH AND SEELENFELD CEMETERIES

The Grove of the Saxons and the two cemeteries of Hilligenloh and Seelenfeld are situated in northern Germany: the Sachsenhain near Verden on the river Aller, the Seelenfeld Cemetery between Minden and Nienburg, and Hilligenloh near Oldenburg. These agricultural regions are characterized by heather-clad landscapes and contain numerous examples of ancient Germanic burial sites. Members of the so-called Tannenberg League and the German People's Parish laid out the cemeteries of Seelenfeld and Hilligenloh in around 1930. Ludendorff's Tannenberg League was part of a movement that 'advocated some form of national socialism which was at times more "*volkish*," more "consciously

German," more "national bolshevist" than the rather vaguely defined nationalization plans of the National Socialist German Worker's Party.'[39] Ludendorff's wife, Mathilde (1877–1966), established the so-called 'German Cognition of God' movement, a pseudo-philosophical–religious sect that rejected the church and sought to transform traditional Christian beliefs into a Germanic Christianity in which nature played an important role. Besides the rejection of the church, anti-Semitism was an important part of the ideological basis of the Tannenberg League and the German Cognition of God.[40]

After 1933, the so-called Tannenberg League was transformed into Das Deutschvolk, 'an organization first launched in 1930 as a philosophical society. Ludendorff finally reached a reconciliation and a *modus vivendi* with Hitler in March 1937 and his wife's German Cognition of God was for a time raised by the Nazis to an equal footing with the Christian sects.'[41] Mathilde Ludendorff's German Cognition of God movement was finally banned in 1961 because of *Verfassungsfeindlichkeit* (hostility to the constitution),[42] but this ban was lifted in 1971 for formal reasons.

The designs of both cemeteries are similar. Although the Hilligenloh site is somewhat more 'designed' than Seelenfeld, both cemeteries clearly reflect the same ideas about nature and the nation. Seelenfeld, which is rectangular in shape, was an ancient German burial site, a megalithic tomb surrounded by heath land. It is described in 1932 in an article entitled 'Place of the Ancestors of the German People's Parish at Seelenfeld,' which was published in the magazine *Deutsche Revolution*:

> Megalithic tombs lie scattered all over German lands … Such a megalithic tomb lies near the village Seelenfeld in the western foothills of a wide heath area, which extends between the villages of Loccum and Seelenfeld. The view from this place wanders far away into the Weser land and gets caught on the quiet brown heathland, which has a particular fascination in its unspoiled state and its solitude. The German People's Parish Seelenfeld chose this marvelous spot of earth as the burial place for its dead … [43]

The overall layout of Seelenfeld was designed by the landscape architect Rudolf Bergfeld (1873–1941). Bergfeld, who came from Bremen, was a follower of Lange's ideas about natural garden design and published a book in 1912 entitled *The Natural Form Garden: An Attempt at the Foundation of Naturalism in the Garden*.[44] It is not known whether Bergfeld also designed the Hilligenloh Cemetery (figure 10.1). The original decree authorizing the construction of the Hilligenloh site begins with a rigid prescription outlining the scope of the design and rejecting 'exotic' plants in favour of 'indigenous' German varieties: 'The Ahnenstätte shall be preserved as uniform heath landscape. The planting of trees and shrubs and the laying out of individual beds on the graves is not allowed.

10.1. Mortuary in the Hilligenloh Cemetery.

Furthermore, it is forbidden to incorporate humus into the soil of the graves. All the vegetation is common property of the Ahnenstätte.'[45] The second paragraph of the decree goes on to specify in even greater detail the exact materials to be used in the site's construction: 'Only natural stones, so-called erratic blocks (*Findlinge*) are allowed as gravestones. Inscriptions should fit in with the character of the place. The inscription should not conflict with the spirit of the sacred place because it serves first of all the followers of the Cognition of God.'[46] The gravestones are not to be inscribed with Christian symbols of birth and death. Instead, they are to be decorated with Germanic runes and pre-Christian symbols, such as the 'Teutonic Sonnenrad, or "sun-wheel," derived from a pre-Christian sun cult among the Germanic tribes.'[47] The emblem of National Socialism, the swastika, at least in a reversed version, was still to be found in the 1990s on a gravestone at Hilligenloh (figure 10.2).

Today, both cemeteries continue to bear testimony to how landscape design was used in the 1930s by a *Volkish* nationalist movement for extreme political ends. The designs laid claim to an ancient Germanic heritage, even while they celebrated an ostensibly 'organic' German culture, which was perceived as wedded to the German soil. Moreover, although the Tannenberg League and the German People's Parish cannot be equated with Himmler's SS, the design of the cemeteries and its underlying ideology relates them to the Grove of the Saxons, which was laid out a few years later.

10.2. Gravestone with reversed swastika in the Hilligenloh Cemetery.

THE GROVE OF THE SAXONS: A COMMEMORATIVE SITE FOR HEINRICH HIMMLER'S SS

In 1934 the Reichsführer SS, Heinrich Himmler (1900–45) (figure 10.3), and Alfred Rosenberg (1893–1946), one of the leading Nazi ideologists who in 1941 was appointed Minister of the Occupied Eastern Territories, decided to commemorate the alleged assassination of 4500 Saxons by Charlemagne in 782 AD by laying out the Grove of the Saxons (figure 10.4).[48] This commemorative project needs to be seen within the context of Himmler's overriding interests in Germanic history. He was, in fact, one of the leading figures in the development of racist myths promoted by the Nazis, and at the time he joined the Nazi Party in 1925 was a member of the Thule Society (Thule Gesellschaft), founded in 1919, which believed in the Aryan supremacy as evinced in the heroic exploits of the Teutonic

10.3. Reichsführer SS, Heinrich Himmler, visiting the exhibition 'Planning and Rebuilding in the East,' 1941. To the left, Rudolf Hess; to the right of Himmler, Martin Bormann. (Photograph, Bundesarchiv, Bild 146/83/12/26.)

tribes in their struggle against the Romans. In 1935 Himmler established a new arm of the SS, Das Ahnenerbe (the Ancestral Heritage Society), whose 'antiquarian warriors,'[49] comprised of academics, supervised German heritage.[50]

The Grove of the Saxons was planned specifically to commemorate 4500 Saxons who were allegedly butchered because they refused to convert to Christianity. It is unclear whether this event actually happened or whether the story is apocryphal and arose because of the misreading of an historical text. If the Latin word *delocare* (to resettle) was confused with *decolare* (to behead), the interpretation would be significantly different. During the reign of Charlemagne, many Franconians were resettled in Saxonia and many Saxons were brought to Franconia.[51] Himmler himself was very much interested in ancient Germanic history and, as we have seen, he established Das Ahnenerbe to promote research in this field. His interests matched those of Rosenberg, who rejected the Catholic Church and wanted to establish a new race-specific religion.

10.4. View of the walkway framing the Grove of the Saxons, c.1936. (Photograph, Stadtarchiv Verden an der Aller.)

The Grove of the Saxons lost its ideological significance for National Socialism when Charlemagne was integrated into Nazi ideology as the great founder of a German Reich who could serve to legitimate the claim for Nazi Germany's aggrandizement. After World War II, in 1950, the Grove of the Saxons was taken over by the Protestant Church and was reopened as the Protestant Youth Farm.[52]

The Grove of the Saxons was designed by the landscape architect Wilhelm Hübotter (1895–1976), a close friend of Wiepking-Jürgensmann and along with him one of the most influential landscape architects during the National Socialist period. Hübotter was a former member of a *Volkish* group of the German Youth Movement, the Wandervogel Völkischer Bund. The Grove of the Saxons is a huge oval clearing framed by a walkway and flanked by two rows of huge erratic blocks, 4500 in number, which serve as reminders of the 4500 Saxons. The edges of the walkway are planted with wild roses, alder dogwood and other indigenous shrubs.[53] The inner part of the site is grazing land.

It was necessary for the walkway to be situated on a slightly raised embankment, on account of the fact that the surrounding area was a natural flood plain for the nearby Aller River, and although the area was protected from the Aller by a dam, it nevertheless continued to flood. The choice of this difficult natural terrain on which to erect the commemorative site is yet another example of the extent to which landscape architects consciously strove to exploit harsh natural conditions in order to emphasize both the hardiness of the Germans and their coexistence with the physical environment.[54]

At the very centre of the Grove of the Saxons stands a small gathering place with the two so-called 'leader's pulpits,' which are overhung by vast beech trees. In front of these pulpits a stream, the Halsebach, flows in the direction of the Aller. Within the site lies a council ring, in the shape of a campfire marked out with boulders. The rest of the meadow was intended to provide a large gathering place for rallies and parades. At the north end of the oval are three farmhouses, which were moved from other parts of northern Germany to the Grove of the Saxons and rebuilt there in 1935.

Both before and during the rise of National Socialism, numerous such memorials and gathering places were designed in Germany according to similar ideas about ancient Germanic heritage and the relationship of the German people to nature. The use of rocks and boulders 'was thought especially apt as a monument, singled out as symbolic of primeval power (*Urkraft*).'[55] Examples of such sites include the Bismarck Memorial at the Bookholzberg and the Landtagsplatz Hösseringen in the Luneburg Heath, built in 1935. As George Mosse has observed: 'The nation represented itself through pre-industrial symbols in order to affirm its immutability.'[56]

References to ancient Germanic history as part of the 'natural' history and heritage of the German nation can also be found in contemporary descriptions of the Grove of the Saxons. Reinhard Berkelmann, the engineer who supervised the site's construction, referred in an article to 'the great spiritual and psychic goods of our Germanic ancestors.'[57] He explicitly linked natural design to history by claiming that a gathering place such as the Grove of the Saxons always evolves organically out of the historic landscape. As he put it: 'The landscape is the dominating element and the whole site is developed out of the natural conditions.'[58] According to the engineer, the aim of the site was to build 'a bridge from our ancestors to today's generation'[59] – from the glories of a prehistoric Germanic past to the ideology of National Socialism. This goal was to be realized by landscape architects such as Hübotter and Bergfeld, who played a leading role during the period of National Socialism. As I have sought to demonstrate, the specific element that made this 'bridge,' in Berkelmann's words, a functioning one, was the overall design conception, as well as details such as the selection of plants and building materials. The overarching design seeks to emphasize the 'embeddedness' of the site in the landscape. Indeed, adorned with indigenous plant varieties, the sites do not resemble highly designed landscapes, but rather areas of natural woodland.

If National Socialism had endured, such landscape design would undoubtedly have become more important. Towards the end of the regime plans were already underway for the implementation of a Landscape Law, which aimed to institutionalize this approach to landscape design. Thus, Wiepking-Jürgensmann, in collaboration with colleagues, produced a draft known as 'Landscape Law', which would form the basis for instructing landscape architects and other professionals on the 'proper' design of German landscapes. An antecedent to this law was the longwinded 'General Order No. 20/VI/42 Regarding the Design of the Landscape in the Annexed Eastern Territories, December 21, 1942.'[60] Himmler officially approved these so-called 'Landscape Rules' in 1942 as a guideline for remodelling the conquered Polish territory according to Germanic landscape ideals. The Landscape Rules were formulated by Wiepking-Jürgensmann, who was Himmler's special representative on landscape design at the time, in collaboration with Erhard Mäding.[61] The design of the Grove of the Saxons and the two Places of the Ancestors complies absolutely with Himmler's Landscape Rules, which give the following instructions for the design of commemorative places:

> The design of gravestones and cemeteries should be a worthy expression of the veneration of the ancestors and of race-specific people's and nature's piety. The creation of graves of the ancestors and families on one's own land is in accordance with Germanic conviction and traditional customs … These places where nature and belief meet each other have to be designed and maintained in a way that they are high points of simple design of the landscape … Tree and grave belong together. For the planting of family graves on one's own land and in the cemeteries of the villages only the use of indigenous species such as oak, linden and birch trees, ash, yew, juniper and other evergreen conifers is possible.[62]

The collapse of National Socialism in 1945 meant that the Landscape Rules were never formally passed as a law.

CONCLUSION

This chapter has explored some of the ways in which 'nature' and 'heritage' have been historically intertwined. More specifically, the focus has been on the ideological construction of 'nature' and of a distinctive 'Teutonic' heritage by nationalist groups in early-twentieth-century Germany. Landscape design, I have suggested, played a vital role not only in providing a theoretical justification for a supremacist ideology, which argued for the deep-rooted nature of an authentic German culture, but also in the practical embodiment of this ideology in a landscape.

The Grove of the Saxons and the cemeteries of Seelenfeld and Hilligenloh serve as important examples of how concepts of natural garden design in

Germany were profoundly influenced by nationalistic and racist ideas. These sites exemplify how nature can be politicized at the same time as politics is naturalized, so that landscape becomes both a symbol of power and an instrument of its perpetuation.[63] They demonstrate that landscape architecture cannot be viewed as a discipline somehow detached from the socio-political contexts that surround it. On the contrary, as Karen Lang argues in a chapter that explores the monumentalization of German history in a different phase, land-scape design continues to remain a highly political and ideological discipline.

CHAPTER 11

A GARDEN OF RETURNS: BERNARD LASSUS AND THE HISTORICAL COMPOSITION OF PLACE

STEPHEN BANN

INTRODUCTION: THE GROUNDS OF HERITAGE

Let me begin by quoting a passage which I wrote five years ago when introducing the recent garden designs of the French landscapist Bernard Lassus in the *Journal of Garden History*:

> In fact, the connecting thread through virtually all of the schemes illustrated in these texts from 1983 to 1993 is the recuperation and reinvention of the historic past. In this connection, Lassus's position is luminously clear, and can serve as a powerful rejoinder to so many of the confused and nostalgic arguments used in defence of 'conservation' and 'heritage' in the contemporary world. The authenticity of the historical object does not reside simply in its identity with itself: as a museum piece ratified by scholarly consensus and detached from the everyday milieu. On the contrary, it becomes authentic to the extent that it communicates within a wider context: it must be made accessible to the senses and this inevitably implies that it should take its place within a continuum of sensory impressions for which the designer assumes responsibility.[1]

As I am writing here specifically about Lassus's gardens within the context of 'heritage' and 'culture', I want to stress from the outset the contrast that I was making at that stage between the 'garden' and the 'museum'. For the museum is the privileged location, which we immediately call to mind when issues of heritage and conservation are raised. The garden seems too fluid, too subject to the vagaries of the seasons – in a word, too irredeemably natural – to be considered as a privileged place of heritage. What I shall argue, by contrast, is that this seeming naturalness can in fact be an asset if it is used effectively by the cunning garden designer. The garden is inevitably grounded, and this will be a literal as well as a metaphorical thread running through this chapter. But whereas the museum may be, metaphorically, grounded in notions of national heritage symbolized by precious objects, the garden has the capacity to bring into play a number of literal and metaphorical levels: the terrain which is an object of archaeological science may also be a place of pleasant, sensuous distraction. Not for nothing did Proust quote towards the end of *Time Regained* the line from Victor Hugo: 'The grass must grow and children have to die.' What Proust sees as the paradigmatic case of the individual suffering that is sublimated in the work of art is capable of being generalized in the garden:

> We ourselves die after exhausting every form of suffering, so that over our heads may grow the grass not of oblivion but of eternal life, the vigorous and luxuriant growth of a true work of art, and so that, thither, gaily and without a thought for those who are sleeping beneath them, future generations may come to enjoy their *déjeuner sur l'herbe*.[2]

Here we have a garden, then, a 'Garden of Returns' as Lassus entitled it, built upon the site of a historic dockyard on the estuary of the Charente at Rochefort-sur-mer. But before I start to discuss a number of images recording its development since work was begun in 1983, I need to explain how it is that the landscapist is formed: how someone acquires the qualifications to cover with innocent grass the deserted scene of a seventeenth-century arsenal. This is not a story of a simple professional formation, since the implication of what I am saying is that this landscapist has to be, first and foremost, a painter and even a poet. The creation of a 'continuum of sensory impressions' which I described as the landscape designer's special responsibility needs to be guaranteed by both of these forms of expertise: poetics – not however the strict sense of words on the page, but in the more general sense of a rhetorical system underlying phenomenal manifestations; painterliness, in the sense of an achieved immediacy of sensuous impact which transcends but does not wholly conceal the poetics.

CREATING ORDER: FROM STILL LIFE TO THE FRENCH GARDEN

Bernard Lassus began his professional development as a painter, in the studio of Fernand Léger. His paintings from around 1956, often involving a simple still-life study such as glasses on a table-top, are already involved with the dialectic of visual and tactile values that he was later to explore programmatically in garden schemes: colour serves not to define the object in relation to its background, but on the contrary to enhance the sense of pure plastic value inherent in the painted surface. Ten years later, Lassus has become a kinetic artist, no longer confined to traditional pigments but using his 'Brise-lumière' to experiment with the vagaries of phenomenal light (figure 11.1). The painted vertical slats create by reflection the impression of nebulous colour shifts on the back plates, thus modelling the possibilities of environmental design that were being undertaken simultaneously by his Groupe de Recherches d'Ambiance.[3]

By the mid-1970s, Lassus is returning again to the basic properties of still life. But he does so in order to offer a model of the contrasts and conflicts existing in the visual environment, in a study financed by the research section of the French Ministry concerned with policies on landscape and urban planning. The aim is to show, through progressive variations in the ordering of the basic elements – glasses and bottles – how both semantic and formal elements are necessarily intertwined in our perceptions of order and disorder within a given

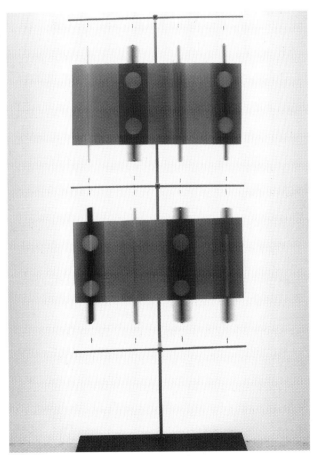

11.1. Bernard Lassus, 'Brise-lumière,' c. 1962.

visual field. If all the glasses and bottles shown are filled with red wine, the sequence is repetitive and monotonous – the one bottle that is not filled right to the top is singled out for vision, and perhaps with a view to possible use. The frame in which some of the bottles are left empty straight away sets up the expectation of an economy of fullness and emptiness, and hence of a foreseeable practical use – though we might prefer to have had just a full bottle and an empty glass! On the other hand, when full glasses and empty bottles sit opposite a row of bottles, which includes a ship in a bottle, the glaring anomaly causes visual and semantic disorder. This can be recuperated, though perhaps only partially, by taking the eccentric bottle out of the series and situating it on its side, with the ship then appearing upright.[4]

The Glasses and Bottles series mirrored, as did Lassus's previous environmental schemes, the contemporary strategies of gallery art. In the 1950s he was a student of Léger and a friend of Giacometti, in the 1960s a kinetic artist, and in the 1970s, as has been seen, a kind of conceptualist in his exploration of identity and difference through seriality. But the further purpose of the Glasses and Bottles was, quite explicitly, to model the extreme complexities of urban and environmental design, all too often neglected (then as now) by the formalist tendencies of modern architecture. Instead of assuming an ideal, utopian order, like the pioneers of the modern movement, Lassus wished to examine the subtle ways through which order tends to be created out of heterogeneity – and indeed the ways in which an initial heterogeneity can be a benefit to the environment, provided that it is intelligently assessed as such. Although not at this point addressed to the problem of working with 'heritage' – with the 'historic' environment – the problematic developed by Lassus in these years seems highly relevant. The ship in the bottle, that particularized cultural signifier, needs semantic as well as physical space in order to establish its identity within the sequence.

Yet the concrete environment is evidently much more complex than any modelled situation, however creatively designed. For one thing, it is not clear what reason can be adduced for drawing the visual and practical boundaries of the field at any one point in space. Are we in fact to assume that the array of bottles might stretch to infinity, or if not, how are the internal relations of the series related to the boundary of the frame, and what is supposed to exist beyond? If Lassus turns his attention at this stage to the specific study of the classic French garden, this is partly because he conceives it to be an historical example of a closed system of physical relations, inserted within another, essentially conceptual, system. As we can see from a contemporary aerial view, a typical garden by Le Notre, such as that at the Château de Champs in the valley of the Marne, extends outwards from the domestic space through a series of graded transitions: the areas closest to the chateau are highly organized from a decorative point of view, and utilize mineral elements to create the characteristic Rococo designs known as *broderie*. Beyond them are the topiary hedges, cut into cubic forms, which prolong the lines of sight up to the circular ponds and the 'eye-catcher,' which is typically a classical statue. The surrounding forest, unconstrained by such linear and geometrical ordering, is both the terrain for hunting – evidently much more extensive and unbounded in the seventeenth century than it will appear today – and at the same time the privileged symbol of an untamed nature, notionally limitless: it signifies an ultimate wildness beyond the determinations of culture.

Lassus has certainly employed what he takes to be the system of the classically French garden in a number of different spheres within his practice. In his work for a school at Guénange in Lorraine, for example, he created what he called 'artificial bushes' out of specially commissioned coloured enamel balls. The concept was that the topiary principle, which combines a geometrical form with a vegetable material, could be shifted slightly, with mineral elements miming the luxuriance of natural vegetation. It should be noted that the aesthetic role of the installation is crucial here, as a mediating element between the utilitarian prefabricated school building and the woodland surrounding. Lassus's work in the 1980s at Uckange in the Metz region employed the vastly greater scale of the façades of numerous reconditioned blocks of apartments to inscribe natural features which were lacking in the schematic environmental planning of the original architect's design. Taking as his principle the creation of a visual continuum, which connected the built forms to their location, he shifted the topiary principle one further stage, by making the concrete block also a support for the image of a tree.[5]

DEEP HISTORY: RETHINKING A LANDSCAPE HERITAGE

These, however, are examples of the principle used punctually, without reference to the garden concept as a whole. In the course of the 1970s, Lassus became convinced that the model of formal order within a world system represented by the classical French garden had to be replaced by another, more closely attuned to the contemporary sense of space and time. It is this conviction that has dominated his planning of major garden schemes from 1980 onwards, including the Garden of Returns, which is especially relevant in the context of this publication. But before introducing this garden at Rochefort-sur-mer, now over a decade old, I should briefly mention its precursor, the Garden of the Planets submitted for the competition for a garden at La Villette, on the outskirts of Paris, in 1980. There has probably been no competition for a landscape scheme in the last 25 years which attracted so much comment in France and elsewhere. The winner of the competition, Bernard Tschumi, thus attracted considerable attention, initially through his scheme involving an assortment of postmodern pavilions. The present state of his project is, however, as much of an embarrassment to the ordinary visitor as it has become to those in charge of the site, and needs no further comment.

Lassus, for his part, saw the competition as an opportunity to demonstrate that the horizontal dimension, which had traditionally provided the garden with its physical characteristics and its mode of closure, now needed to be supplemented by a vertical scale. In a period when the ocean has become a lake that we fly across, and the whole of the Earth has been criss-crossed with tracks of exploration, so that 'terra incognita' can no longer be found on the map, it is the vertical that still offers scope for the imagination – whether through the infinite dimensions of interstellar space, or the unplumbed depths of the earth itself. Consequently the La Villette scheme is designed to be a Garden of the Planets, incorporating a planetarium inserted deep down in the earth itself.[6] That such a concept could have been actually realized seems to me beyond doubt. Indeed it would have been a powerful successor to the Moscow planetarium by Bartsch – perhaps the culminating achievement of Constructivist architecture in post-revolutionary Russia – and a companion piece to Hans Hollein's projected Musée des Volcans in the Auvergne, a museum which is planned to exist almost completely underground, reaffirming the priority of the natural landscape.

History can also be understood as a vertical dimension. I say this in the certainty that my readers will respond by saying that history is neither horizontal nor vertical, but a concept without any spatial implications. My answer is that, precisely in the cultural conditions of Europe since the eighteenth century, there is a close semantic bind between the notions of historical and physical depth. The rapid development of archaeology from the eighteenth century onwards, coupled with the extraordinary growth of popular archaeology in the recent period, have made it not just an abstruse fact, but a generally shared imaginative perception, that what lies beneath the soil is an earlier layer of historical data, which can be brought to light and made meaningful. Now that the notion of the 'primitive' has been uncoupled from its link with geographically distant – and thus 'horizontal' – regions, the association of the vertical with deep time, so to speak, appears all the more compelling.

But how can this historical depth be recovered in the form of the garden? As Lassus demonstrated in his design for the 'reinvention' of the Tuileries Gardens in 1991, the simultaneous existence of different, chronologically foliated layers in a historic garden poses an insoluble problem if it is desired to make all of them simultaneously apparent in the restored garden. The best that can be hoped for is a 'reinvention' manifesting several of the different layers through an astute interplay of levels. But this must be strictly adjusted to the existing urban context which, as it has changed irreversibly over the past five centuries, requires new problems like traffic noise from the 'voie exprès rive droite' to be taken into account. Lassus's scheme for the Tuileries is thus a 'stratified' garden, which reaches downwards as far as the foundations of Le Notre's original design and those of his predecessors, on the one hand, but maintains its upward emphasis, on the other, in consolidating the raised terraces that tower above the Seine.[7]

The Garden of Returns at Rochefort-sur-mer also has to resolve these two complementary questions of historical depth and environmental accommodation, so to speak. A bird's-eye shot shows the garden in its early stages, with the relationship of the site to the town obviously posing a real problem. The history of Rochefort is essentially that of a naval base, built on a grid of wide streets around a central square. The 'Corderie Royale' (constructed in the seventeenth century, probably to designs by Mansart) is located by the Charente River, where the forms for construction of warships also came to be situated. There was no reason at the period of its development for the naval base to be integrated with the town, or for the corderie to display itself as anything but a factory – one which appeared excessively long in its dimensions because of the practical problems of fabricating the lengths of cordage for ships' rigging. Having been abandoned as a factory in the nineteenth century, and left to go to ruin throughout the period of World War II, when the German occupying troops built a concrete block-house there to command the estuary, the site called for complete renovation in the 1980s, when Lassus won the open competition with his scheme for The Garden of Returns (figure 11.2).[8]

11.2. Bernard Lassus, 'Jardin des Retours,' Rochefort-sur-mer. Plan.

It will be apparent straight away that he did not adopt the simplest solution: merely to integrate the area around the Corderie with the rather dilapidated *jardin à la française* constructed on the axis of the naval commander's residence. In this case, the Corderie, however eccentric in its proportions, would have emerged as a kind of honorary *château*, with the conventional flowerbeds and fountains axially related to it. Instead, two decisions with very different consequences were taken. The view of the building from the river was to be interrupted by new planting along the banks, with the effect that river traffic and the visitors to the garden would see it only intermittently (like the eighteenth-century view of the Abbey of Rievaulx in North Yorkshire from the so-called Rievaulx terraces). At the same time, from the opposite side of the Corderie, the change of levels between the garden of the naval commander and the area around the main building was to be positively emphasized, rather than eliminated by a sloping transitional space. Lassus decided to build up the stone retaining wall so that it would extend along the whole length of the rear access, with a broad ramp leading in parallel down the eastward side.

We can understand this insistence on an unambiguous change of levels from a number of different aspects. On the one hand, it is a restatement of the principle which goes back to Lassus's earliest garden schemes (and indeed to his paintings of the 1950s): that the visual and the tactile should be dissociated, in other words, that we should initially observe the garden from a privileged viewpoint where actual access is denied.[9] When (and if) we do choose to descend by the ramp, we are all the more prepared for the effect of estrangement created by the presence of the array of exotic plants: Virginian tulip trees descend in close ranks along the ramp itself and a row of palm trees extends along the ground level. This is called a Garden of Returns primarily because Lassus intends to create a vivid reminiscence of the various exotic species that first entered Europe through the port of Rochefort. In fact, two of its naval intendants gave their name to incoming plants that took this path of access: De la Galisonnière gave his name to a type of magnolia and Michel Bégon's name was used to christen the begonia.

This disorientation which occurs in gaining access to the garden does not, of course, prevent the visitor from moving in to enjoy the profusion of exotic plant forms. However, it seems to me that Lassus has staked a great deal, in his Garden of Returns, on the sheer, uninterrupted extent of the green turf that covers the entire riverward side of the Corderie. Nothing could be more natural, it could be said, than a greensward. And yet, at the same time, nothing is more difficult to create and maintain, in climates less favourable than the collegiate enclaves of Oxford and Cambridge. Lassus certainly wants us to feel that a carpet of green turf is not a naturally occurring phenomenon but, on the contrary, an historically more recent level superimposed upon the paving of cobbled stones that surrounds the monument. But he also insinuates that this is not an inaccessible and protected region. People can – and do – walk regularly across it in both directions.

This attention to the garden as a place of individual trajectories, to be seen but also to be walked – at various speeds and with differing preoccupations – comes across also in the planning of the two different pathways that run parallel to the Charente. The path which is closest to the building is a straight one, with bluish tiles bordering a firm tarmac walkway, and a line of formal trees aligned on the side of the Corderie. The path close to the river is, by contrast, serpentine; it loses itself in the thick bushes, and offers direct access to the riverbank, where extensive replanting of shrubs has taken place, so as to convey the impression of a comparatively untouched environment. It is at the end of the serpentine river path that we first see the rigging of what appears to be an early sailing ship, placed in a position which suggests that it must be moored beside the riverbank. Finding it impossible to dislodge the mass of German concrete commanding the riverbank, Lassus has built this garden feature on its foundations: the Garden of Returns thus possesses a ship returned from the ocean, its rigging authentic and to scale, and its decks loaded with the 'tontines' that protect tender exotic plants from the salt sea on their journey back to France.

CONCLUSION: HERITAGE AS HISTORICAL REINVENTION

My description of the Garden of Returns has focused specifically on the site and its history. Another way of approaching it would be to analyze the substantial, though perhaps unsuspected, political stakes involved in the creation of this garden, which are in one way specific to the French context, but would doubtless have their parallels in other countries. One factor to be emphasized would be the unremitting hostility to Lassus of a powerful sector of the French architectural profession, which had been used to seeing its nominees undertake the design of such important landscape features, and was intensely suspicious of a project so foreign to the architect's way of thinking. Another would be the role played in the planning of the garden by the local mayor, who could not however find the total funding for the project, and the subsequent, necessary injection of national subsidies when Rochefort was personally adopted by President Mitterand as one of his presidential '*grands projets.*' It is inevitable and appropriate that a garden should take its place as a stake in the combination of political and professional interests that underlie planning decisions in contemporary society. But it is also worth acknowledging the uniquely inventive features of such a

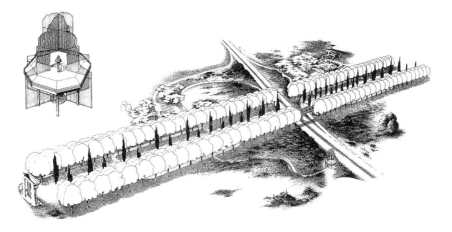

11.3. Bernard Lassus, 'Nîmes-Caissargues,' motorway rest area. Plan showing theatre façade on extreme left and Tour Magne belvedere in detail.

project, when compared with more frequently publicized objects of conservation such as museum objects and historic buildings. Lassus's long-term plan, it should be added, was to develop the garden's historic connection with the name of Bégon to the stage of creating a national centre for the propagation and cultivation of begonias.

Yet in one sense, we could forget, – for the purposes of this debate on 'heritage' – that it is a garden involved here: we could say instead that this is a case of historical reinvention that simply takes as its materials natural as well as man-made forms, with a cultural objective that is educational and recreational at the same time. This would also apply to a number of subsequent projects which Lassus has undertaken more recently, involving what in French are termed *'aires d'autoroutes,'* and in America something like 'vehicular rest areas:' in other words, what you find if you decide to stop for a while on a journey along a motorway. The particular structure for financing such sites in France – involving as it does distinct and regionally based *'Sociétés d'autoroute'* – has stimulated intense competition, with the effect that we now have some truly grandiose achievements like Lassus's 'Aire de Nîmes – Caissargues,' which has an axial length to rival Versailles, and puts the adjacent motorway into shade (figure 11.3). The game with history in this case is a very subtle one. Nîmes has some of the finest Roman monuments outside Italy. It also possessed until recently a neo-classical theatre, sited just opposite the famous Maison Carré, which was scheduled for demolition when Norman Foster erected his own 'Carré pour l'Art.' The colonnade on the theatre façade was, however, a classed monument, and Lassus prevailed upon the mayor to have it moved from its now superfluous position in the centre of the city to the new motorway area, where

11.4. Bernard Lassus, 'Nîmes-Caissargues,' the relocated theatre façade.

it has rapidly acquired a much enhanced authenticity as the only 'classical' feature around. The former poor relation of the Roman structure, displaced by the arrival of the contemporary high-tech box, is now prestigious enough in its new context to be a frequent point of photograph opportunities for newly married couples (figure 11.4).[10]

History as representation, suggests Lassus, is always a matter of relativity in a scale, which must be determined by the immediate environment. Far from the *aire d'autoroute*, in the middle distance, the city of Nîmes itself shimmers in the sunlight, with the silhouette of the Roman Tour Magne rising above it. We may not be able to see as far as this from ground level, but Lassus offers us a place to ascend and admire the view. The point from which we can make our observation, and the monument that we know to be nearby, are both prefigured in the traditional landscape form of a belvedere.

PART IV:

THE DISINHERITANCE
OF HERITAGE

CHAPTER 12

THE MUSEUM OF WHAT YOU SHALL HAVE BEEN

DONALD PREZIOSI

INTRODUCTION: MUSEUMS AND MODERNITY

What indeed is heritage if it could be 'displayed?' In the pages that follow I want to explore this question from a number of different perspectives. Why is it, for example, that the modern pursuit of identity invariably contrives to make identity ultimately impossible? What it is that museums do to persuade us that what they are doing is not what they are, in fact, denying? And why are we unable to exit them once we have entered, even though we imagine that we have?

Contemporary museums are recent versions of an ancient European tradition of using groups of objects as instruments for the production of knowledge about the world and its history, and thus about ourselves as individuals and communities. They are among the most powerful and subtle of modern rein-ventions: coyly masquerading as mere representational artefacts, as microcosmic reflections of the world, they in fact are psycho-political instruments for reflecting on (and thus changing) the world. They have long provided us with unparalleled means for fabricating and transforming whole worlds, for fac-tualizing our realities and for fictionalizing the realities of others.

Museums arose two centuries ago as one of a series of complementary solutions to social, political and intellectual problems surrounding the birth of the modern nation-state. The museum was a method of posing questions masquerading as answers, and the answers it inevitably provided were as simultaneously specific and ambiguous as the little strips of writing handed out to petitioners by the Delphic oracle herself. It was a product of the European Enlightenment reinterpretation and reinvention of earlier arts of memory and traditions of knowledge production and accumulation, some of which, since the Renaissance at least, also had the name 'museum.'

The modern museum is not comprehensible except as one of a set of complementary social practices, including, of course, language itself. These would include things that today are commonly classed as distinct phenomena, professions or disciplines. Among these are exhibitions, fairs, the tourist and heritage industries, the fashion and design industries, certain facets of modern consumerist ceremony, from art-making and marketing to shopping centres and department stores, and certain disciplines, not the least of which are history and art history. All of these professions and institutions are centred upon very specific modernist concerns with fabricating, preserving, communicating and transforming individual and group allegiances and identities. Museums are one of the central institutions of our modernity, and in a very important way the keystone of the whole modernist edifice. No museums, no modernity.

The claims that I have been making may seem exaggerated and in the remaining sections of this chapter I will clarify a number of complementary issues, which should highlight some of the implications of what I have just been discussing: namely, the relationship between the museum and modernity.

LEGIBLE IDENTITIES: THE SEARCH FOR A STYLE

The American academic philosopher and erstwhile East Coast art critic Arthur Danto once remarked, at the conclusion of a *Nation* magazine review of the 1997 biennale at the local Whitney American Art Museum: 'You may not like the art, but it is probably closer to the heart of our period than other art we might prefer.' He then added: 'Not knowing what we are looking at is the artistic counterpart of not altogether knowing who we are.'[1] This is a claim breathtaking in its innocence of both art and Freud.

Four years earlier there was an article in the *New York Times* entitled 'In France, It's How You Cross the t's.' It concerned the case of a former sales manager of a Parisian furniture company who, after being unemployed for six months, decided to have his handwriting analyzed by an 'expert.' After several attempts to find a job, he began to fear that his handwriting was somehow 'suspect.' The article went on about the increasing use by French corporations of 'graphological tests' in narrowing the field of applicants, particularly for managerial positions. As one corporate representative stated, 'You may suddenly find that a person you are about to hire as an accountant has a tendency toward deviousness,' a personality trait, the article went on to say, that might be clearly evidenced in the loops, slants, margins and flourishes of the applicant's handwriting. Almost all adverts for jobs in France today, the article claimed, require a handwritten letter, for, as one recruiter was quoted as saying, 'it would be very badly viewed if a job applicant sent a typewritten letter.' Commenting on this whole phenomenon, the Parisian current affairs magazine, *Le Nouvel Observateur*, concluded: 'Americans use figures... while we prefer impressions. We like grace, emotion, approximation, instinct. We are probably not made for the modern world.'

But in fact, it has been precisely this belief in a close and telling linkage between individuals and their productions, the idea that the form of your work is the succinct and honest figure of your truth, that is central to the modernities we have built ourselves into over the past two centuries. But these have been more than just telling linkages; they are linkages which can be delineated by others outside of the consciousness of the producing person or people, and even beyond their own capacities to articulate such connections. In other words, identity and individuality in modernity are closely linked to external prostheses. Of such prostheses, the central and key technology is that astonishing invention of the European Enlightenment that we call 'art' – that psycho-semiotic fiction that has long since colonized every corner of the planet.

Such beliefs have been essential to the modern professions of museology, art history, art criticism and connoisseurship, not to speak of the graphology that achieved its modern synthesis in the work of the nineteenth-century French priest Jean-Hippolyte Michon, who in fact coined the term *graphologie* in 1875 to refer to his systematic method for determining individual character and personality traits through the study of handwriting. This modern 'science' had early precedents in the theses of the seventeenth-century Italian physician at the University of Bologna, Camillo Baldi, who may have been one of the first to articulate a correspondence not only between a writer's identity and her style of penmanship, but more importantly between a person's writing and her moral character. Graphological science developed further in the eighteenth century, notably in the work of the Swiss physiognomist Caspar Lavater (who at the end of that century further concluded that there were indeed intimate and demonstrable homologies between handwriting, speech and gesture).[2] The idea, in short, and as we might more commonly say today, was that each person and people, each nation and race, each class or gender, had a distinct and distinguishable 'style:' a quality that permeated everything palpable about a person or people.

Lavater was the contemporary of the Enlightenment philosophers, historians, philologists, collectors and connoisseurs who were fashioning the systematic foundations of art history and museology as we know them today. For example, for Winckelmann, the most influential eighteenth-century progenitor of modern art history and archaeology, the glory of classical Greek art was a direct consequence of the ancient Greek diet, climate, moral character, homosocial appetites and (male) physical beauty – traits that he argued could be read clearly and concretely in all the best works of art. For subsequent art historians and critics, the scientific task was to render the visible properly legible – so starkly and fully legible that objects could assume a physiognomic, even 'graphological,' relationship to their makers, and to the times and places of their production and reception. Virtually all of what museology and its ancillary professions such as art history have been since the end of the eighteenth century follows from this.

In imagining the uniqueness and private inner truths of the individual subject, modern disciplinary institutions have constructed that inwardness and singularity as most truly (scientifically) knowable (even by those to whom it refers) through its invasion and exposure; by rendering it public and hence susceptible to classification, comparison, and thus control. As the secular descendent of religious confession, this came to be achieved in modernity by the creation of a new optical or perspectival technology; a new system of topological relations among individuals, environments and communities; a landscape designed both to echo and enable the performance of individuals' inner truths; a new technology for articulating and factualizing individualities. The eighteenth-century invention of the modern museum was precisely such a technology.

Museums are part of a network of eclectic modern institutions designed explicitly to illuminate and illustrate important 'truths' about individuals, peoples, nations, genders, classes and races – in short, about precisely those things that museums are simultaneously complicit in fabricating and factualizing. The artefacts are the modernist fictions, if you will, of race, gender, nationality, ethnicity and identity. These fantasms have for two centuries been key instruments of power and control in the massive enterprises of nationalism and imperial and global capitalization.

In point of fact, the history of the institution effectively ended, and the museum itself, as a full-blown 'exhibitionary complex' dependent on new discourses of display,[3] was frozen in its final, unsurpassable modern state, on 15 October 1851, at 4.30 in the afternoon, with the closing of the Crystal Palace exhibition by Queen Victoria. There has been nothing substantively new in museum and exhibitionary practice for a century and a half, except perhaps for the very recent admission that the evolution of museology may well be cyclical rather than linear, and that the posteriorities (the self-described 'post'-modernisms) we may have avidly imagined ourselves to be desirous of a couple of decades ago (and that still survive in a dreary and hectoring half-life in our moribund art journals) have been little more than our modernity's own avant-gardist shell game. Such an admission could lead, belatedly, to a rather more nuanced and realistic understanding of the history and prospects of the institution than has been the case in the past couple of decades, during which museology has been argued in the predictable accents of intellectual fashion, economics, politics, information management, marketing, or 'infotainment' and 'edutainment.'

Museology, art history, art criticism, aesthetic philosophy, connoisseurship, curatorship, commodification and art-making – which I will refer collectively to by the term 'museography' – are performative 'genres' in the theatre of modernist nationalism and hypermodernist globalization. Common to the practices just mentioned is the project of the modern corporate state in defining and prescribing disciplined and predictable linkages between citizen-subjects and their object-worlds. In our world, you are made desirous of being convinced that you are your 'stuff,' so that you will be even more desirous of becoming that which even better stuff can say even more clearly to others and to yourselves about your continually greater truth. (Or, in Lacanian terms, the future anterior of what you shall have been for what you are in the process of becoming.) This linkage of psychology and physiognomy is no mere accident of modernity, but its very essence – and it is connected to the necessity of discovering and articulating the individual citizen-consumer as a marked site; as the locus on and upon which meaning and purpose are constructed and inscribed. To sin in modernity is to be untrue to your 'style,' as any modern teenager knows perfectly well without having to read Proust.

Some argue that changes in our social conditions require that the nature of museums must change. Others continue to argue, with equally partial cogency, that museological institutions should not be linked immediately or directly to external conditions, but should take a more preservative or archival role in society. Both positions are only opposed insofar as the two sides of the same coin are in conflict, since both take it as given that museums really are representational artefacts, and should be organized as 'faithful' microcosms, as symbolizations, of particular worlds, histories or peoples.

THE TEMPLE AND THE EXPOSITION

Underlying such presumptions are more fundamental attitudes toward objects themselves, and about our relationships to the world of objects as human subjects. Such attitudes in modern times have crystallized around the problem of 'art' itself. I do not mean problems with art – whether someone thinks this or that art is good or bad, or politically correct or incorrect, or should or should not be displayed or debated or analyzed, or does or does not get to the heart of our current historical condition, to echo Arthur Danto's rather unfortunate if nonetheless telling words – but rather the problem that is 'art' as such; the problematic status of this Enlightenment fantasm.[4] Modern conceptions of art are inextricably linked to our unquenchable desire to imagine art as a universal, pan-human phenomenon; the essential mode of symbolization; the (one might say purely graphological) idea that every distinguishable people 'has' its own 'art.' The idea, in effect, that art is a universal language, exemplified (and legible) in the artefacts of every people. The fiction, in other words, that one can 'display' heritage – which always somehow seems rather obscene, like unbuttoning one's trousers to reveal testimonials of one's character.

We have been living in an age (for over two centuries) when virtually anything can properly be displayed (as 'art' or as 'history') in a museum, and when virtually anything can cogently be designated and serve as a museum.[5] Trying to understand just what kind of world that is may bring us closer to seeing what is more deeply at stake today in attempting to deal with heritage, culture and politics. If virtually anything can be museological in intention and function, then we are going to have to find ways of dealing with and talking about the institution – and, equally, about art and architecture – in ways that depart from not a few of our received ideas, including, for a start, the para-doxical oppositions between historiography and psychoanalysis, as the late Michel de Certeau so poignantly illustrated some time ago.[6] The more useful question might be not 'What is a museum?' but rather 'When is a museum?' When is heritage? Or culture?

As I have already pointed out, the historical evolution of the modern museum effectively came to an end on 15 October 1851, the implication being that what we have seen since that time is an ongoing oscillation between what I call the two 'anamorphic states' of museological practice. One is the 'temple of art' (which is to say the 'shrine of and for the self'), intended to 'cure' (that is to say discipline) individuals, and transform them into citizen-subjects of the nation-state or members of the *Volk* by imagining individuality, citizenship, as that which can be self-fabricated through optical and kinesthetic experience in museum space. The other is the 'exposition' or 'expo,' which was intended to transform citizen-subjects into consumers, to induce individuals to conceive of their lives with the fantasy-language of capitalism, to imagine oneself and others as commodities in every possible sense of the term. Figure 12.1 is a view of the interior of Sir John Soane's Museum in London, which I argue in a new book was a veritable astrolabe of the Enlightenment project.[7]

12.1. Sir John Soane's Museum, London. View of the Dome.

Crystal Palace (figure 12.2) opened on May Day 1851, and was officially closed by Queen Victoria at 4.30pm on 15 October of that year. It was here that the enterprises of capitalism, orientalism, aestheticism, fetishism and patriarchy were stunningly and powerfully put in their full and proper perspective and interwoven for all to see, for the first time. That momentary, six-month exposition (whose interior is shown in figure 12.3) was like a brief and blinding flash at mid-century that revealed, as would the quick shine of a torch in the night, an unexpected and uncanny landscape. The real landscape, as Walter Benjamin observed in speaking of the 1937 Paris exposition, of the capitalism that had blanketed nineteenth-century Europe. What the Crystal Palace exhibition also revealed with unparalleled lucidity was the massive European co-construction of aestheticism and orientalism in its de-othering of 'others.'

12.2. The Crystal Palace, London, 1851. Lithograph of the exterior façade.

EGYPTIAN MUSEUMS

This absorption of every corner of the earth into the matrix of modernity was poignantly illustrated along the eastern and southern margins of late-nineteenth-century imperial Europe. The institutions established by Europeans and native elites in the Islamic Middle East very sharply highlighted what their episte-mological and sociological prototypes within Europe itself often too easily masked, at least to most Europeans. The Victorian-age museums founded in Cairo during the last two decades of the nineteenth century, for example, were places within which the dramaturgy of the nation's origins and evolution could be staged in the most encyclopedic and synoptic manner, and also in the most dense and minute detail, at the level of the juxtaposition of the newly imagined individual citizen-subject with object-relics staged so as to be read as 'representing' moments in the evolving spirit, mentality, will and mind of the nation. Each such staged and framed object was indeed an object-lesson, and an object of intense desire for natives and foreign visitors.[8]

The new museums of Cairo were instruments for the manufacture, the bodying forth, of that virtual entity, the modern state called 'Egypt.' Each museum's contents were arranged to reveal a pre-existing evolutionary journey in the unfolding of identity. Each object staged as a sign, and each sign a link, in a vast archival consignment system in which all the elements might articulate a

12.3. The Crystal Palace, London, 1851. Lithograph of the interior.

synchronic slice (or a diachronic moment) of 'Egypt.' The museums, in effect, were pantographic machineries for projecting up that larger abstraction of the nation from its fragmented relics. The museum gallery embodied a *genius loci* – it being one of those places within the envelope of urban space where the confusion of time and history might be seen to be banished in favour of legibility and narrative and causal sense. These optical-theatrical instruments retroactively constituted that which they purported to simply reflect and re-present.

One of the problems peculiar to Egypt was that to European eyes there was more than one authentic, historical 'Egypt' – the original or native Pharaonic civilization with its own 4000-year history, a Greco-Roman civilization just less than 1000 years long and succeeding and overlapping and partially assimilating the first; a Christian (Coptic) culture, now itself 2000 years old (Egypt being the first officially Christian state), partly coterminous with the Greco-Roman, and tracing its ethnic and linguistic roots to the older native Pharaonic society, and an Islamic civilization, introduced by invaders from the Arabian peninsula, and now itself over 1300 years old. Egypt was historically a multi-ethnic and polyglot country, the home to not insignificant numbers of various different peoples: Arabs, Copts, Greeks, Italians, Armenians, Jews, Turks and others, in Cairo and Alexandria. The art-historical and museological 'solution' to representing this social and cultural amalgam, projected in the 1880s largely by the Committee for the Conservation of Arab Monuments (the Comité), and realized over the following 25 years, was the formation of four different museum institutions housing the artworks and material culture of the Pharaonic, Greco-Roman, Coptic and Muslim Arab 'facets' of, or 'stages' in, the modernizing nation's history.

The first museum, still bearing the name 'The Egyptian Museum,' originally housed artefacts of all periods and cultures. Founded under French patronage in 1835 near the Giza pyramids, it was relocated twice before being refounded in its present neoclassical form (with dedicatory inscription in Latin) in 1902 on one of the modern city's immense central squares (Midan al-Tahrir), itself at the time bounded on the west and south by the barracks of the British military. Its location gave it pride of place among all the cultural institutions of the new city, in a neighbourhood of major government ministries and foreign embassies. By designating it as The Egyptian Museum, its patrons projected an indigenous national authenticity, distinctiveness and autochthonous originality, in comparison to which the cultural institutions and museums dedicated to other facets of the country's immensely long history – Greek, Roman, Christian and Muslim – could be imagined (and continue to be imagined by most tourists) to be somehow less 'authentic,' less 'truly' Egyptian.

From the year of its founding in 1882, the Comité undertook a massive project of (in its own words) 'separating out' the artistic monuments of different ethnic and religious communities, and dedicated itself to 'exchanging' artefacts of what to their eyes were 'distinct aesthetic categories' ('des objets purement musulmans contre les objets purement coptes') so as to 'relieve the confusion' of (foreign) visitors. This resulted in the foundation of separate 'ethnically' marked museums in the 1890s: the Museum of Arab Art in 1893 (today the Islamic Museum), originally formed by the Comité as a collection in 1883 in (what at the time was) the ruined mosque of Al Hakim in the old city, the Coptic Museum, created in 1895 in the older Christian quarter of the city, and the Greco-Roman Museum, founded in 1892 in the Mediterranean city of Alexandria (the Greek and Roman capital of Egypt). The latter is referred to in twentieth-century guidebooks as the 'link' between the Egyptian and Coptic Museums in Cairo – texts, which simultaneously rescripted and refashioned the geography of the country into an itinerary of 'sites' or moments in a 4000-year 'history' re-enacted by walking through.

The urban landscape was itself a disciplinary instrument, with its very striking juxtaposition of two fantasmatic artefacts – a 'new' city and an 'old.' The new city with its long, broad boulevards, intersecting at squares or roundabouts, on which were sited major governmental institutions and ministries as well as hotels. The Museum of Arab Art was situated in a liminal zone, on a new major boulevard separating older and newer quarters. The Coptic Museum was situated in the old Christian quarter to the south, adjacent to several ancient churches, and near the remains of the Roman settlement of Babylon, the immediate precursor to the first colony of the Arab invaders, Fustat (641). (And yet, in fact, the Islamic and Coptic museums contain objects which are not infrequently identical – like the identical doors in Lacan's famous sketch of the doors of men's and women's restrooms, whose only difference is in their labels.) The museums had as their primary function the representation of the country's history by the reformatting of its complex and, to modern European eyes, confusingly miscegenated (and hybrid) identity as a succession of stages or periods leading inexorably to the presentness and modernity of the new Westernized nation-state. In this regard, the 'new' city and the 'old' were art-historicist and museological artefacts. The new Egypt was in the process of becoming a nation-state controlled by European-educated native elites – both Muslim and Christian – endowed with cultural, financial and technological aspirations, partnered with their European mentors and advisors, and tied more and more tightly to the global economies of the British and French Empires.

The weekly meetings of the Comité in Cairo were primarily devoted to the proper disposition of the hundreds of thousands of artefacts and monuments being unearthed and circulated among the newly founded Cairo museums. The discussions invariably centred upon the worth or value of objects destined for display, and there was a very clear (and unanimously shared) attitude toward the role of the Cairo museums in exhibiting only the 'best' works of art, by which was very specifically meant those works that the members of the Comité regarded (one might say with clear graphological rigour) as the 'truest' representations and the most authentic effects of a people's spirit or mind. All the rest were to be sold, given away as souvenirs to foreign dignitaries or discarded. The Cairo museums in fact contained 'sale rooms' precisely for such a purpose, to aid the ongoing refinement of their collections. The more aesthetically distinct the collection, the more distinctively legible the identities of the various communities. Aesthetic cleansing and ethnic cleansing are of course two sides of the same coin.

CONCLUSION: THE MUSEOLOGICAL FANTASY

Let me conclude by returning to the broader contexts of all this. The invention of the modern museum as an instrument of individual and social transformation was, as we now know more clearly, a specifically masonic idea. Virtually every single founder and director of the new museums in Europe and America in the late eighteenth and early nineteenth centuries was a Freemason, and the idea of shaping spatial experience as a key agent of the shaping of character was central to the museological mission from the beginning. The institution was also a masonic realization of a new form of fraternization not dependent upon political, religious or kinship alliances – that is to say, citizenship. In that regard, these new early modern museums constituted a version of the ideal or heterotopic landscapes animated and operated by these new citizens.

Sir John Soane's Museum in London is virtually unique (because of its actual physical preservation, mandated in Soane's bequest of it to the nation) in retaining today some flavour of the articulation of the masonic programme that it shared with the Freemasons who founded the post-Revolutionary Louvre (very explicitly organized for the political task of creating republican citizens out of former monarchical subjects), the original Ashmolean, and, in part, the British Museum during its Montague House period, prior to the opening of the core of the present neoclassical confection of 1847. In America, Peale's Museum in Philadelphia was the foremost masonic heterotopia of the new republic in the 1790s: the place (in this case, literally on the floor above the seat of the new government) where the new citizen of the new American Republic might imagine him or herself into existence, thanks to its revelation of the history of the earth and its creatures and races (including stuffed animals, Indians and Negroes), culminating in the present moment of the new (white) republic. Of all these masonic foundations, only Soane's retains the character that all these others (where they still exist) have lost.

In the summer of 1851 in London, you would have seen the two purest forms of this paradoxical object, this anamorphic museological artefact. Soane's retained its final form upon his death in 1837, and the Crystal Palace was the final evolved state, the complete summation, of the expositionary practices that had begun earlier in the century in a smaller and more fragmented fashion with the arcades of London and Paris, here orchestrating together the whole world of peoples and their products; of objects and their subjects. Replacing the ubiquitous prostitutes found in all the arcades was the ubiquitous figure of Queen Victoria, whose virtually daily arrival in the Crystal Palace (she visited some 60 times) galvanized thousands, and whose gaze encatalyzed the desires of the multitudes. In seeing Victoria seeing, a whole world learned how and what to desire. The subsequent development of the museum as an institution constitutes an ongoing oscillation between these two equiprimordial poles, one or the other of which has been dominant or subordinate at any one time. To imagine that museums (or art) have evolved is to participate in a museological fantasy.

It is in this regard that the new museums of Cairo of half a century later can begin to make real sense as instruments for conjuring up and appearing to 'embody' nationality, ethnicity, citizenship, heritage and history itself. As an institution and as an idea, the museum is a social phenomenon precisely on the order of an optical illusion; perpetually oscillating between the temporary stabilities of one 'type' and the other; one mode of exhibition and display and the other; one protocol of relating together objects and the subjects that seem to haunt them; subjects and the objects that appear to represent them – artefacts or artworks which themselves for 200 years have had a similarly 'anamorphic' character, alternating between aesthetic commodities and fetishes. These oscillations are complex in ways we are really only beginning to be able to articulate. Museums and expositions are not simply two different 'styles' of display or forms of content: they coexist in the same frame, as it were; each presupposing and conjuring up the other; each the other's shadow.

We have never really left the Crystal Palace, the very emblem of modernity's 'unconscious,' and still cling to its brilliant memory.

Modern museums (and their ancillary and complementary technologies such as history or art history) are the heirs to an ancient European, ultimately Hellenic, tradition of using things to reckon with, fabricate and factualize the realities that in our modernity they so coyly and convincingly present themselves as simply representing. A museum, like a city, is a theatre for staging realities. No art, no history; no museums, no modernity; no us. Taking museums seriously entails appreciating them in their historical mission as modernity's paradigmatic artifice, as the active, mediating, enabling instrument of all that we would wish to have become. Any progress in understanding here would entail – to use the example I have cited – lucidly seeing ourselves seeing Egypt imagining Europe seeing Egypt – which is precisely what the museums of Cairo were designed to do in their 'display' of 'heritage' – in ways that can foreground what we see when we see ourselves seeing museums imagining us.

But first we need to acknowledge that museums bear the mark of an irreducible dissonance between the affirmation and suspension of the symbolic identity of subjects – sites, in fact, of 'mortification,' where subjects are simultaneously petrified into immortal representations and alienated; where the price of immortality is precisely the mortality of the subject. Museums, in sum, are the sites par excellence of absent, lost and impossible signifieds; sites for the manufacture of what they purport to simply re-cite.

CHAPTER 13

HERITAGE AND INHERITORS: THE LITERARY CANON IN TOTALITARIAN BULGARIA

ALEXANDER KIOSSEV

INTRODUCTION: THE SEARCH FOR A HERITAGE

This chapter examines debates in nineteenth-century Bulgaria surrounding the idea of a national Bulgarian literary 'heritage.' It traces the evolution of these debates into the middle decades of the twentieth century, focusing particularly on the formative influence of the Communist activist, writer, poet and critic Todor Pavlov. My aim in what follows is to explore emergent nineteenth-century preoccupations with 'heritage' within the context of Bulgarian nationalism and, more specifically, within the context of literature as an increasingly important cultural institution for negotiating national identity. At the same time, I argue that the concept of 'heritage' in Bulgaria, as well as the controversies that have surrounded its formulation, was framed by an overarching anxiety about Bulgaria's 'lack' of heritage. If a nation, in order to be recognized as a nation, required a heritage, what were the consequences of Bulgaria's absent heritage? In short, this chapter endeavours to throw light on the political and contested nature of heritage, as well as on its importance in the creation of the Bulgarian nation-state.

It was not until the final decade of the nineteenth century that concerted efforts were made to establish a Bulgarian literary canon. Prior to that, literary production had been minimal. What literary works there were, were slavishly imitative of foreign, European models. In the decades between 1820 and 1850, before the foundation of the modern state in 1878, Bulgarian literature consisted for the most part of school textbooks, patriotic and educative poems, sentimental popular poetry, journalism and some short stories and dramas. Literary production was impeded by institutional weaknesses. While the level of literacy remained at around three per cent, there was only a handful of printing and publishing houses, no significant public libraries, and the distribution network linking the country was, at best, patchy. The only literary institutions were the emergent non-specialized presses and the *chitalishta* or 'reading rooms,' community centres that provided the population with books and newspapers, as well as a place for people to gather.

Bulgaria's literary life was precarious and characterized by passionate debates which centred on the very existence and nature of 'Bulgarian literature' and, more generally, on the definitions of a Bulgarian 'literary heritage.' For the most part, literature was presented in negative terms: as a deficiency or absence, as the consciousness of an essential lack. The 'missing Bulgarian classics' were experienced as a genuine trauma and mourned in countless complaints, appeals, laments, public programmes designed to promote literary activity and textbooks of rhetoric and poetics. It was not until well into the 1880s and 1890s, as we shall see, that this feeling of 'lack' gave ground to other, more complex cultural moods and ideas. As late as 1883 in his article 'The Bulgarian Popular Theatre,' the celebrated poet Ivan Vazov responded to the censorious pronouncement of Russian reviewers who condemned the Bulgarian theatre, by claiming that such criticism undermined the very existence of Bulgaria itself. 'What have we got which is Our Own and Eternal?' Vazov enquired, before concluding that before long hostile critics would be claiming that even 'the Bulgarian people do not exist!'[1]

In the last two decades of the century, however, as the state consolidated its independence, this negative topos of the Bulgarian literary *Oeffentlichkeit* began to be questioned. The role of an academic establishment was crucial, here, and substantially enhanced with the foundation of the University of Sofia in 1888. Yet there was also an earlier tradition – the historians and philologists responsible for establishing Bulgarian studies in the middle of the nineteenth century challenged a widespread opinion that Bulgaria lacked a cultural heritage and that, as a consequence, the most urgent task confronting the nation was the construction of such a heritage. Conversely, academic ethnographers, linguists, philologists and literati argued that the Bulgarian heritage had simply been forced underground. Accordingly, the scholar's task was to disclose and reactivate a buried heritage. Dedicated research would reveal a glorious, age-old Bulgarian literature and language, from which an unenlightened general public, after centuries of subservience to Ottoman rule, had become estranged. In this way, academic historians and philologists produced reverse ideologems: positive figures, which, paradoxically, served only to underscore the idea of an absent culture.

Later philologists such as Alexander Teodorov-Balan, Benyo Conev and Ivan Shishmanov, to name but a few, succeeded in shaping a clearly delineated disciplinary field called 'Bulgarian literature.' This field was characterized by a rigid taxonomic approach and by strategies of collecting, storing, preserving and cataloguing the literary heritage, as well as by pedagogical activities, which involved the interpretation of 'great works' and the writing of literary histories for educational purposes. Meanwhile, a non-academic literary culture continued to dispute the very concept of the 'Bulgarian classic.' Leading writers and critics outside the university perceived the majority of literary texts composed up to 1915 as being narrowly ideological and hence undeserving of either the appellation 'literature' or 'classics,' or for that matter, 'heritage.'

This 'second party' became much stronger after 1890 when a younger, well-educated generation returned from its studies in Europe. The group consisted of radical writers, intellectuals and critics such as Pentcho Slaveykov, Krastyo Krastev, Petko Todorov, Peyo Yavorov and Ivan Radoslavov. Once again, its members declared that Bulgarian literature, at least up until 1895, was non-existent. They claimed that existing works were no more than pale reflections of a national literature, which had been produced purely for patriotic and political purposes, and as a consequence, these works were devoid of any aesthetic merit. Writers such as Slaveykov, Yavorov and Todorov, as well as literary critics such as Krastev, dreamed of a fundamental Nietzschean 're-evaluation of the values.' They saw themselves as the genuine future 'classics' of a Bulgarian literature that was waiting to be born. Moreover, they invented the idea of an 'authentic' literary tradition; a tradition founded upon the oral culture of the Bulgarian *Volk*, a national 'folklore' which was imbued with metaphysical depths. This 'hidden tradition,' they declared, needed to be continued and developed by the classics of the future, since it alone could express the national spirit and give voice to Bulgaria's 'restless soul.'

The third party in the debate over the nation's literary heritage was the Bulgarian left. Indeed, the interpretation and evaluation of a Bulgarian cultural heritage by leftist critics constituted another alternative project. As we shall see, this was a different approach, hostile to the official academic tradition, as well as the Nietzschean vision promoted by the radical modernists. Between 1885 and 1939, at exactly the same time as the academic establishment was founding and promoting its particular version of Bulgaria's literary canon with a codified national language and shared national values, Communists and Socialists were developing an alternative literary culture of their own.

After the violent political turmoil in Bulgaria during the early 1920s, when Alexander Tzankov's government crushed a Communist uprising, leftist literature became further removed from the officially sanctioned canon. Left-wing works were published in Communist journals, newspapers and publishing houses, whose editors and directors were often closely connected to the Communist Party leadership or to the various rival leftist factions. This literature advanced aggressive counter-values, and promoted entirely different poets and writers, as well its own revered critics, who were ready to fight for their alternative ideological ground. Young writers who engaged with the official Bulgarian literati or who dared to publish their work outside the party press were considered renegades. The prominent critics of this leftist tradition, such as Dimitar Blagoev and Dimitar Dimitrov, struggled on several fronts. They fought against the official patriotic literature, as well as against what they construed as 'decadent' writings. They were strongly opposed to 'Agrarian Fascism' and to any literature which reflected bourgeois individualism and aesthetic formalism.

Leftist criticism searched for the so-called 'social equivalent' of the literary work. Social content, here, was equated in a mechanistic way with literary meaning, and the aims of art, in this sense, were socially orientated and practical. During this early period, Bulgarian Communists castigated many of the best-known Bulgarian writers and condemned prominent figures such as Vazov, Pencho Slaveikov, Stojan Mihailovski and Peyo Yavorov as bourgeois writers who were intrinsically opposed to Bulgaria's proletarian tradition. These authors, who had been institutionalized in school and university textbooks, were viewed as the representatives of an embattled and fundamentally decadent intellectual elite. From this point of view, they were certainly not worthy of incorporation into 'the great Bulgarian tradition' or, for that matter, of being assigned a place among the pantheon of the nation's literary heritage.

TODOR PAVLOV AND THE RECONSTRUCTION OF THE BULGARIAN LITERARY CANON

In the decades after 1930, the cultural policy of the Bulgarian left became embodied in the charismatic figure of Todor Pavlov (1890–1977), who redirected the left away from its self-imposed isolation. Pavlov's early career as a Communist activist and literary critic began conventionally enough. In the 1920s and 1930s he was a prominent member of the Bulgarian Communist Party and was imprisoned several times for terrorist activities. Pavlov's early collection of prison essays, poems and short stories, entitled *Beams in Hell*, which was written between 1923 and 1929, but published officially in 1947,[2] was a typical leftist attempt to create an alternative tradition. Here, he juxtaposed an ecstatic 'cosmic' vision of the future with the hellhole of the prison where he was incarcerated. Pavlov euphorically envisioned new 'bright stars on the sky of the people's soul' and conjured up a radically new, Communist pantheon of 'immortal poets' and 'heroic classics.' According to Pavlov these 'new stars' personified authors such as Christo Smirnenski, Christo Yasenov, Geo Milev, Sergei Rumyancev and Tzanko Tzerkovski, names that, far from being recognized as 'great writers' in conventional accounts of Bulgarian literature, were omitted altogether from academic textbooks. Pavlov's list was highly political and, indeed, was intended as an attack on bourgeois writers within the establishment. His list of the 'new stars' was a critique of individualist poets and literary critics such as Pencho Slaveikov, Krastev and Yavorov who, as we have already seen, sought to promote themselves as the new classics of modern Bulgarian literature.

Nonetheless, Pavlov's alternative constellation of Communist classics was linked to the Bulgarian national tradition in an important way. The poet and revolutionary Christo Botev, for example, was appropriated by Pavlov in his refashioned canon, along with some of the key ideological metaphors and heroic imagery which were popularly associated with the Bulgarian national movement. Thus, Pavlov claimed Botev, who died during the struggle for liberation in 1876, as the founding father of his Communist literary history. Botev's poetry, he maintained, articulated an authentic Bulgarian national spirit in contrast to the dry textbooks and unexceptional literary works produced by bourgeois Bulgaria. As Pavlov observed in characteristically hyperbolic terms:

> Botev…is an extreme manifestation of the deepest essence, of the unconscious drive and of the conscious goal of the whole revolutionary spirit of the Bulgarian People and of Human Spirit in general! This is the reason for the force, greatness, beauty and irresistible charm of Botev's poetry! This is the reason for its genuine immortality![3]

Significantly, Pavlov's newly invented literary tradition reflected, albeit in an inverse way, conventional histories. This appropriation and inverse reflection of the very values it contested, characterized Communist criticism in the 1920s and early 1930s.

In the mid-1930s, the central Committee of the Bulgarian Communist Party posted Pavlov to the Soviet Union in order that he could continue his political education. This was a crucial juncture in his life, as well as a decisive moment, as it turned out, in the formation of a Bulgarian literary canon. Much to his own surprise, Pavlov was elected a professor of philosophy. A year later he was awarded an honorary doctorate and made Dean of the Faculty of Philosophy, History and Literature at the Moscow University. His meteoric rise was not only the result of the political favour he curried within the Communist hierarchy, but a reflection, too, of his intellectual abilities. In Moscow he wrote a seminal work of Stalinist philosophy entitled *The Theory of Reflection* (1936; in Russian),[4] as well as completing his monumental *General Theory of Art* (1938) and a collection of outspoken critical essays aimed at undermining Communist intellectual heavyweights such as the Hungarian critic Georg Lukás.

By the time he returned to Bulgaria, Pavlov had acquired a near-mythic status as a pre-eminent Communist intellectual with an international reputation, who wielded considerable political power within the party. This was a particularly productive phase and saw the publication of numerous tomes, which sought to map out an all-encompassing ideological system. The titles speak for themselves: *Metaphysics and Dialectics, Nation and Culture, Freedom of Will, What is a Democracy?, What is a Nation?, What is Patriotism?, What is Art?* and *Contemporary Philosophical Trends.* Pavlov was no less active in the field of literary criticism, publishing works such as *The Poetry of Venko Markovski, The Literary Critic Georgii Bakalov, The Poetry of Vladimir Mayakovski and Some Important Questions on Literary Theory and Practice,* and *Christo Botev: Poet, Critic and Philosopher.*

The range of subjects tackled by Pavlov in his publications is indicative: rejecting what he considered to be the blinkered vision of Bulgaria's previous leftist tradition, he challenged the left's policy of 'self-isolationism.' His writings from this period were preoccupied with elucidating concepts such as 'heritage,' 'national tradition,' 'preservation' and 'continuity.' He ceased to search for an alternative, proletarian literary canon. Instead, his primary goal as a theoretician, critic and historian, became the 'scientific' evaluation of the national literary heritage in its entirety, including those bourgeois writers whom, on ideological grounds, he had previously excluded.

Pavlov's new rhetoric of 'inclusivity' appropriated the national literary heritage in two ways. Firstly, in a series of articles dedicated to his 'forefathers' such as Blagoev and Bakalov, Pavlov reconsidered traditional leftist criticism and rid it both of its reductive sociological methodology, and its cultural nihilism.[5] Ultimately, his ambitious aim was to synthesize leftist and rightist theory. In so doing, he sought a privileged position for himself above narrow partisan lines. Escaping from both the excesses of a bourgeois ideology and of leftist extremes, Pavlov crowned himself the legitimate heir and interpreter of an 'authentic' literary legacy. His status left him in full command of Bulgaria's cultural heritage.

After the Red Army's victory on 9 September 1944, the Anti-Fascist, Democratic National Front assumed power in Bulgaria. A few years later this coalition regime was transformed into an outright Stalinist dictatorship. The totalitarian state imposed an officially sanctioned literary culture on Bulgaria, repressing any counter-visions. This new culture was introduced both by overt force and direct repression, as well as by more subtle methods of manipulating Bulgaria's already much-contested literary heritage.

The regime's repression was not limited to any single area, but spanned the gamut of cultural fields. First, it masterminded brutal attacks on any dissenting voices, especially those who had possessed any credibility or prestige in the past. Prominent writers, literary critics and academics were denounced as the pawns of Bulgaria's previous 'Fascist' governments. Some were jailed, while others were exiled to the provinces. Publishing was effectively prohibited for any group that was judged 'ideologically suspicious.' The threat of terror silenced many or induced them to become Communist themselves, obedient members of the new 'artistic' Communist unions who colluded, in turn, with the repression. The complete domination of all forms of communal and professional literary life in Bulgaria – from universities and schools to writers' and journalists' unions, as well as reading and publishing houses – proved to be one of the most effective tools of the Communist regime's cultural policy. An ostensibly 'public' domain was subject to ideological control. Communist criticism went hand in hand with various forms of censorship and self-censorship of radio broadcasts, broadsheets and magazines. Some books were relegated to special library departments with restricted access, while library catalogues were purged of all suspicious titles.

This was the era of the People's Republic, and once again Pavlov played a crucial role. A member of Parliament's Presidium, he was also elected one of the three regents of Bulgaria (1944–46). Within the Communist leadership he was vested with the power to oversee the entire 'superstructure,' that is to say the cultural arena. Between 1945 and 1950 he occupied, at one time or another, almost all of the crucial positions in the field of ideology and cultural policy. Thus, he was Honorary Chairman of the new Union of Bulgarian Writers, Chairman of the Union of Journalists, Chairman of the Bulgarian Academy of Science, Founding Director of the Institute of Philosophy, Professor and Head of the Department of Philosophy at the University of Sofia, Doctor Honoris Causa of the University of Sofia and Chairman of the Union of the Bulgarian-Soviet Unity.

There is no evidence to suggest that during that period Pavlov was involved in any direct or indirect form of repression against the Bulgarian literati. That job was left to other, lesser figures. Nonetheless, he was instrumental in the state's new cultural and literary policy-making process. Between 1945 and 1948 he wrote a new series of books and pamphlets: *The Tasks of the National Literary Front*, *The Congress of the National Front's Writers*, *Our National Front's Intelligentsia*, *The Intelligentsia*, *Our Students and Their Task in National Front's Bulgaria*, *The Bulgarian Academy of Sciences in 1947 and its Scientific Plan for 1948*, *Science and Party Policy*, and *Our People's Teachers*.

Pavlov was especially concerned with the question of Bulgaria's cultural and literary heritage, hence the numerous books and speeches he devoted to the subject. Between 1945 and 1946, his views on these matters had begun to lose their abstract, philosophical orientation. Contemporary political events were crucial in the revision of Pavlov's ideas: Communist victory in September 1944 followed in the wake of the heroic battles of World War II, and was in turn succeeded by the first five-year plan and by the immense practical challenges posed by the building of a Socialist state. History was equated with the development of the Communist Party. References both to momentous historical events and to the official party 'narrative' constituted a mandatory rhetoric in Pavlov's speeches. Thus, his speech on the occasion of Vazov's anniversary began with a characteristic panegyric to Communist victory:

> After completing their heroic Anti-Fascist Revolution on 9 September 1944, and after their liberation with the decisive help of the Soviet Army, the Bulgarian People had to cope in a short time with all their external and internal enemies and went on, under the banner of the National Front and the leadership of the Bulgarian Communist Party, to build the economic and cultural basis of Socialism in our country.

It was only after this stock introduction that the question of heritage could be addressed. As Pavlov added:

> It is an established fact that the country's economic and cultural foundations have been successfully laid, and the Five Year Plan satisfactorily implemented. It is also a fact that Socialist culture needs to be erected on sturdy foundations; it is impossible to build Socialism without creating a new culture, national in its form and Socialist in its content. Hence, the unprecedented importance attached today to our cultural heritage, which can and must be included (although on an altogether new basis) in the building of our new People's Socialist culture. By the same token, it follows that today all democratic, progressive national figures from our near or distant past are objects of the People's affection, respect and devotion. They never enjoyed (and never could enjoy) such respect and affection under the previous reactionary, Monarchist and Fascist regimes.[6]

The oft-repeated claim in these Communist mantras was that history should be considered as a great march towards an inevitable Communist victory. In this essentially teleological vision, Communist history was construed as a fundamental revision of the past: it disclosed new meaning in Bulgaria's cultural heritage. Importantly, however, as we have seen in Pavlov's writings, this heritage was reconstructed on radically new grounds.

Because of the unprecedented importance invested in cultural heritage as a crucial component in the building of Socialism, cultural policy was a state and party concern. Along with the struggle for a new, proletarian 'literary front,' and in order to achieve the ideological unification of all 'progressive intellectual forces,' heritage remained a priority. While Pavlov presided over Bulgaria's cultural policy-making as Chairman of the Academy of Science and Head of the Writer's Union, an army of Communist *kulturträgers*, activists and Party *apparatchiks* carefully examined and 'dealt with' the management of the state's valuable heritage.

The ideological and institutional appropriation of this heritage was far from simple. An interpretative, ideological framework was put in place which regulated the canon and prescribed a hierarchy of Bulgaria's literary 'classics.' New political norms were introduced in public debates. The party organized jubilee ceremonies, commemorative ceremonies and festivities dedicated to 'classic' authors and their work, such as Vazov, Botev and Polyanov. Party activists intervened in drawing up new school and university curricula. They carried out blatant and covert censorship, dictating which authors could be published in the new party-controlled publishing houses. Pavlov himself wrote several articles dedicated to the 'correct' Communist understanding and evaluation of the Bulgarian classics. In his papers and jubilee speeches he officially codified the ideological norm, laying down the ways in which they should be properly read and understood. He enumerated their 'great and immortal contributions' and, while noting minor 'mistakes' in their work, he established the official hierarchy between the two 'greatest' authors Botev and Vazov. The former was, he argued, the greater owing to his revolutionary life, heroic death and utopian Socialism. Pavlov was even personally involved in editing and publishing a new, 'standard' edition of Vazov's work.

CONCLUSION: THE TOTALITARIAN LEGACY

The 'genius' and 'immortality' of Bulgaria's classics had been established. They were elevated to the pantheon of world greats and likened to Shakespeare, Goethe, Pushkin, Balzac and Tolstoy. Now officially canonized and policed by the *apparatchiks* of the party, the nation's heritage remained closed to debate. Thus, the ideological dictatorship imposed by the party stabilized Bulgarian literature, fixing it within the parameters of an authoritative literary history, but silencing all dissenting voices.

Mass action required a mass language. If it can be said that 'the style is the man,' then the changes discernible in the style and content of Pavlov's writing serve as a good example of how an individual can lose his own sense of self. As the official spokesperson of the party, Pavlov could now only speak in an impersonal and institutional Communist style. The language of his Marxist philosophy gradually descended towards the 'wooden,' dogmatic idiom of Stalinist totalitarianism. A price had to be paid for the creation of a mass rhetoric suitable for public meetings, with all its slogans and rallying cries to whip up the crowds. The philosophical dialectics of Hegel and Marx were distorted and then hardened into the doctrinaire clichés and rituals of party propaganda.

Yet the creation of a mass language by an elite gave rise to a number of interpretative problems. How could the meaning and emotion contained within the rhetoric be conveyed? How could the party ensure that its intentions were correctly understood? How were the writings of a prominent Marxist philosopher such as Todor Pavlov to be interpreted? How was orthodoxy, in party terms, to be defined? Such questions led, in turn, to a new, self-reflexive preoccupation with their own rhetoric: the language of the party became the focus of their concerns. The shift in emphasis from defining a 'heritage', to the very medium itself, was an index of changes in the power structure. During this period, Pavlov's own writings became more important than those of Vazov or Botev, the 'classic' authors he wrote about.

Thus a much-contested Bulgarian literary canon was fixed by totalitarian means: centralization, bureaucratization and the stringent power of a Marxist ideological discourse, which degenerated into a mechanical mass ritual. This process coincided with the violent subjugation of all alternative cultural institutions and authority, the censorship of any public debate and the repression of all nonconformist literary voices.

After this successful appropriation of the nation's symbolic capital, the Bulgarian classics – ideologically fixed and incontestable – became a metonym for the language of totalitarian power. More than 15 years passed before a new generation of commentators was able to attempt any kind of criticism. Yet even this new generation was unable to escape from the entrenched and regulated set of values which made up Bulgaria's literary heritage, and which came replete with an unquestionable genealogy of 'great authors' and 'classic texts.' In short, they were unable to see the stony ghost of the Communist commander who held their literary field together.

CHAPTER 14

DISINHERITANCE POLITICS: SPATIALIZING ABJECT HISTORIES OF WORLD WAR II SWEDEN

MICHAEL LANDZELIUS

INTRODUCTION: AN ARCHITECTURE OF REPRESSION

This chapter develops the concepts of 'disinheritance' and 'dis[re]membering' as tools for a critical, non-essentialist rethinking of heritage issues.[1] While the focus of the chapter is on the Swedish internment camps established by the military in the late 1930s or, as they were euphemistically called in military terminology, 'labour companies,' the implications of this 'disinheritance politics' are not limited to any one particular case. On the contrary, I will argue that the theoretical approach developed here has widespread and general implications for the construction and display of 'heritage.'

The labour-company camps were temporary constructions, erected for the detention of 'subversive' conscripts by the Swedish military in the late 1930s, with approval from the Social Democratic government and, during the war, from the broad-based coalition cabinet comprised of Social Democrats, Liberals, Conservatives and members of the Agrarian Party.[2] The camps were not explicitly intended to function as a way of encroaching on civilian citizens' political rights, but were envisaged as a measure to safeguard the military against destabilizing, subversive activities. However, in the case of individuals imprisoned for their political affiliations, many of the draftees were either drafted directly from civilian life to a labour-company camp, or pre-emptively removed from their military units on the basis of allegations of being 'Communists' – even though they had not engaged in any 'subversive' activities within the military, which was the legal justification for their incarceration.³ In the case of incarcerated civilians, they should obviously have been prosecuted in civilian courts had they trespassed against the law. Disregarding such legal checks and balances, democracy was undermined under the pretext of national security.

In this context, Giorgio Agamben's remark on the Prussian institution of *Schutzhaft* in the 1920s is suggestive. As he observes:

> The first concentration camps in Germany were the work not of the Nazi regime but of the Social-Democratic governments, which interned thousands of communist militants in 1923 on the basis of *Schutzhaft* and also created the *Konzentrationslager für Ausländer*…which housed mainly eastern European refugees and which may, therefore, be considered the first camp for Jews in this century.⁴

There are manifest similarities between the *Schutzhaft*, which authorized the retention of citizens without formal charges, and the labour camps established by the Swedish military in the 1930s and during World War II. The Swedish camps were part of a comprehensive civilian and military strategy of surveillance and detainment planning. They were deeply entangled in governmental practices aimed at producing a compliant, domesticated population, and any investigation of the camps thus involves an examination of 'governmentality,' in Michel Foucault's words.⁵ Representing what might be called an 'architecture of repression,' the camps force us to consider the political issues of social regulation and the practices through which power and control are constituted.

In employing terms such as 'hot interpretation,' 'contested heritage,' and 'dissonant heritage,' recent debates have shown a great interest in past objects and environments that have been excluded or marginalized in official discourses, and that raise questions related to the ones addressed in this chapter.⁶ However, a key problem repeatedly encountered in these debates is the assumption that everyone should have a right to his or her 'roots' and 'heritage,' as if these catchwords somehow represented entities existing prior to their social and cultural construction and appearance in identity struggles. Even inclusive espousals of 'multiculturalist' approaches in politics, however, are not necessarily founded upon democratic premises, as Iris Marion Young explicitly concedes when she inquires: 'But does not such affirmation of group identity itself express an ideal of community, and is it not subject to exclusionary impulses?'⁷ This is important to remember in discussions of heritage issues. Thus, accepting the notion that there is no objective position from which to know, evaluate, judge, rule or remember the world, and applying this notion to our relationships with the past, I argue here for a radical questioning and uprooting of heritage's 'imaginary lineage.'

Perhaps not surprisingly, the Swedish labour-company camps continue to be a sensitive topic in Sweden. Apart from an academic book-length study,⁸ they have been displaced by a politics of institutionalized amnesia, non-representation and non-display. The camps do not feature in publications or exhibitions by local, regional or national museums, and on the whole, critical inquiries into the Swedish camps have been brushed aside by the Swedish governments of the day. In April 2000, for example, in response to a query from a member of the Left Party (previously the Communist Party), the deputy prime minister rejected further research into the camps, simply stating: 'I share the view previously taken by Cabinet and Parliament.'[9] Three years earlier, the then defence minister of the Social Democratic cabinet responded to similar cross-questioning by referring to a decade-old document which discarded a proposed further investigation of the camps on the grounds that they were established because of 'prevailing opinions about what constituted a threat against the country. Attempts to keep Sweden out of the war were put before civil rights issues in a way that would not be tolerated in contemporary society.' Thus, while acknowledging that from a late-twentieth-century perspective the camps were unacceptable, the defence minister nevertheless concluded that there was nothing to be gained from a retrospective investigation. 'It makes no sense,' he declared, 'to scrutinize today the measures taken in the early 1940s in order to assess whether or not they were legitimate.'[10]

Despite the reluctance to address the specific issue of the camps in Sweden, a thorough examination of the camps is crucial. There is substantial proof, for example, that the consensus claimed by the defence minister in his description of 'prevailing opinions' is disingenuous. At the time of their construction there was vigorous opposition to the camps.[11] Furthermore, an assessment of how such 'prevailing opinions' are socially constructed and come to affect certain kinds of de-humanizing and exclusionary practices has important implications in the present for the way we think about the past and its preservation. In short, the experience of the Swedish military labour-company camps has much to teach us about the writing of history and the management of the past.

This chapter is divided into four principal sections. Section one gives a brief historical background to the construction of the camps, while section two proceeds to consider the discourse that framed and enabled the creation of the camps. In section three, I turn to questions of heritage in relation to overarching issues of democracy, citizenship and the role of the past in the present. I suggest that David Held's concept of the 'democratic thought experiment'[12] and Cornelius Castoriadis's concept of 'autonomy'[13] are essential tools for a reconfiguration of a case such as the Swedish camps. In section four, I elaborate the concept of 'dis[re]membering' as a different way of approaching the past, one which results in a permanent replacement of the imaginary lineage of heritage with a 'rhizome history' of 'disinheritance.' I thus argue for a politicized deployment of the past along much more radical lines than those of multicultural inclusivism. In specific relation to the Swedish labour-company camps, I will suggest that a democratic politics of disinheritance could be exemplified and promoted through a reconstruction of a labour-company camp outside the Royal Palace in Stockholm.

THE SWEDISH MILITARY INTERNMENT CAMPS

In 1930, the Stockholm Exhibition, created by avant-garde architects and supported by the government, politicians on both the left and right, labour unions, leading entrepreneurs and companies, staged a vision of the future of Sweden based on principles of rationality, social reform, industrial mass-production and functionalist architecture.[14] It was a vision shared by many. However, 1931 saw social disruptions culminate in open and violent confrontation, with the military gunning down demonstrating workers. The 1930s continued to be fraught, with open class conflict alongside periods of reformist co-operation, and the implementation of a number of important social reforms.[15] In the 1940s, Sweden adopted a pragmatic foreign policy, following the slogan 'neutrality in war as a continuation of freedom from alliances in peace,'[16] the actual contents of which were hidden from public scrutiny through a secretive handling of information including a pre-censoring State Information Board, which included several influential newspaper editors as members.[17] In this context, some Liberal but especially Communist newspapers were suppressed. Arson by police and military officers against one Communist newspaper resulted in the loss of five lives, including those of women and children. Other events during the war included a nationwide police raid against the offices of the Communist Party, while national borders were opened to allow for the transport of 2.14 million German troops through 'sovereign' Swedish territory on trains that also provisioned German military brothels in Norway and Finland with sex-workers. Finally, concessions by the Swedish government to German demands allowed for extensive and profitable exports of iron ore, high quality steel, machinery, ball bearings and the like.[18]

Given the war situation, the management of social tensions and discontent was of utmost importance. During the war, the Swedish military and the government, as well as much of the press, were complicit not only in identifying threats, but in actually fabricating problems and dangers. In 1940, reporting from a meeting of the State Information Board, one newspaper ran the headline: 'Propaganda: an Important Issue in Times of Crisis.' The article quoted a speaker of the board with approval as saying: 'Perhaps the most important task today is the creation of a real spirit of Swedishness in the nation.'[19] Means were created to control this Swedishness through an extensive politics of surveillance, involving police and military officers, as well as ordinary citizens who acted as informers. During the war itself, millions of telephone calls were recorded, while 6000 individual telephones were tapped continuously, and more than 40 million letters and packages were opened.[20] This institutionalized distrust in citizens, and suspension of civil rights and of privacy, indicates a fundamental destabilization of society. When understood in this context, the targeting of alleged 'Communists' and the creation of military internment camps for their detention, seem to confirm the observation that:

> ... practices of modern statecraft work not primarily by solving problems and dangers in the name of a domestic population already given, but by inscribing problems and dangers that can be taken to be exterior to sovereign man and whose exteriority serves to enframe the 'domestic population' in which the state can be recognized as a center and can secure its claims to legitimacy.[21]

Having thus framed the population and targeted certain individuals, the comprehensive strategy for detainment included detailed plans for the seizure of civilians by joint forces of military and police personnel.[22] There were two broad categories of camps. The first kind consisted of eight separate camps, dispersed throughout the country, for people on the political left, who were as a rule labelled 'Communists.' Those incarcerated, however, further included Anarchists, Syndicalists and Swedish volunteers from the civil war in Spain, as well as a few Social Democrats who were also erroneously identified as 'Communists.' The second kind of camp comprised one single camp organized by the army to contain so-called 'undisciplined elements,' a blanket term that encompassed people who had been found guilty of 'antisocial' behaviour such as theft, drunkenness, maltreatment and late return from military leave.

In this chapter both incarcerated groups will henceforth be referred to within inverted commas as 'undisciplined elements' and 'Communists,' respectively, since a core issue here concerns the legitimacy of those practices of marginalization and homogenization that led to this labelling, exclusion and imprisonment of Swedish citizens. With regard to the 'Communists,' it is imperative to 'de-collectivize' the notion of threat and 'otherness.' Rather than imagining the interns as an aggregate mass, they should be thought of as a collection of individuals. Indeed, it is crucial to bear in mind that the exclusion practices took place within particular situated practices of power and involved the interaction of individuals, not of some undifferentiated mass. Thus, individuals reported on other individuals, while individual personnel were responsible for processing the detainees through the system. Moreover, the categorization by the commander-in-chief of certain conscripts as 'undisciplined elements,' also needs to be qualified. In the authoritarian society of Sweden before and during the war years, which, as we have seen, saw the suspension of many democratic rights, notions of 'discipline' and 'indiscipline' have a particular meaning: the 'undisciplined elements' were 'undisciplined' only in relation to a norm that was upheld and promoted by an intolerant military system, which was characterized by its rigid class distinctions and inflexible hierarchy.

The total number of alleged 'Communists' incarcerated in the Swedish military internment camps amounted to some 700 individuals, and the corresponding figure for the 'undisciplined elements' totalled some 120. The length of incarceration corresponded to the normal draft period, but several conscripts were incarcerated more than once. Significantly, not one single National Socialist was detained during the period when the camps were operative. In 1941 a proposal was drafted for 3500 'Communists' to be dispatched to 10 proposed labour camps pending a general mobilization. In the event, however, only two of these camps were ever set up.[23] In this context, it should be noted that the military security service and the secret police kept a so-called Communist Register, which contained the names of between 36,000 and 60,000 civilians.[24] With regard to the possible implications of the surveillance and detainment planning carried out, it should be noted that co-operation between the Swedish secret police and the Gestapo has been disclosed with regard to the handing over of names of Swedish dockworkers who were suspected, largely on the grounds of their political affiliations, of planning to sabotage cargo shipments to Germany.[25]

THE CAMPS AND THE SOCIAL IMAGINARY

The 1930s in Sweden witnessed the implementation of a number of social reforms initiated by the workers' movement, women's rights activists and the Social Democrats. These formed part of a modernizing process, which conventionalized key social practices[26] and ultimately contributed to the imposition of a distinct sense of Swedish 'normality.' In relation to this social construction of normality, the particular conditions of governmentality in the war context brought about the victimization of a particular section of the population, which under the circumstances was more likely to be perceived as a threat than other marginalized groups.[27] However, the sinister 'sameness' of this group of alleged 'Communists' seems to have made them particularly threatening. The construction of them as an 'abject' threat relied upon a conflation of political and medical discourses and served as a means for the self-affirmation of Swedes in general, as well as for giving legitimacy to the particular governmental practices adopted.[28] This psycho-medicalization of the social imaginary and of governmental practices is illustrated by the fact that, in 1931, one in every twenty people facing criminal charges was ordered to take a mental health examination. By 1940, this figure had increased exponentially to one in five.[29] The camps should thus not be seen simply in the context of military threats, national security issues, and the aggressive Stalinist rhetoric articulated by the Swedish Communist Party. Rather, the Swedish military internment camps of the war brought together interdependent psychological, medical, political and geographical factors that were related to other developments in 1930s Sweden.

In the tense wartime situation, the drive for national unity was summed up in the jingoistic assertion: 'A Swede Keeps Quiet.' However, the obsession in the contemporary press and in political debate with the 'Communist threat' shows how, in Mark Wigley's words, 'that which has no place in the space reenters it, takes an illegitimate place, but does so at the invitation of the police of the space, the representatives of its law,' and hence, how 'the illegal alien is recalled by the law, returning to cover over some kind of embarrassing deficiency in the space, to shore it up and articulate the very borders it violates.'[30] In effect, what was involved was a purification ritual. Objectionable thoughts and deviant behaviour were de-legitimated and classified as 'unnatural.' In promoting racialized and de-humanizing thinking, Swedish 'scientific' research and 'medical' practice laid claim to the 'scientific' frontline. In brief, governmental practices were influenced by this imagery and the camps cannot be understood outside of the Swedish state's attempt to impose a regime that would regulate the 'hygiene' of all citizens within the body politic.[31]

There is evidence that biological and medical discourse, which under-scored the need for hygiene, came to structure the camps. Inasmuch as this 'hygienism' was applied to and prescribed the same treatment for both types of incarcerated conscripts, it amounted to a metaphorical condensation of the two different categories. Both the 'Communists' and 'undisciplined elements' were imagined as an indistinguishable aggregate of degenerates. Thus, while the 'Communists' were variously vilified as 'infectious hotbeds,' 'vermin,' 'slimy animals' and 'lunatics,' in the press and military documents, the 'undisciplined elements' were labelled 'infantile egocentrics' and 'spineless psychopaths' suffering from 'moral insanity.' In short, this 'medicalization' homogenized the incarcerated conscripts and facilitated an exclusionary politics of detainment, cleansing and containment.[32]

The alleged otherness of the detainees troubled the imagined integrity and purity of the Swedish body politic in much the same way that discarded elements of an individual's body such as hair, nail clippings or menstrual blood disturb and provoke awkward avoidance or disgust.[33] In this regard, the camps were sites of ambiguity, where prisoners were de-personalized as well as de-humanized in the attempts to police the boundary between inside and outside, between the healthy body politic and unhealthy sources of dangerous infection. The abuses of civil rights that took place in the camps were thus justified in a language that drew upon an imagery of degeneration, repellent bodily discharges and infectious disease. From this perspective, the camps demonstrate how, in the imaginary constitution as well as actual construction of modern Sweden, particularly during World War II, the body politic was invested with an imaginary homogeneous identity through exclusionary practices legitimated in terms of de-humanized 'otherness.'

THEORIZING DISINHERITANCE: THE 'DEMOCRATIC THOUGHT EXPERIMENT'

So far I have sketched a general social and political background to the Swedish labour camps and I have briefly explored some of the strategies that were mobilized to legitimate the detentions within the camps. But the questions remain. What makes this case particularly challenging with regard to the needs and possibilities of rethinking heritage issues and the politics of the past? How can the preservation and display of the past be freed from deadening institutional apparatuses and contribute to a critical public re-engagement with democracy? First, a 'multiculturalist' approach cannot easily be adopted since the alleged 'undisciplined elements' and 'Communists' shared a common culture with their fellow Swedes and prosecutors. It is thus not a case of a dominant cultural group rejecting marginalized cultural expressions. Second, the case is not solely one of rectifying a false account of the past. It is thus neither a straightforward case of a scholarly mistaken understanding of the past, nor simply one of a political repression of facts. In this chapter I argue that considerations of such questions play a crucial role in a reconfiguration of the camps, yet, the case also represents a situation of irresolvable polysemy, where not only party politics, but also different scholarly principles and theories, lead to radically different historical accounts.[34]

Accordingly, in the second half of this chapter my aim is to explore a number of theoretical issues that arise from a consideration of the camps, before concluding with a specific suggestion as to how a reconstruction of the camps might be usefully put to the services of a democratic politics. Let me here introduce Held's theorizing of the 'democratic thought experiment' and Castoriadis's discussion of 'autonomy.' In outlining his 'democratic thought experiment,' Held is concerned with establishing 'the conditions of an ideal autonomy, that is, the conditions, rights and obligations people would accept as necessary for their status to be met as equally free members of their political community.'[35] The key notion here is of course that the freedom of any one citizen presupposes that equal conditions, rights and obligations apply to any other member of society. Similarly, Castoriadis emphasizes the interdependence between the autonomy of self and other when he states that 'the Ego of autonomy is not the absolute Self, the monad cleaning and polishing its external-internal surface in order to eliminate the impurities resulting from contact with others,' but rather the subject 'traversed through and through by the world and by others.'[36] This is in itself important to consider in relation to the purifying and exclusionary practices of Swedish politics discussed above. However, Castoriadis further distinguishes between 'autonomy' as 'self-legislation or self-regulation' and 'heteronomy' as 'legislation or regulation by another.'[37] The democratic notion of autonomy as a matter of 'equally free members' of a political community has never been achieved. In practice, it has always been displaced by heteronomy through 'a mass of conditions of privation and oppression,' reflected 'in the impersonal nature of the "economic mechanisms of the market" or in the "rationality of the Plan," [or in] the law of a few presented as the law as such.'[38] As we have seen, some such 'conditions of privation and oppression' were particularly clearly manifested in Sweden during the 1930s and the war years. It is thus clear that not only should the relationship between state and citizens be considered in discussions of democracy, but also all institutions and agencies in society should be made accountable with regard to the furthering of democracy and autonomy. In Held's words, this necessitates that

> …the articulation of political institutions with key groups, agencies, associations and organizations of the economy and civil society, national and international, be re-formed so that the latter become part of the democratic process – adopting a structure of rules and principles compatible with those of democracy.[39]

In fully interrogating the process of 'othering' that imposed a particular kind of heteronomy in Sweden during the 1930s and the war, one should thus also articulate the role and interests of the different political parties, of the medical establishment, of the press, of labour unions, of businesses making profits from the war economy, and so forth.

The insights of Castoriadis and Held, I contend, can be usefully applied to the present as well as the past, including the challenging case of the Swedish military labour-company camps. Heteronomy, rather than autonomy, is and has been the all-pervasive form of political experience in democracies as well as other kinds of state formations. Accounts of the past as a linear linkage of events that put everything in order, and thus to rest, contribute to this heteronomy. The notion of heritage is deeply implicated in such an understanding of the past, and should be permanently uprooted. The only legitimate democratic relation to the past in a time of globalization is to strive for 'conditions of an ideal autonomy.'

History cannot but be an imagined reconstruction, and individuals as well as organizations such as museums, I argue, should actively engage in a politics of 'dis[re]membering.' The idea of the past as a construction or reconstruction, needs to be radicalized and politicized from the point of view offered by the democratic thought experiment. The objective would be to involve people in the process of relating to the past in a way that makes them acknowledge their own 'situatedness' both within society and history, as well as positively affirm the unavoidable human condition of distance and estrangement in relation to the past. In this view, we do not inherit a 'heritage,' but a 'disinheritance.' This idea is contrary to notions of 'living history,' as well as to the position taken by critics such as John Tunbridge and Gregory Ashworth, who conceptualize disinheritance as a dilemma when they state that: 'The problem of disinheritance is not simple, therefore it admits of no simple solution. The attempted creation of a universal heritage which provides an equal but full inheritance for all is not only essentially illogical but the attempt to approach it rapidly creates its own problems.'[40]

In contrast to this reasoning, I argue that disinheritance, to paraphrase Tunbridge and Ashworth, is not a problem but, on the contrary, simply the universal democratic solution. Thus, sectarian claims upon the past in terms of heritage and identity should be incisively critiqued and deconstructed with the aim to subvert and deny all claims of an immediate linkage to the past, and to thus actively disinherit each and every one. The interpretation and management of the past should not be left in the hands of quasi-neutral bodies, but should take place through what Henri Lefebvre characterizes as 'the permanent participation of the "interested parties," with their multiple, varied and even contradictory interests.'[41] The objective would be to construct disinheritance objects/assemblages/sites of a sufficiently complex nature, on the one hand, to affirm our inevitable estrangement from the past, and on the other, to make appropriation for any one particular purpose, except for the furthering of global democracy, impossible.

THE POLITICS OF 'DIS[RE]MEMBERING' THE PAST

The remains of the past have for too long been given over to homogenizing and legitimating strategies. For example, the notion of a homogeneous 'Swedishness' is no more justified or democratic today than when imposed through governmental practices upon a heterogeneous population during the 1930s and the war years. A progressive disinheritance politics, as a tool for democratic development, should explicitly acknowledge the complexity of the past and highlight the continuous and open-ended process of struggle around political rights as well as cultural identities. Hence, disinheritance politics should not be seen merely as a matter of pointing out the self-evident fact that people in the past lived under conditions of political heteronomy, but rather as a way of re-inscribing into the past the undetermined and open-ended, and thus deeply political, character of that particular moment understood as a past/passed present.

As a radical critique of the inherently 'historicizing' notion of heritage, disinheritance should be thought of as a matter of 'spatializing' the past. The distinctive difference between heritage and disinheritance can be illustrated with reference to Gilles Deleuze and Felix Guattari's conceptualization of 'rhizome,' which should be understood as 'a map and not a tracing.'[42] A rhizome establishes connections not 'vertically' across time, but 'horizontally' across space between diverse forms of social phenomena in a ceaseless process. The qualities of a rhizome therefore question notions of stable meanings, firm identities, and territorial boundaries, and subvert the idea that stability could be achieved through a historicizing strategy.[43] Critical of any such idea of roots, Deleuze and Guattari have stated that 'Values, morals, homelands, religions, and these private certitudes that our vanity and our complacency bestow generously on us, have as many deceptive sojourns as the world arranges for those who think they are standing straight and at ease, among stable things.'[44]

In articulating the notion of a 'rhizome history' of disinheritance as bound up with a spatial strategy, inspiration can also be gained from recent discussions of 'counter-monuments'[45] and 'spaces of resistance,'[46] as well as of 'geographies of exclusion.'[47] Indeed, an important aspect of conceptualizing 'dis[re]membering' is an interdisciplinary engagement with spatiality, which brings together approaches developed across fields, from politics, architecture, geography, heritage and preservation. The potential of such an approach is to disclose further the constitutive ways in which processes of othering and conditions of heteronomy are related to physical measures, such as exclusion and detainment, and thus deeply embedded in spatial practices and organization.

Before considering how the Swedish military labour-company camps could be reconstructed as what we might call a disinheritance site, we should ask: What value do the Swedish military labour-company camps represent in the present if we were to employ the conventional criteria that determine heritage policy? They would be significant in a number of ways: the camps are historically as well as architecturally unique (even if they were not consciously designed); they represent an important historical event in Swedish history and, more specifically, in the personal histories of prominent individuals, such as leading members of the radical Swedish left; they functioned, as we have seen, as important sites around which national, as well as individual, identities were formed; they are war monuments with significant symbolic meanings; finally, the camps have an important educational role in teaching how citizens' rights and democracy have been negotiated in the formation of Swedish modernity.

Yet there are clear problems involved in fitting the camps into a conventional heritage discourse. The core problem concerns the uncanny and foundational character of the camps as located on the border between legal and illegal procedures, between the rule of law and arbitrary injustice.[48] In an uncanny fashion this border location concerns both perpetrators and victims, both governmental power and incarcerated conscripts. Indeed, these very distinctions become ambiguous. The camps therefore represent a recalcitrant past not immediately possible to 'domesticate' and purge of all ambiguity. However, this recalcitrance should not make us fall victim to the quantitative, 'choose your own story,' approach of liberalism. Instead, the aim should surely be to achieve an unsettling experience, in which immediate closure is forestalled, and which would encourage us to engage in the creative act of thinking the social differently, of realizing the possibility of a different 'constitutive social imaginary,' in the words of Castoriadis.[49] As I have argued in this chapter, the camps represent a number of essential possibilities for achieving such an unsettling experience.

The strategy of 'dis[re]membering' that I propose would include temporary critical interventions aiming at a spatial implosion of the past into the present. The notion of the 'counter-monument' shows some affinities with this idea, since it refers to 'attempts to visually complement or change the appearance of earlier monuments,' in order to 'register protest or disagreement with an untenable prime object and to set a process of reflection in motion.'[50] The objective should not be to simply invert meanings or in other ways freeze signification. Gilles Deleuze, commenting on Walt Whitman's writing, remarks suggestively that '...a kind of whole must be constructed, a whole that is all the more paradoxical in that it only comes after the fragments and leaves them intact, making no attempt to totalize them.'[51] I suggest that the 'kind of whole' to be constructed should be a disinheritance assemblage. In the case of the Swedish camps, de-humanizing social abjection was entangled in spatial dispersal: the camps were located far away from the sites of power where they were conceived, and invisible to most Swedish citizens. In this fashion, spatial interdependencies between social phenomena were hidden by powerful textualizations that purified centres of power through dislocation of its actual effects. A politics of dis[re]membering would counter this disjunction by a method of implosion, whereby abjected fragments would be made to reappear as disinheritance assemblages in key sites whence abjective textualizations emerged and were enforced.

OPENING/CONCLUSION

In the case of the Swedish military labour-company camps, one strategy of dis[re]membering would entail building a disinheritance assemblage in the form of a reconstructed camp in the courtyard of the Royal Palace in Stockholm, where the Nazi sympathizer, King Gustav V (1858–1950), resided during the war. In this way, the marginalized past would be critically relocated to the centre, while the silencing authority behind the exhortation 'A Swede Keeps Quiet' would be crucially de-centred. 'Dis[re]membering' the past would involve the temporary erection of such disinheritance assemblages in attempts to subvert and disrupt the 'normal flow of things,' and to de-naturalize the social imaginary with the aim to critically open up the past and promote much-needed principles of autonomy, cosmopolitan democracy and citizenship.

CHAPTER 15

MOURNING HERITAGE: MEMORY, TRAUMA AND RESTITUTION

ROBERT SHANNAN PECKHAM

> Lest we forget.
> *Rudyard Kipling*

INTRODUCTION: THE LOSS OF HERITAGE

Although heritage is associated with the preservation of artefacts, buildings, and landscapes that have survived from the past, in many cases heritage performs the obverse function: it preserves things that have already been destroyed. In effect, it manages a loss. War cemeteries are one extreme example of heritage sites that are also sites of mourning.[1]

There is a close connection between heritage, memorials and the elaborate commemorative rituals that surround them, such as the laying of wreaths at cenotaphs. The memorial to the Unknown Soldier serves as an example of the way in which loss is located at the centre of heritage and functions as a cornerstone in the construction of national identities:[2]

> No more arresting emblems of the modern culture of nationalism exist than cenotaphs and tombs of Unknown Soldiers. The public ceremonial reverence accorded these monuments precisely because they are either deliberately empty or no one knows who lies inside them, has no true precedents in earlier times.[3]

The connections between heritage and war commemorations are made explicit in war museums, where the museum itself functions as an overarching memorial.[4] 'Museum and mausoleum,' Theodor Adorno remarked, 'are connected by more than phonetic association.'[5]

Commemorative rituals associated with war have been central in shaping our understanding of heritage in Europe. The cemeteries in northern France are a case in point. They are memorials that elicit grief and have functioned as the focal point for the bereaved to articulate their loss. They serve as sites of pilgrimage, too, where visitors marvel at the heroism and noble sacrifice that is localized and objectified in the war cemetery. Although the bodies of fallen soldiers were collected together and interred in the cemetery at Gettysburg (1863) during the American Civil War,[6] World War I represented 'a new era of remembrance' since 'for the first time in British military history scattered bodies were to be gathered together, reinterred, and individually marked.'[7] Guidebooks of the battlefields were published as early as 1919. Following George V's visit to the scene of war in 1922 on the so-called 'King's pilgrimage,' tours of the cemeteries became commonplace.[8]

An Imperial War Graves Commission, which included Sir Edwin Lutyens, the architect of the Cenotaph in London (1919–21), and the Nobel Laureate Rudyard Kipling, deliberated on the form and style of the commemorations. Kipling's words from the poem 'Recessional' composed for the 1897 Jubilee – 'Lest we forget' – were chosen as 'the emblematic phrase of remembrance.' The rituals of remembrance elaborated in the aftermath of World War I largely 'defined what was to be remembered in post-war Britain.'[9] The war cemetery became an important component of a British national heritage, a place where national memories were enshrined in material form.[10]

'The rituals of remembrance' that surround the experiences of war and mass death in the twentieth century suggest that loss and its commemoration are important dimensions of heritage. My aim in this chapter is to develop this insight and to explore how attitudes to history and memory are changing within the context of a new 'moral politics,' where the emphasis is on testimony, trauma and restitution. Significantly, the concept of 'trauma,' from the Greek word for wound, acquired new meanings in both world wars, where it came to be equated with 'shell shock' and 'battle fatigue;' an understanding of 'trauma' as a psychological category merged, in complex ways, with trauma's physiological meanings. Moreover, the critical reappraisals of heritage from the point of view of the 'abject,'[11] which James Duncan and Michael Landzelius discuss elsewhere in this volume, suggest that within cultural studies ethico-political interventions are being increasingly advocated and can be considered, in some sense, as extensions of this moral politics.

'Heritage' is exposed in such cultural approaches as an 'invention;' a state-sponsored fabrication designed to silence dissenting voices and experiences. As such, heritage involves the perpetuation of historical injustices and the systematic erasure of other people's memories. Accordingly, museum exhibitions, it is argued, must be made to negotiate historical discriminations and provide ways of redressing the past. In the words of Elazar Barkan, 'moral issues [have come] to dominate public attention and political issues.'[12]

In the pages that follow I suggest that memories of trauma are taking the place of an increasingly discredited heritage. At the same time, the concept of trauma is appropriating the 'loss' that has haunted heritage and making use of the institutional apparatuses, such as museums, that have underpinned heritage. The problems of remembrance and restitution posed by the experiences of the Holocaust and World War II have been crucial in this reinterpretation of heritage and have been largely responsible for the ongoing re-evaluation of history.[13] Whereas history has conventionally been construed as an 'objective' account of the past, in opposition to memory, today the opposite is becoming true. History is increasingly viewed as partial and memory as authentic. The concern with trauma, reflected in blockbuster films such as Steven Spielberg's 1993 adaptation of the Australian writer Thomas Keneally's book, *Schindler's Ark*, forms part of a growing preoccupation with personal and collective trauma in popular culture.

Heritage, as we have seen in the case of war commemorations, celebrates a heroic loss that preludes a greater victory. The unknown soldier dies so that the nation can live on. Here, loss is re-inscribed with a positive meaning as 'sacrifice,'[14] and becomes a precondition for victory. The language in which heritage is championed is often triumphalist, as Walter Benjamin recognized when, speaking of 'cultural treasures,' he wrote in his 'Theses on the Philosophy of History:' 'Whoever has emerged victorious participates to this day in the triumphal procession in which the present rulers step over those who are lying prostrate. According to traditional practice, the spoils are carried along in the procession.'[15] As Benjamin concluded: 'There is no document of civilization which is not at the same time a document of barbarism.'[16] 'Heritage,' it could be argued, is usually the prerogative of the vanquisher. For the defeated, 'lying prostrate' under 'the triumphal procession,' remembrance takes a different form: trauma.[17]

'As living memory dies out,' the sociologist and cultural historian Paul Gilroy remarks, 'the idea of [a] just, anti-Nazi war is being recovered, comm-emorated, and struggled over, but we must ask hard, uncomfortable questions about the forms this commemoration takes.'[18] Growing up as a black child in postwar London, Gilroy experienced the tension at first hand between an enthusiastic patriotism and the realization that non-whites were being expurgated from the heroic narrative of war. Indeed, as Gilroy concedes, the memory of World War II provides 'ethical resources' that have consequences for our thinking about identity and heritage today.[19] Drawing upon his youthful experience of prejudice, Gilroy is concerned primarily with how a democratic, cosmopolitan viewpoint might be promoted, which nurtures trans-cultural identification and eludes entrenched national, racial and cultural camps. How is this 'planetary humanism' with its radical cosmopolitanism to be created?[20] The disavowal of heritage and its implosion by a political rhetoric of difference, I argue in this chapter, cannot provide the answer. All too often, one essentialist version of identity is replaced by another, so that authoritarian and anti-democratic outlooks are reaffirmed.

In pursuit of redress, the 'victims' replicate the segregationist politics they set out to undermine, propagating 'a repertory of power that produced their sufferings in the first place.'[21] The Greenwich exhibition is a good example, too, of the way in which critiques of racist politics can themselves perpetuate forms of 'ethnic absolutism,' forging what might, perhaps harshly, be called 'pseudo-solidarities.'[22] This discourse of differentiation, between 'white' and 'black,' like the nationalist discourse that has grounded heritage, propagates the absolute incompatibility of race it claims to supersede. As Iris Young has observed:

> The categorical opposition of groups essentializes them, repressing the differences within groups. In this way the definition of difference as exclusion and opposition actually denies difference. This essentializing categorization also denies difference in that its universalizing norms preclude recognizing and affirming a group's specificity in its own terms.[23]

HISTORY AND MEMORY

Some 40 years ago, Ernest Gellner argued that national cultures were imaginatively engineered and that nations were 'invented' – as he put it – by nationalism.[24] Since then, the idea that traditions are 'inventions' that sustain the 'imagined community' of the nation has become a commonplace.[25] Accordingly, heritage is viewed as an ideological construct, a social fantasy, which masks, naturalizes, and legitimates the authority of the state.

It is this political context of heritage-building that the French historian Pierre Nora explores in his mammoth compilation *Les Lieux de Mémoire* (1984), a work that informs many of the contributions in the present volume. Nora distinguishes 'history' from 'memory' and argues that the former is a recent construct, manufactured by the institutions of the state in order to compensate for the loss of what he calls a 'real' and 'spontaneous memory' associated with peasant culture, 'that quintessential repository of collective memory:' '*Lieux de mémoire* arise out of a sense that there is no such thing as spontaneous memory, hence that we must create archives, mark anniversaries, organize celebrations, pronounce eulogies, and authenticate documents because such things no longer happen as a matter of course.'[26]

In short, history is a response to a crisis of memory, which modernity has precipitated. New technologies and economic conditions, fuelled by the gathering pace of globalization, mean that people are uprooted and severed from the social and cultural foundations that anchor memory and provide social cohesion and continuity. Nora's 'sites of memory' (*lieux de mémoire*) are nodes in a comprehensive mnemonic network designed to prevent citizens from forgetting. 'History,' as opposed to this 'real memory,' is one way that 'modern societies organize a past they are condemned to forget because they are driven by change.' Heritage, in essence, is viewed as a coherent, state-sponsored strategy of forceful remembrance.[27] As Michel de Certeau remarks, in contrast to the formal consecration of an historical past in the museum, 'memory is a sort of anti-museum: it is not localizable.'[28] The creation of an 'archive' culture, replete with museums and heritage sites, is not an indication of society's healthy state of memory; on the contrary, it is a symptom of a debilitating amnesia.

Implicit in the idea of invented traditions is the assumption that somewhere beyond this construction resides a world of legitimate 'memory.' And precisely because these memories have been forcefully suppressed, they must necessarily entail trauma. The emphasis on slavery in the permanent exhibition at the Maritime Museum in Greenwich discussed by Duncan, or on military camps in the 'democratic thought experiment' proposed by Landzelius, serve as examples of this tendency to deconstruct official versions of 'history' and 'heritage' as works of imaginative labour in order to privilege the traumatic experiences of slavery and incarceration, which have been obscured.

The debates surrounding Maya Lin's design of the Vietnam Veterans Memorial on the Washington Mall and a projected exhibition of the atomic bomb and the origins of the Cold War at the Smithsonian Institution in Washington serve as other examples of the way in which contested versions of the past are increasingly colliding and making the construction of public commemorative monuments and museum displays contentious. Originally erected in 1982, the Vietnam Memorial provoked a violent reaction from those who saw the black granite wall engraved with the name of nearly 60,000 men and women killed or missing in the war as undignified – 'a black gash of shame.' The ostensible purpose of the memorial was to set apart the sacrifices of the veterans from the US's calamitous military policy in Vietnam. However, a conventional statue depicting three soldiers in action was subsequently added to the site in response to condemnation from critics who regarded the wall as unworthy of those who gave their lives for their country.[29]

Central to the exhibition of the atomic bomb and the beginning of the Cold War, entitled The Crossroads, at the Smithsonian, was the display of the Enola Gay, the B-29 aircraft that dropped the atomic bomb on Hiroshima. The controversy that surrounded the proposed exhibition in 1994 and 1995 under-scored conflicting ideas about how the past should be represented and about which version of the past was the 'balanced' one. Discussing the episode, one commentator has recently observed: 'How will history be represented in public museums when it must become the conjoint product of several competing epi-stemic cultures with incongruent standards of evidence, argument and purpose?'[30]

Heritage, which is increasingly viewed as an ideological reworking of the past that serves to bolster and promote political interests, has become a field of political struggle around the issue of 'Whose past?' 'What kind of represen-tation?' 'In whose name?' Moreover, if heritage is construed as the preservation and management of an 'historical' past, 'trauma' calls for the resolution of repressed 'memories'. Today memory has become a site of power where restitution turns the losers into winners.

In the final sections of this chapter I look at some of the ways in which heritages are being deconstructed and reconfigured as memory within a new moral politics where the emphasis is on guilt and forgiveness. Today sites of victory are being re-inscribed as sites of defeat, so that heritage and trauma are being fundamentally realigned. Europeans are being asked to remember what they were taught to forget: the acts of violence and the losses upon which Europe's prosperity has been dependent. As James Young has argued in the context of the Holocaust, as different collective memories compete with national self-images and political interests, remembrance itself has become problematic. What form should remembrance take?[31] This is the question being addressed in the aftermath of 11 September 2001 bombing of the World Trade Center in New York, where different forms of memorializing a 'global' trauma are being debated.[32]

THE NEW MORAL POLITICS

Mass atrocities have haunted twentieth-century Europe with the experience of Nazi Germany. Recent events in Bosnia and Kosovo have once again brought the issues of genocide, restitution and the institution of war-crimes tribunals to the forefront of public debate. The indictment of the Serb leader Slobodan Milosevic for masterminding a policy of 'ethnic cleansing' in Bosnia, and his trial at the UN International Criminal Tribunal at The Hague, marks the rise of an increasingly influential and self-proclaimed 'moral' politics. It is precisely the high moral ground of this politics that Milosevic has challenged in claiming that NATO's direct involvement in the Balkan conflict in 1999 was not dictated by humanitarian concerns, but was, in effect, an imperialist intervention.

The Treaty of Versailles in 1919 had reaffirmed the principle of enforced retribution. The so-called 'war guilt clause,' in Article 231, forced a defeated Germany to accept responsibility for 'causing all the loss and damage to which the Allied and Associated Governments and their nationals have been subjected.' Article 232 compelled Germany to pay hefty reparations.[33] Yet the response by the Allies to Germany in the aftermath of World War II represented a shift away from the punitive and vindictive approach. The Marshall Plan effectively reversed traditional demands for indemnity by instigating an economic development programme. As such, it marked a radical break with a recriminatory politics – or so it is maintained.[34] And in the late twentieth and early twenty-first centuries the drive to recompense the victims of war has given rise to numerous different restitution agreements.[35]

This contemporary emphasis on restitution has led a number of commentators to argue that today we are witnessing a new international morality and the demise of traditional *Realpolitik*. Yet, it could be maintained that this politics of restitution needs to be understood primarily as an attempt to reaffirm the historical unity of the nation; it may be less about negotiating historical injustices than it is about confirming the integrity of the national group who is asking for forgiveness and accommodating a diverse, post-colonial and postmodern nation.

Although it has become conventional to think of heritage as the selective celebration of a collective past, heritage has often been linked to the expiation of past crimes and past suffering. The Irish commemorations of the Great Famine in 1996 might serve as one example. In the words of Roy Foster, ' "survivor guilt"and "cultural loneliness" stalked the land, famine museums were opened, famine diaries rediscovered and published.'[36] As the Irish commemorations suggest, guilt and suffering can provide the foundations of a new solidarity. Identities are made not only through victories, but also through the trauma of defeats.

Germany's recent history reminds us, as well, how the experience of genocide can provide powerful cohesive material to bind a modern nation-state together. The Holocaust has been central to definitions of the German Federal Republic since its creation in 1949.[37] Konrad Adenauer's policy of restitution and making reparations to the Jewish community were crucial components of Germany's reconstruction. The concentration camps, many of which have been turned into 'historical centres,' have become part of an industry that promotes a German heritage founded upon a public avowal of the nation's abhorrent past.

Here, it could be argued, an official state-sponsored identity has been built upon a public commitment 'never to forget.' From this perspective, the new Jewish Museum designed by Daniel Libeskind in Berlin, a city reinstated as capital of the unified Germany, occupies a position of considerable symbolic importance. Indicatively, the museum's website declares that the Jewish Museum is 'a major tourist attraction' of the capital.

As Duncan's chapter reminds us in the present volume, however, the institutionalization of guilt in heritage sites and museum exhibitions is not a uniquely German phenomenon. In Britain, as elsewhere, new curatorial practices are asking the public to remember the horrors that their ancestors perpetrated. Exhibitions are conceived as explicit ethico-political interventions. Museums are increasingly recording the dark side of public history, rather than the celebratory.

VICTIMIZATION AND FORGIVENESS

Abject histories require both a perpetrator and a victim. And just as the politics of restitution is becoming more prevalent, as Ian Buruma has recently observed, so victimization is becoming an important factor in the formation of contemporary identities. There are many cases in which national identity is popularly imagined as a history of victimization, be it of the Scots by the English, the Greeks by the Turks or the Poles by the Russians. Similarly, many minority groups 'have come to define themselves as victims.' Traumatic events in the past can become so deeply imprinted on a group's collective memory that they become an indelible part of its identity, as the genocide of 1915 has for the Armenians. As Buruma notes, there are dangers 'when a cultural, ethnic, religious, or national community bases its communal identity almost entirely on the sentimental solidarity of remembered victimhood. For that way lie historical myopia and in extreme circumstances, even vendetta.'[38]

Increasingly, national governments are seeking forgiveness for the iniquitous acts that their 'nations' have committed in history. Shortly after assuming office, on the 150th anniversary of the Potato Famine, Tony Blair issued what was tantamount to an apology for Britain's failure to come to Ireland's aid in the 1840s. Blair's apology reflected a more general tendency.[39] Since the 1980s political apologies have become widespread.[40] In 1988 Ronald Reagan apologized to Japanese-Americans interned in camps during World War II, and in 1992 a monument to these people was erected.[41] Boris Yeltsin apologized for Stalin's acts of genocide and the forceful displacement of populations within the Soviet Union. Former President Frederick W. de Klerk apologized, albeit ambiguously, for the 'pain and suffering' that apartheid had caused the black population. In 1997 President Clinton contemplated issuing an apology for slavery, following his apologies to the victims of the Tuskegee syphilis experiments and the American victims of the Atomic Energy Commission. Although Clinton's slavery apology was never proclaimed, a Reparation Assessment Group is preparing to sue the US government. As the leader of the group has declared: 'We want a change in America. We want full recognition, and a remedy, of how slavery stigmatized, raped, murdered and exploited millions of Africans through no fault of their own.'[42] As the slavery debate in the US underlines, the issue of apology is intertwined, in complex ways, with the question of financial reparations.

The concept of 'apology' – understood as a public expression of regret – is indebted to Judaeo-Christian notions of confession, repentance and forgiveness. This was accentuated in 1999 by the self-proclaimed members of the 'Pilgrimage of Apology' who visited Jerusalem for the 900th anniversary of the city's sacking at the hands of the first crusade and declared: 'We deeply regret the atrocities committed in the name of Christ by our predecessors. Forgive us for allowing His name to be associated with death.'[43] Moreover, the Truth and Reconciliation Commission instigated in South Africa in 1995 under the chairmanship of Archbishop Desmond Tutu, underscored the links between the Christian principle of forgiveness and social healing.[44] Significantly, however, the commission 'has mobilized a version of the history of apartheid that accentuates its political affinities as well as its concrete historical connections to the criminal governance of the Nazi period.'[45] In a chapter of his autobiography entitled 'Nuremberg or National Amnesia? A Third Way,' Tutu argues explicitly against a response to apartheid along the lines of the Allies' handling of the defeated Nazis at Nuremberg.[46]

CONCLUSION: REMEMBERING TO FORGET

But the question remains – when Blair apologizes for the past, in whose name is he speaking? Can a multi-ethnic society be held accountable for the past of an imperialist Britain? It could be argued that the politics of reconciliation promotes an essentially nineteenth-century conceptualization of the nation as a distinct body possessing a reformable moral 'character.' The demand for restitution presupposes an essentialist idea of the national population as an undifferentiated aggregate.[47]

In a reversal of Ernest Renan's dictum that the process of nation-building is contingent upon a population remembering many things, and also forgetting many things, it could be maintained that heritage sites are increasingly reconstructed as places where people are being asked 'to remember to forget' through an admission of complicity. Contemporary moral politics and its assumptions are reflected in European heritage institutions such as museums, or in universities where 'counter-factual' approaches to history promote historical events as collective 'choices.'[48] 'This national self-reflexivity,' writes Barkan, 'is the new guilt of nations.'[49]

The assumptions that underlie contemporary preoccupations with apologizing are numerous, as Roy Foster has written. Apologizing for perpetrating crimes in the past suggests that it is possible to overcome, control and finally close off the consequences of the past from the present. Restitution renders the past irrecuperable, relinquishing it to 'the cold storage of history.'[50] The representation of traumatic memory that has come to fill the vacated space of a discredited national heritage reproduces the essentialist view of the world it claims to displace. And it does so because it assumes heritage's commemorative rituals, ultimately trivializing the past. Gilroy takes as an example the representation of slaves in Spielberg's drama *Amistad*, who arrive at their Cuban auction from the horrors of the Middle Passage 'apparently fit and gleaming with robust good health' as though they have enjoyed 'the worked-out and pumped-up musculature that can only be acquired through the happy rigors of a postmodern gym routine.'[51] The tension identified by Gilroy is manifest elsewhere in memorial sites where past sufferings are commodified for mass public consumption.[52]

Histories of suffering throw into relief the lack of consensus over interpretations of the past and the forms of its commemoration. The Vietnam Memorial in Washington is one example. Another is the tension between African Americans and Ghanaians over the meanings invested in the fortified slave-trading depots that have been preserved as heritage sites for a lucrative cultural tourism.[53] The inability to reach any kind of consensus over the past means that increasingly the past cannot be integrated into historical narratives. One consequence of this may be the dissolution of a unified past into multiple local pasts, where ghettoized and antagonistic styles of remembrance, reflecting different group interests, compete.[54] It may be that when heritage has gone, we will learn to mourn its loss.

NOTES ON THE TEXT

NOTES ON INTRODUCTION

1 See the report in *The Times*, 'I'm Danish and I want to stay Danish,' 29 September 2000.

2 Andrew McClellan, *Inventing the Louvre: Art, Politics, and the Origins of the Modern Museum in Eighteenth-century Paris* (Cambridge, 1994).

3 James Clifford, *The Predicament of Culture: Twentieth-Century Ethnography, Literature, and Art* (Cambridge MA, 1988), pp. 216–29.

4 'Authenticity, as we shall see, is produced by removing objects and customs from their current historical situation - a present-becoming-future.' See Clifford, *The Predicament of Culture*, p. 228; Arjun Appadurai and Carol A.Breckenridge, 'Museums Are Good to Think: Heritage on View in India' (1992), reprinted in *Representing the Nation: A Reader. Histories, Heritage and Museums*, eds D.Boswell and J.Evans (London and New York, 1999), pp. 404–20 (p. 406).

5 Gilles Deleuze and Félix Guattari, *Anti-Oedipus: Capitalism and Schizophrenia*, trans. R.Hurley, M.Seem and H.R.Lane (New York, 1977), pp. 200–61.

6 See Jean-François Lyotard, *The Postmodern Condition: A Report on Knowledge*, trans. G.Bennington and B.Massumi (Manchester, 1984) [1979].

7 Sharon Macdonald and Roger Silverstone, 'Rewriting the Museums: Fictions, Taxonomies, Stories and Readers' (1990), reprinted in *Representing the Nation*, pp. 421–34 (pp. 420–21).

8 Appadurai and Breckenridge, 'Museums Are Good to Think,' pp. 406–7.

9 See Douglas Crimp's essay 'On the Museum's Ruins,' which argues that the heterogeneity of postmodern texts marks an epistemological break with the archive of the museum, in *Postmodern Culture*, ed. H.Foster (Trowbridge, 1985) [1983], pp. 43–56.

10 Appadurai and Breckenridge, 'Museums Are Good to Think,' p. 406. On the 'exhibitionary complex,' see Tony Bennett, 'The Exhibitionary Complex,' *New Formations* 4 (1988): 73–102. Bennett uses the term to describe the museum, which he links to a range of other institutions, including arcades and department stores, which formed 'a complex of disciplinary and power relations.' Drawing on Foucault, Bennett argues that objects in the museum 'formed vehicles for inscribing and broadcasting the messages of power.' See Chapter One in the present volume and the catalogue for the recent exhibition at the Victoria and Albert Museum, *London A Grand Design* (1999), which seeks to explore the function of the museum and to suggest ways in which the museum might evolve.

11   Appadurai and Breckenridge, 'Museums Are Good to Think,' p. 407 and Arjun Appadurai and Carol A. Breckenridge, 'Why Public Culture?' *Public Culture* 1/1 (1988): 5–9.

12   Appadurai and Breckenridge, 'Museums Are Good to Think,' p. 407.

13   David Batchelor, 'Unpopular Culture' (1995), reprinted in *Art and Its Histories: A Reader*, ed. S. Edwards (New Haven CT and London, 1999), pp. 295–97 (p. 297).

14   Julian Barnes, *England, England* (London, 1999), pp. 39–40.

15   David Lowenthal, *The Past is a Foreign Country* (Cambridge, 1985).

16   Robert Hewison, *The Heritage Industry: Britain in a Climate of Decline* (London, 1987).

17   Eugen Weber, *Peasants into Frenchmen: The Modernization of Rural France, 1870–1914* (London, 1976).

18   See Chapter Eight in the present volume.

19   Eric Hobsbawm and Terence Ranger, eds, *The Invention of Tradition* (Cambridge, 1983).

20   Hewison, *The Heritage Industry*; for general information see Patrick Wright, *On Living in an Old Country: The National Past in Contemporary Britain* (London, 1985).

21   Wright, *On Living in an Old Country*.

22   Karen E. Till, 'Reimagining National Identity: "Chapters of Life" at the German Historical Museum in Berlin,' in *Textures of Place: Exploring Humanist Geographies*, eds P. C. Adams, S. Hoelscher and K. E. Till (Minneapolis MN and London, 2001), pp. 273–99 (p. 272). Till examines a recent show, Chapters of Life in Germany, 1900–1993, at the German Historical Museum, which was conceived 'as a tangible expression of national history housed in an official place of memory during a period of postunification transition' (p. 274).

23   Pierre Nora, ed., *Les Lieux de Mémoire*, 3 vols (Paris, 1997) [1984–1993]. An English translation is available by A. Goldhammer, *Realms of Memory: Rethinking the French Past. Vol I: Conflicts and Divisions*, ed. L. D. Kritzman (New York, 1996).

24   Pierre Nora, 'General Introduction: Between Memory and History,' in *Realms of Memory*, pp. 1–23 (p. 7).

25   Jean Baudrillard, *Simulacra and Simulations*, trans. S. F. Glaser (Ann Arbor MI, 1994) [1981]; Guy Debord, *The Society of the Spectacle*, trans. D. Nicholson-Smith (London, 1994) [1967].

26   See Barnes, *England, England*, p. 53.

27   Baudrillard, *Simulacra*.

28   Pierre Bourdieu and Alain Darbel, *The Love of Art: European Art Museums and their Public*, trans. C. Beattie and N. Merriman (Cambridge, 1991) [1966].

29   See http://www.artscouncil.org.uk/wider/whose

30   However, in focus-group interviews, black communities expressed the exclusion they felt from England's historical environment.

31   Raphael Samuel, *Theatres of Memory Vol I: Past and Present in Contemporary Culture* (London and New York, 1994).

32   Samuel, *Theatres of Memory*, pp. 259–73 (p. 265). See also John Urry, *The Tourist Gaze: Leisure and Travel in Contemporary Society* (London, 1990). Urry argues

that the extension of the term 'museum' to include all kinds of displays of the past will make the term 'museum' redundant: 'The very term "museum" stems from a period of high art and auratic culture well before "heritage" had been invented' (p. 134).

33   Annie E. Coombes, 'Inventing the "Postcolonial": Hybridity and Constituency in Contemporary Curating' (1992), reprinted in *The Art of Art History: A Critical Anthology*, ed. D. Preziosi (Oxford, 1998), pp. 486–97 (p. 491); Avtar Brah and Annie E. Coombes, eds, *Hybridity and its Discontents: Politics, Science, Culture* (London and New York, 2000).

34   Ernest Renan, 'What is a Nation?' trans. M. Thom, in *Nation and Narration*, ed. H. K. Bhabha (London and New York, 1990), pp. 8–22 (p. 11).

35   Maryon McDonald, quoted in Loring M. Danforth, *The Macedonian Conflict: Ethnic Nationalism in a Transnational World* (Princeton NJ, 1995), p. 21.

36   See Wright, who discusses the relationship between heritage and danger within the context of what he evocatively calls 'Trafficking in History,' *On Living in an Old Country*, pp. 33–93.

37   Maurice Halbwachs, *On Collective Memory*, ed. and trans. L. A. Coser (Chicago IL and London, 1992), p. 173.

38   On the distinctive features of this new politics of difference and how it stands out from other cultural critiques, see Cornel West, 'The New Cultural Politics of Difference,' in *Out There: Marginalization and Contemporary Cultures*, ed. R. Ferguson (New York and Cambridge, 1990), pp. 19–36 (p. 19); Iris Marion Young, *Justice and the Politics of Difference* (Princeton NJ, 1990), pp. 156–91.

39   Coombes, 'Inventing the "Postcolonial."'

40   See M. Christine Boyer, *The City of Collective Memory: Its Historical Imagery and Architectural Entertainments* (Cambridge MA, 1994), pp. 24–29.

41   See Young, *Justice and the Politics of Difference*.

42   See Till, 'Reimagining National Identity,' p. 274.

NOTES ON CHAPTER 1

1   Joseph Conrad, *The Heart of Darkness* (Harmondsworth, 1994), pp. 31–32.

2   Maya Jaggi, 'Comment and Analysis: Casting off the Shackles of History,' *Guardian*, 3 November 1999.

3   Jaggi, 'Comment and Analysis.'

4   Joseph Conrad's *The Secret Agent* (Harmondsworth, 1994), although set in 1886, describes an attempt made in 1894 to blow up the Greenwich Observatory, the symbolic centre of the empire. See Martin Seymour Smith, 'Introduction,' pp. 9–36 (pp. 14–15).

5   James Clifford, *The Predicament of Culture: Twentieth-Century Ethnography, Literature, and Art* (Cambridge MA, 1988).

6   Brian Graham, G. J. Ashworth and J. E. Tunbridge, *A Geography of Heritage: Power, Culture and Economy* (London, 2000), p. 222.

7   Graham et al., *A Geography of Heritage*, pp. 222–23.

8   Martin Prosler, 'Museums and Globalization,' in *Theorizing Museums: Representing Identity and Diversity in a Changing World*, eds S.Macdonald and G.Fyfe (Oxford, 1996), pp. 21–44 (pp. 24–29).

9   Prosler, 'Museums and Globalization,' p. 31.

10   A.Gilette, 'One world, Not Enough Voices,' *Museum* 3 (1990).

11   Sharon Macdonald, 'Theorizing Museums: An Introduction,' in *Theorizing Museums*, pp. 1–20 (p. 8).

12   Peter Virgo, ed., *The New Museology* (London, 1989).

13   Eric Hobsbawm and Terence Ranger, eds, *The Invention of Tradition* (Cambridge, 1983).

14   Letter to Gershom Scholem (1963) in the Hannah Arendt Papers, Library of Congress, Washington DC.

15   David Batchelor, 'Unpopular Culture,' (1995) reprinted in *Art and its Histories*, ed. S.Edwards (New Haven CT and London, 1999), pp. 295–97; Kobena Mercer, 'Art of Africa' (1995), reprinted in *Art and its Histories*, pp. 298–99.

16   C.Duffy, 'Letter to the Editor: Empire Gallery is a Disgrace,' *Daily Telegraph*, 18 August 1999.

17   J.G.Mallett, 'Letter to the Editor: Spinning History,' *Daily Telegraph*, 28 August 1999.

18   J.Catton, 'Letter to the Editor: Empire Gallery is a Disgrace,' *Daily Telegraph*, 18 August 1999.

19   S.Bush, 'Letter to the Editor: Empire Gallery is a Disgrace,' *Daily Telegraph*, 18 August 1999.

20   E.Kean, 'Letter to the Editor: Empire Gallery is a Disgrace,' *Daily Telegraph*, 18 August 1999.

21   T.Pocock, 'Letter to the Editor: Empire Gallery is a Disgrace,' *Daily Telegraph*, 18 August 1999.

22   Richard Ormond, 'Letter to the Editor: Aims of the National Maritime Museum,' *Daily Telegraph*, 20 August 1999.

23   Ormond, 'Letter to the Editor.'

24   A.Couper, 'Letter to the Editor: All at Sea Over Slavery,' *Guardian*, 25 August 1999.

25   Jaggi, 'Comment and analysis.'

26   David Spence, 'The Wolfson Gallery of Trade and Empire: A Display Debate at the National Maritime Museum,' National Maritime Museum website, 7 August 2000.

27   For a discussion of the links between heritage and economic interests, see Graham et al., *A Geography of Heritage*.

28   Graham et al. argue that contestation lies at the centre of heritage and remembrance more generally: see *A Geography of Heritage*.

29   Vera Zolberg, 'Remaking Nations: Public Culture and Postcolonial Discourse,' in *Paying the Piper: Causes and Consequences of Art Patronage*, ed. J.H.Balfe (Chicago IL, 1993), pp. 234–50.

30   Vera Zolberg, 'Museums as Contested Sites of Remembrance: The Enola Gay Affair,' in *Theorizing Museums*, pp. 69–82 (p. 77). See Chapter Fifteen in the present volume.

31   Henrietta Riegel, 'Into the Heart of Irony: Ethnographic Exhibitions and the Politics of Difference,' in *Theorizing Museums*, pp. 83–104. This exhibit is also

discussed by James Clifford in *Routes: Travel and Translation in the Late Twentieth Century* (Cambridge MA, 1997), pp. 206–7.

32   Mary Louise Pratt, *Imperial Eyes: Travel Writing and Transculturation* (London, 1992). Clifford has an extended discussion of museums as 'contact zones' in *Routes*, pp. 188–219.

NOTES ON CHAPTER 2

1   José Saramago, *Viagem a Portugal* (Lisbon, 1999) [1981], p. 279.

2   Portaria de 29 de Agosto de 1938, Diário do Governo s.2 203–II (1 September 1938), quoted in *Boletim da Direcção Geral dos Edifícios e Monumentos Nacionais* 25–26 (September–December 1941): O Castelo de S.Jorge, p. 5.

3   António Maria Zorro, *Honra de Ser Português* (1955), p. 15.

4   Henrique Gomes da Silva, 'Monumentos Nacionais; orientação técnica a seguir no seu restauro' [1934], cited in Jorge Custódio, 'Salvaguarda do Património – Antecedentes Históricos,' in *Dar Futuro ao Passado* (Lisbon, 1993), p. 57.

5   Jorge Rodrigues, 'A Direcção Geral dos Edifícios e Monumentos Nacionais e o Restauro dos Monumentos Nacionais durante o Estado Novo,' in *Caminhos do Património* (Lisbon, 1999), pp. 69–82 (p. 73); see also Custódio: 'Salvaguarda,' p. 59.

6   'Oitocentos Anos de Independencia,' [1940] in *Salazar, Discursos e Notas Políticas* III (Coimbra, 1959), pp. 255–59 (p. 255).

7   Zorro, *Honra*, p. 14.

8   Saramago, *Viagem*, pp. 56–58.

9   'Palavras para uma cidade,' in José Saramago, *Folhas Políticas* (Lisbon, 1999), pp. 178–82.

10   José Saramago, *History of the Siege of Lisbon* (London, 1996), p. 279.

11   The symbolic significance of the call to prayer lies not only in the fact that it contains the proclamation of the faith, and can therefore function as a synecdoche of Islam itself, but in the specificity of its silencing in the history of Christian Muslim polemic. See Norman Daniel, *Islam and the West* (Oxford, 1993), pp. 233–34.

12   J.P.Oliveira Martins, *História de Portugal*, ed. I.Faria de Albuquerque (Lisbon, 1988), p. 339.

13   'Entrevista com José Saramago (Diálogo com Manuel Gusmão),' *Vértice* s.2 14 (May 1989): 85–99 (88).

14   José Augusto de Oliveira, *A Cruzada* (Lisbon, 1949), p. 125; in the above cited interview, Saramago has identified this author as the 'innocent victim' of his pastiche of 'the historian,' 'Entrevista,' *Vértice*: 97. On the document in question see *The Conquest of Lisbon/ De Expugnatione Lyxbonensi*, trans. Charles Wendell David with a foreword and bibliography by Jonathan Phillips (New York, 2001).

15   José Mattoso, 'No 850º Aniversário da Conquista de Lisboa,' *Arqueologia Medieval* 7 (2001); Actas do Colóquio, 'Lisboa: Encruzilhada de Muçulmanos, Judeus e Cristãos,' pp. 11–13 (p. 12).

16   See Urbano Rodrigues's description of the planned festivities in the *Programa Oficial das Comemorações do VIII Centenário da Tomada de Lisboa* (Lisbon, 1947).

17 A.Teixeira da Mota, *Guiné Portuguesa* I (Lisbon, 1954), p.257.

18 José Garcia Domingues, 'Presença Árabe no Algarve,' in *Islão e Arabismo na Península Ibérica* (Évora, 1986), pp.113–30 (p.113).

19 See Ana Maria Ramalhete, 'Ficcionalização de Contactos Culturais e Especificidade Nacional: Olhares Românticos sobre Modelos, Cristãos e Mouros,' in *Literatura Comparada: Os Novos Paradigmas*, eds M. Losa et al. (Oporto, 1996), pp.67–74 (p.74).

20 *Leonardo* 1/4 (December 1988), pp.25–35; 2/5–6 (March–September 1989), pp.69–71.

21 On the Archaeology and archaeological collections in the Algarve, see the relevant chapters in *Noventa Séculos entre a Serra e o Mar* (Lisbon, 1997).

22 F.Xavier Athaide de Oliveira, *As Mouras Encantadas e os Encantamentos no Algarve* (Tavira, 1898); António Maria de Oliveira Parreira, *Os Luso-Árabes (scenas da vida mussulmana no nosso país)*, 2 vols (Lisbon, 1898–1899), I, pp.v–xiv.

23 Parreira, *Os Luso-Árabes*, II, pp.228–29.

24 Adalberto Alves, *Al-Mu'tamid Poeta do Destino* (Lisbon, 1996), pp.26–29.

25 Adalberto Alves, *Arab-Islamic Memories in Portugal* (Lisbon, 1997), p.57.

26 In, among others, *O Meu Coração é Árabe: A Poesia Luso-Árabe* (Lisbon, 1987); *Arabesco: Da Música Árabe e da Música Portuguesa* (Lisbon, 1989); *Portugal e o Islão escritos do crescente* (Lisbon, 1991); *Nítido Crescente: Ensaios* (Lisbon, 1997).

27 Maria Rosa Menocal, 'Al-Andalus and 1492: The Ways of Remembering,' in *The Legacy of Muslim Spain*, ed. S.K.Jayyusi (Leiden, 1994), I, pp.483–87; *The Arabic Role in Medieval Literary History: A Forgotten Heritage* (Philadelphia PA, 1987).

28 Adalberto Alves, *Portugal - Ecos de Um Passado Árabe* (Lisbon, 1999), p.65.

29 Alves, 'Introduction,' *Arab-Islamic Memories in Portugal*, pp.13–16.

30 Adalberto Alves, *Portugal, Ândalus e Magrebe: Um contexto de Tolerância* (Lisbon, 1995).

31 On this issue see AbdoolKarim Vakil, 'Guinean Princes and Portuguese Pilgrims: Race, Religion and Politics in the Forging of a Portuguese Colonial Culture' (forthcoming).

32 António da Silva Rêgo, *O Oriente e o Ocidente* (Lisbon, 1939), Chapter 3.

33 Rodrigues Junior, *Quando se Pensa nos que Lutam* (Lisbon, 1970), pp.52–53.

34 Francisco José Velozo, 'Portugal, os Árabes e os Muçulmanos da Costa Oriental de África,' *Gil Vicente* s.2 XVI/7–8 (July–August 1965): 106–13 (110).

35 Rogério Seabra Cardoso, 'Islamitas Portugueses,' *Panorama* s.IV 33/34 (March/June 1970): 49–62 (49, 52, 53).

36 Mattoso, 'No 850° Aniversário da Conquista de Lisboa.' On the relation between the revisionist historiography of the Gharb Al-Andalus and the shifting cultural and political context of post 1974 Portugal, see AbdoolKarim Vakil, 'Novos (Ante) Passados: Portugal pós-colonial, multiculturalismo e a re-descoberta do Gharb Al-Andalus' (forthcoming).

37 Jorge Sampaio, 'Jornadas Memórias Árabe-Islâmicas,' *Portugueses* II (Lisbon, 1998): 337–40.

38 Cited in 'Tirar o Legado Islâmico do nevoeiro: Jorge Sampaio 'apadrinha' releitura do islamismo na cultura portuguesa,' *Jornal de Notícias* (22 November 1998): 8.

39 'Pelas Ruas e Lugares de Loures,' *Museu Municipal de Loures*, 19 July 1996–16 March 1997.

40 On the principles of eco-museology, see Nancy J. Fuller, 'The Museum as a Vehicle for Community Empowerment: The Ak-Chin Indian Community Ecomuseum Project,' in *Museums and Communities: The Politics of Public Culture*, eds I. Karp, C. Kreamer and S. Lavine (Washington DC, 1992), pp. 328–33; António Nabais, 'Nova Museologia – novas práticas museológicas,' *Vértice* s.2 54 (May–June 1993): 46–50.

41 Rui Mateus, 'Mértola - Reflexões sobre um projecto de desenvolvimento local,' in *Encontros Cem Anos de Antropologia 'O Archeólogo Português' – Actas*, eds M. I. Silva et al. (Vila do Conde, 1998), pp. 109–27; Rosa Amaral, 'Uma Entrevista com Cláudio Torres,' *Pedra & Cal* 2:6 (April/May/June 2000): 16–19.

42 See the exhibition catalogue, *Portugal Islâmico: Os últimos sinais do Mediterrâneo*, Museu Nacional de Arqueologia (Lisbon, 1998).

43 See, for example, *O Islão Entre o Tejo e o Odiana* (Mértola, n.d.); 'O Garb Al-Andaluz,' in *História de Portugal* I, ed. J. Mattoso (Lisbon, 1992); as well as the exhibitions *Arab-Islamic Memories in Portugal* (Lisbon, 1998); *O Legado Islâmico em Portugal* (Lisbon, 1998); *Portugal Islâmico: Os últimos sinais do Mediterrâneo*; 'O Extremo Ocidente Ibérico;' *Marrocos-Portugal: Portas do Mediterrâneo* (Lisbon, 1999); Janus (1999–2000); *Terras da Moura Encantada: Arte Islâmica em Portugal* (Oporto, 1999).

44 Cláudio Torres and Santiago Macías, *O Legado Islâmico em Portugal*, pp. 10–11; Santiago Macías, 'Aspectos do Quotidiano no Ocidente Islâmico,' in *Marrocos-Portugal*, p. 61.

45 Quoted by Jacinto Rego de almeida, 'Portugal e o Islão no Brasil,' *Jornal de Letras* (7 April 1999).

46 Eva-Maria von Kemnitz, 'O Pânorama das colecções museológicas islâmicas em Portugal,' in *Portugal Islâmico*, pp. 307–19 (p. 314).

47 The diversity of contemporary claims upon the heritage of Al-Andalus is well mirrored in a tortuous history ranging from nineteenth-century Turks and subcontinental Indians discovering the Al-Andaluz, through French Romantic writers (Bernard Lewis, 'The Cult of Spain and the Turkish Romantics,' in *Islam in History* [New York, 1973]), to African American 'Moors' laying claim to the heritage of Medieval Iberia on the inspiration of masonic rituals (Ivan van Sertima, ed., *Golden Age of the Moor* [New Brunswick NJ, 1992]); Peter Lamborn Wilson, 'Lost/Found Moorish Time-Lines in the Wilderness of America,' in *Sacred Drift* [San Francisco CA, 1993]). Today, with voices as diverse as the internationally celebrated Francophone and Commonwealth writers from the Indian and Middle-Eastern diaspora (Amin Maalouf, Salman Rushdie, Tariq Ali), King Faisal of Saudi Arabia, obscure Pakistani immigrants in Britain (Khola Hasan, *The Crumbling Minarets of Spain* [London, 1988]), or proselytizing American Muslims (Yahiya Emerick, Isabella, *A Girl of Muslim Spain* [New York, 1998]), UNESCO officials promoting intercultural dialogue or ordinary Brazilians and Mexicans festively re-enacting the battles of the Iberian Reconquest (Max Harris, *Aztecs, Moors and Christians* [Austin TX, 2000]), the heritage of Muslim Iberia is there for the taking.

48 For an illuminating discussion of some of the issues involved, see Seán McLoughlin, 'In the Name of the Umma: Globalization, Race Relations and Muslim Identity Politics in Bradford,' in *Political Participation and Identities of Muslims in Non-Muslim States*, eds W.A.R.Shadid and P.S.van Koningsveld (Kampen, 1997), pp.206–32.

49 In the period 1997–99, for example, no less than 13 of its quota airtime slots on public television were given over to historical aspects of the Islamic past in Portugal. Both the Cultural Association Al-Furqan and the administrative organization Comunidade Islâmica de Lisboa have commemorated their anniversaries with cultural events focusing on the Islamic contributions to Portuguese history and Portugal's Islamic heritage. The Ismaili Muslim community, for its part, has been more directly involved in the sponsorship of archaeological excavations of Islamic sites in Portugal through the Agha Khan Foundation. On Portuguese Muslims' negotiation of identity and belonging, see AbdoolKarim Vakil, 'Muçulmanos em Portugal/Muçulmanos Portugueses: Imaginários e identidades trans-/nacionais' (forthcoming).

50 www.aliasoft.com/postcards/cardrack.html

NOTES ON CHAPTER 3

1 Gianfranco Folena, 'Volgarizzare e Tradurre,' in *La Traduzione: Saggi e Studi*, ed. G.Petronio (Trieste, 1973), pp.57–120.

2 Benedict Anderson, *Imagined Communities: Reflections on the Origin and Spread of Nationalism* (London and New York, 1991) [1983], pp.12–19.

3 Quoted and discussed in Kevin Robins, 'Tradition and Translation: National Culture in its global Context,' in *Representing the Nation: A Reader - Histories, Heritage and Museums*, eds D.Boswell and J.Evans (London and New York, 1999), pp.15–32 (pp.15–16).

4 Lawrence Venuti, 'Translation as Cultural Politics: Regimes of Domestication in English,' *Textual Practice* 7/2 (1993): 208–23 (209).

5 James Clifford, *The Predicament of Culture: Twentieth-Century Ethnography, Literature, and Art* (Cambridge MA, 1988), pp.23–24. For an account of the violence involved in the 'translation' of the 'Third World,' see Talal Ada and John Dixon, 'Translating Europe's Others,' in *Europe and Its Others*, eds F.Barker et al. (Colchester, 1985), pp.170–93.

6 L.P.Hartley, *The Go-Between* (London, 1953). See David Lowenthal, *The Past is a Foreign Country* (Cambridge, 1985), p.xvi.

7 See Itamar Even-Zohar and Gideon Toury, eds, *Translation Theory and Intercultural Relations* (Tel Aviv, 1981); Gideon Toury, ed., *Translation Across Cultures* (New Delhi, 1987).

8 Walter Benjamin, 'Theses on the Philosophy of History,' in *Illuminations*, ed. H.Arendt, trans. H.Zohn (London, 1973), p.254.

9 Jacques Derrida, 'Des Tours de Babel,' in *Difference in Translation*, ed. and trans. J.F.Graham (Ithaca NY, 1985), pp.165–207 (p.188).

10   Walter Benjamin, 'The Task of the Translator: an Introduction to the Translation of Baudelaire's Tableaux Parisiens,' in *Illuminations*, p.71.

11   Benjamin, 'Theses on the Philosophy of History,' pp.257–58.

12   Benjamin, 'The Task of the Translator,' p.70.

13   Benjamin, 'The Task of the Translator,' p.75.

14   Homi K.Bhabha, 'DissemiNation: Time, Narrative, and the Margins of the Modern Nation,' in *Nation and Narration*, ed. H.Bhabha (London, 1990), pp.291–322 (p.314).

15   Wolfgang Iser, 'Coda to the Discussion,' in *The Translatability of Cultures: Figurations of the Space Between*, eds S.Budick and I.Wolfgang (Stanford CA, 1998), pp.296–97.

16   Claude Lévi-Strauss, *The Scope of Anthropology*, trans. S.Ortner and R.A.Paul (London, 1967) [1960], p.80.

17   James Clifford, *Routes: Travel and Translation in the Late Twentieth Century* (Cambridge MA, 1997), p.11.

18   Susan Bassnett, *Translation Studies* (London, 1991), pp.xiii–xv.

19   Roland Barthes, 'Authors and Writers,' in *A Barthes Reader*, ed. S.Sontag, trans. R.Howard (London, 1993) [1972], pp.185–210; Michel Foucault, 'What Is An Author?' in *Textual Strategies*, ed. and intro. J.Harari (Ithaca NY, 1979), pp.141–60.

20   Lawrence Venuti, *The Translator's Invisibility* (London and New York, 1995), p.16.

21   James Clifford, 'The Translation of Cultures: Maurice Leenhardt's Evangelism, New Caledonia 1902-1926,' in *Contemporary Literary Criticism: Literary and Cultural Studies*, ed. R.C. Davis and R.Schleifer (New York, 1994), p.627.

22   Clifford, *The Predicament of Culture*, pp.117–51.

23   Sérgio Luiz Prado Bellei, 'Brazilian Anthropophagy Revisited,' in *Cannibalism and the Colonial World*, eds F.Barker, P.Hulme and M.Iversen (Cambridge, 1998), pp.87–109 (p.93). For an excellent collection of essays which explore the place of the 'primitive' in modernism, see Elazar Barkan and Ronald Bush, eds, *Prehistories of the Future: The Primitivist Project and the Culture of Modernism* (Stanford CA, 1995).

24   Richard M.Morse, 'The Multiverse of Latin American Identity, c.1920-c.1970,' in *The Cambridge History of Latin America: Volume X: Latin America Since 1930: Ideas, Culture and Society*, ed. L.Bethell (Cambridge, 1995), pp.1–128 (pp.18–19).

25   Bellei, 'Brazilian Anthropophagy Revisited,' p.95.

26   Quoted in Sérgio Luiz Prado Bellei, 'Brazilian Anthropophagy Revisited,' pp.87–109 (p.100).

27   See Else Ribeiro Pires Vieira, 'Liberating Calibans: Readings of Anthropofagia and Haroldo de Campos' Poetics of Transcreation,' in *Post-colonial Translation: Theory and Practice*, ed. S.Bassnett and H.Trivedi (London and New York, 1999), pp.95–113.

28   On the cannibal trope in Brazilian film, see Luis Madureira, 'Lapses in Taste: "Cannibal-Tropicalist" Cinema and the Brazilian Aeshetic of Underdevelopment,' in *Cannibalism and the Colonial World*, pp.110–25. Madureira discusses Rocha on p.119.

29   Quoted in Bellei, 'Brazilian Anthropophagy Revisited,' p.106.

30   Fredric Jameson, *Postmodernism, or, the Logic of Late Capitalism* (London, 1991), p.96. See the discussion in Bellei, 'Brazilian Anthropophagy Revisited,' pp.108–9.

31   Works of contemporary Greek literature also explore the cross-cultural or multicultural subject in its Ottoman or Balkan context. For example, Rea

Galanaki, *The Life of Ismail Ferik Pasha Spina Nel Cuore*, trans. K.Cicellis (Paris, 1996) [1989].

32   Tahar Ben Jelloun, *French Hospitality*, trans. B.Bray (New York, 1999).

33   Edouard Glissant, *Caribbean Discourse*, ed. and trans. M.Dash (Charlotteseville VA, 1989), pp.163–65.

34   Salman Rushdie, *Imaginary Homelands: Essays and Criticism, 1981-1991* (London, 1991).

35   Rushdie, 'Errata,' in *Imaginary Homelands*, p.24.

36   'Imaginative Maps' (Interview with Una Chaudhuri), *Turnstile* 2/1 (1990): 36–47.

37   This phrase from Rushdie inspires the title of Homi K.Bhabha's chapter 'How Newness Enters the World: Postmodern Space, Post-colonial Times and the Trials of Cultural Translation,' in *The Location of Culture*, ed. H.Bhabha (London and New York, 1994), pp.212–35.

38   Salman Rushdie, *Shame* (London, 1983), p.29.

39   Benjamin, 'Theses on the Philosophy of History,' p.255.

40   Rushdie, *Shame*, pp.87–88.

41   Rushdie, *Shame*, p.28.

42   Sara Suleri, *The Rhetoric of English India* (Chicago IL, 1992), p.192.

43   Wilson Harris, *Jonestown* (London, 1996), p.100.

44   Quoted in Sandford Budick, 'Crises of Alterity: Cultural Untranslatability and the Experience of Secondary Otherness,' in *The Translatability of Cultures*, pp.1–22 (p.20).

45   Budick, 'Crises of Alterity,' p.22.

46   Clifford, *Routes*, p.10.

47   Wilson Harris, *Jonestown*, p.130.

48   Clifford, *Routes*, pp.213–19. The concept of the 'contact zone' is taken by Mary Louise Pratt from linguistics and used by her to signify a shift away from the notion of 'frontier.' See, in this context, *Imperial Eyes: Travel Writing and Transculturation* (London, 1992), pp.1–11.

NOTES ON CHAPTER 4

1   The Convention's Article 1 defines 'cultural heritage' strictly in this sense as 'monuments…groups of buildings…[and] sites.' Full text at http://www.unesco.prg/whc/nwhc/pages/doc/main.htm

2   Decision No 2228/97/EC of the European Parliament and of the Council of 13 October 1997 establishing a community action programme in the field of cultural heritage (the Raphael Programme), Article 2 (Official Journal L 305, 08/11/1997, pp.0031–0041).

3   Introduction, note 15.

4   See, in this context, Harold Bloom's *The Western Canon: The Books and School of the Ages* (New York, San Diego and London, 1994). The literatures of 'small' nations like the Poles, the Czechs, the Danes or the Swedes only appear in Bloom's appendices to the 'Western Canon' (Dutch literature does not figure at all), and

with entirely random selections showing that the key criterion for admission to the 'Canon' is not so much literary quality as the presence or absence of an English translation.

5   John Slater, *Teaching History in the New Europe* (London, 1995), p. 8.

6   Jeremy Boissevain, 'Towards an Anthropology of European Communities?' in *The Anthropology of Europe: Identities and Boundaries in Conflict*, eds V.A.Goddard, J.R.Llobera and C.Shore (Oxford, 1994), pp. 41–56 (p. 52).

7   David Gress has called this 'the Grand Narrative of Western Civilization,' and summed it up in the title of his book: *From Plato to NATO* (New York, 1998). The choice between the labels 'Western' and 'European' to some extent reflects different national traditions: the former is more used in a British or American context whereas the latter prevails in continental European accounts. Of course, the two differ significantly in their connotations, a discussion that cannot be broached within the confines of the present chapter.

8   Norman Davies, *Europe: A History* (Oxford, 1996), p. 98; Jacques Le Goff, *La Vielle Europe et la Nôtre* (Paris, 1994).

9   Johannes Sløk, *Europas Sjæl* (Viby, 1994). Sløk is the author (with Erik Lund and Mogens Pihl) of the influential standard textbook *De Europæiske ideers historie* (Copenhagen, 1962), translated into English as *A History of European Ideas* (London, 1971).

10   A similar argument about the Classical roots of European culture, and about its historical uniqueness, can be found in the German philosopher Hans-Georg Gadamer's collection of essays, *Das Erbe Europas: Beiträge* (Frankfurt am Main, 1989). In the German tradition – perhaps more than in English usage – *Europäisches Erbe* ('heritage') often refers to a philosophical or spiritual tradition said to be constituent of Europe or the Abendland.

11   Norman Davies recounts how an EU-sponsored European history of Europe, written by the French historian Jean-Baptiste Duroselle, *L'Europe: Histoire de ses Peuples* (Paris, 1990), aroused Greek fury for neglecting the achievements of Ancient Greece and Byzantium. Ironically, the main problem of Duroselle's account was not so much the downplaying of Greek history as his reduction of European history to the history only of the present member states of the EC, erasing everything east of the (then vanishing) Iron Curtain. See *Europe*, pp. 43–44. Contemporary Greek sensitivities are understandable, given the supercilious Western discourse on 'modern Greece' since the nineteenth century. As the anthropologist Michael Herzfeld argues: 'Romanticism has given way to deconstruction, and those whom romanticism had once "constructed" as true Hellenes now feel, in every sense, undone.' *Cultural Intimacy: Social Poetics in the Nation-State* (New York and London, 1997), p. 106.

12   Gress, *From Plato to NATO*, especially Chapters 1 and 2. Gress writes on p. 75: 'Of course, the West inherited a legacy from the Greeks, as it did from the ancient Near East, Rome, Judaism, early Christianity, medieval Islam, China, and other civilizations. But the West was more than the sum of these legacies, nor were the legacies necessarily representative of the civilizations that spawned them.'

13   Søren Mørch, *Civilisationen (Det europæiske hus 1)* (Copenhagen, 1991), p. 256.

14   Martin Bernal, *Black Athena: The Afroasiatic Roots of Classical Civilization*, 2 vols (London, 1987–91). On Bernal's partiality and his factual errors, see Mary A. Lefkowitz and Guy MacLean Rogers, eds, *Black Athena Revisited* (Chapel Hill NC, 1996).

15   Robert Bartlett, *The Making of Europe. Conquest, Colonization and Cultural Change, 950-1350* (Princeton NJ, 1993).

16   Explanatory Statement, p. 9 – Document listed as DOC_EN\RR\352\352418. The Danish historian Lars Hedegaard argues in his polemical article, 'Da Europa var muslimsk' ('When Europe was Moslem'), that if Europe is defined in terms of values like universalism, relativism, humanism, tolerance, and reason the Arabic, Islamic empire of Córdoba represented 'the most European society' to be found at that time (in the tenth and eleventh centuries), *Samvirke* (December 1994): 70–73.

17   Several such histories have been written in recent decades. See Denys Hay's pioneering study, *Europe: The Emergence of an Idea*, 2nd ed. (Edinburgh, 1968), or Kevin Wilson and Jan van der Dussen, eds, *The History of the Idea of Europe* (London, 1995).

18   For an excellent discussion of Ancient Greek ideas about 'Europe,' and the absence of any Greek 'Euro-consciousness,' see Jörg A.Schlumberger, 'Europas Antikes Erbe,' in *Europa - aber was ist es?*, eds J.A.Schlumberger and P.Segl (Köln, Weimar and Wien, 1994), pp. 1–20. See also Arnold Toynbee, 'Asia and Europe: Facts and Fantasies,' in *A Study of History*, vol. VIII (Oxford, 1954), pp. 708–29. This contains a stimulating discussion of the origin and function of the names of the continents, and provides a vehement critique of the idea of any cultural divide along the European–Asian border.

19   On developments in the Russian usage of the word, see Ekkehard Klug, 'Europa und europäisch im russischen Denken vom 16. bis zum frühen 19. Jahrhundert,' *Saeculum* 38 (1987): 193–224.

20   See the following volumes: Hay, *Europe*; Wilson and van der Dussen, *The Idea of Europe*; John Hale, *The Civilization of Europe in the Renaissance* (London, 1993), especially Chapter 1.

21   See Jan Ifversen's fine account, 'The Meaning of European Civilization - a Historical-Conceptual Approach,' *European Studies Newsletter* 1/2 (Aarhus 1998): 20–38.

22   On Hegel, see Dieter Groh, *Rußland im Blick Europas* (Frankfurt am Main, 1988), pp. 175–85 and Heinz Gollwitzer, *Europabild und Europagedanke - Beiträge zur deutschen Geistesgeschichte des 18. und 19. Jahrhunderts* (Munich, 1964), pp. 212–14.

23   Sløk, *Europas Sjæl*, p. 32. Less bluntly, but with a similar conviction that only European culture possesses a truly history-making dynamism, the British Marxist archaeologist Gordon Childe writes: 'If our own culture can claim to be in the main stream, it is only because our cultural tradition has captured and made tributary a larger number of once parallel traditions. While in historical times the main stream flows from Mesopotamia and Egypt through Greece and Rome, Byzantium and Islam to Atlantic Europe and America, it has been repeatedly swollen by the diversion into it of currents from Indian, Chinese, Mexican, and Peruvian civilizations, and from countless barbarisms and savageries. Chinese and

Indian civilizations have indeed not failed to absorb currents from one another and from further west. But, on the whole, they have hitherto discharged these into placid unchanging backwaters.' *What Happened in History* (Harmondsworth, 1942), p. 23.

24   Ivan Hannaford, *Race: The History of an Idea in the West* (Washington DC, 1996), p. 233.

25   Duroselle's unfortunate attempt has already been mentioned. Davies's monumental oeuvre programmatically seeks to challenge this Western bias, identifying it with the erroneous doctrine of 'Western civilization:' *Europe, A History,* pp. 19–32, 39–42. However, Davies's own ideas about the function of history writing are, in the final analysis, quite similar to those of Duroselle: 'Sooner or later, a convincing new picture of Europe's past will have to be composed to accompany the new aspirations for Europe's future.' *Europe, A History,* p. 45. On Ranke, see Herbert Ludat, *Deutsch-Slawische Frühzeit und modernes Polnisches Geschichtsbewusstsein* (Cologne and Vienna, 1969). On the construction of an 'Eastern Europe' serving as an 'internal Other' for a Western Europe usually simply calling itself 'Europe,' see Larry Wolff, *Inventing Eastern Europe: The Map of Civilization on the Mind of the Enlightenment* (Stanford CA, 1994), and Larry Wolff, 'Voltaire's Public and the Idea of Eastern Europe: Toward a Literary Sociology of Continental Division,' *Slavic Review* 54/4 (1995): 932–42. For a later dating of the emergence of a discourse on Eastern Europe, however, see Hans Lemberg, 'Zur Entstehung des Osteuropabegriffs im 19. Jahrhundert - Vom 'Norden' zum 'Osten' Europas,' *Jahrbücher für Geschichte Osteuropas* 33/1 (1985): 48–91. A sharp, witty, critique of post-1989 stereotypes of Eastern Europe can be found in Adam Burgess, *Divided Europe: The New Domination of the East* (London, 1997).

26   Morgens Trolle Larsen, 'Europas Lys,' in *Europas Opdagelse: Historien om en Ide,* eds H. Boll-Johansen and M. Harbsmeier (Copenhagen, 1988), pp. 9–37 (pp. 18–20).

27   Sløk, *Europas Sjæl,* p. 22; Le Goff makes similar statements in his *La Vielle Europe.*

28   Gress, *From Plato to NATO,* pp. 84–86; Pim den Boer, 'Europe to 1914: The Making of an Idea,' in *The History of the Idea,* p. 74. See also Davies, *Europe, A History,* p. 131 on how Athenian-style democracy had for centuries been forgotten or dismissed as harmful.

29   Moses Finley, *The Ancient Economy,* 2nd ed. (London, 1985), p. 28. As Larsen remarks – and I borrow the Finley quote from him – this assertion is incorrect. Thus, Finley's pronouncement testifies to the way in which prejudices predetermine scholarly investigations or interpretations of the past.

30   Edgar Morin, *Penser l'Europe* (Paris, 1987). Morin espouses a vision of Europe conceived in terms of a 'cohesive' multiplicity, see pp. 234–36.

31   Milan Kundera, 'The Tragedy of Central Europe,' *The New York Review of Books* (26 April 1984): 33–38.

32   See Iver B. Neumann, *Uses of the Other: The East in European Identity Formation* (Manchester, 1999); Peter Bugge, 'The Use of the Middle: Mitteleuropa vs. Střední Evropa,' *European Review of History* 6/1 (1999): 15–35. See also Katherine Verdery, *What was Socialism, and What Comes Next?* (Princeton NJ, 1996), especially

Chapter 5, Susan Gal, 'Bartók's Funeral: Representations of Europe in Hungarian Political Rhetoric,' *American Ethnologist* 18/3 (1991): 440–58, Peter Bugge, 'Longing or Belonging? Czech Perceptions of Europe in the Inter-War Years and Today,' *Yearbook of European Studies* 11 (1999): 111–29; Maria Todorova, *Imagining the Balkans* (Oxford, 1997).

33 Quoted from B.de Witte, 'Building Europe's Image and Identity,' in *Europe from a Cultural Perspective*, eds A.Rijksbaron et al. (The Hague, 1987), p.134.

34 Quoted from de Witte, 'Building Europe's Image,' p.136.

35 There is a growing literature on EU identity policies and their impact. See, for example, Bram Boxhoorn, 'European Identity and the Process of European Unification: Compatible Notions?' in *Culture and Identity in Europe*, ed. M.Wintle (Aldershot, 1996), pp.133–45; Chris Shore, 'Inventing the People's Europe: Critical Approaches to European Community: A Cultural Policy,' *Man* 28/4 (1993): 779–800; Chris Shore and Annabel Black, 'Citizens' Europe and the Construction of European Identity,' in *The Anthropology of Europe*, pp.275–98; Thomas Wilson, 'An Anthropology of the European Community,' in *Cultural Change and the New Europe - Perspectives on the European Community*, eds T.Wilson and M.Estellie Smith (Boulder CO, 1993), pp.1–23; Klaus Eder, 'Integration durch Kultur? Das Paradox der Suche nach einer europäischen Identität,' in *Kultur, Identität, Europa*, eds R.Viehoff and R.T.Segers (Frankfurt, 1999), pp.147–79.

36 Decision No 508/2000/EC of the European Parliament and the Council of the EU of 14 February 2000 establishing the Culture 2000 Programme, Introductory remarks, notes 1 and 5. The last paragraph is a far cry from the crude function-alism of the 1973 declaration, and seems to reflect the shift towards cultural paradigms discussed above. Now, culture, more than economy, has to carry through European integration, and so quite a heavy burden of responsibility is put on it. According to a summary of the Current State and Prospects in the field of culture, 'culture must contribute to European citizenship, to personal and human development (through education), to economic and social cohesion among Member States, to job creation in Europe, to eliminating exclusion, and generally to enriching the quality of life in Europe.' Such prescriptions, although hardly to be taken seriously, are in their scope and style remarkably similar to the demands made on culture in Communist cultural policies. Text found at http://europa.eu.int/scadplus/leg/en/lvb/l29001.htm

37 The teaching of history has also recently been included in this new offensive with the Council Resolution of 28 October 1999 integrating history into the Community's cultural action (1999/C 324/01).

38 See Maitland Stobart, 'Der Europarat und die Bildungsforderungen im "Neuen Europa,"' in *Realisierung der Bildung in Europa*, eds K.Schleicher and W.Bos (Darmstadt, 1994), pp.19–45. Margaret Shennan's *Teaching about Europe* (London, 1991) is both an outcome of and an introduction to these new initiatives. John Slater, whose book quoted above is published in the same series (the Cassell Council of Europe Series), is actually critical of many of the assumptions and the rhetoric (including allusions to a so-called 'European cultural heritage')

that has prevailed in earlier Council of Europe initiatives, see Slater, *Teaching History*, p. 4.

39   Published on the Internet at http://culture.coe.fr/postsummit/pat/en/eguide.htm

40   See the promotional literature for the book published on the Internet at http://culture.coe.fr/infocentre/book/eng/epubroutes.htm

41   Slater, *Teaching History*, pp. 8–9.

NOTES ON CHAPTER 5

1   See http://www.europe-heritage.net

2   Ernest Gellner, *Nations and Nationalism* (Cambridge, 1983), p. 1.

3   Jürgen Habermas, 'The European Nation-State - Its Achievements and Its Limits. On the Past and Future of Sovereignty and Citizenship,' in *Mapping the Nation*, eds G. Balakrishnan, intro. B. Anderson (London and New York, 1996), pp. 281–94 (p. 293).

4   See, for example, Ernst B. Haas, *The Uniting of Europe: Political, Social, and Economic Forces 1950–57* (London, 1958), p. 16.

5   Dominic Abrams and Michael A. Hogg, eds, *Social Identity Theory* (New York, 1990); Samuel N. Eisenstadt and Bernhard Giesen, 'The Construction of Collective Identity,' *European Journal of Sociology* 36 (1995): 72–102; Bernhard Giesen, 'National Identity and Citizenship: The Cases of Germany and France,' in *European Citizenship. National Legacies and Transnational Projects*, eds K. Eder and B. Giesen (Oxford and New York, 2001), pp. 36–58.

6   Benedict Anderson, *Imagined Communities. Reflections on the Origin and Spread of Nationalism*, rev. ed. (London and New York, 1991) [1983], p. 6.

7   Anderson, *Imagined Communities*, p. 7.

8   William Bloom, *Personal Identity, National Identity and International Relations* (Cambridge, 1990).

9   Penelope J. Oakes, S. Alexander Haslam and John C. Turner, *Stereotyping and Social Reality* (Oxford, 1994), p. 100.

10   The following is an abbreviated and revised version of Thomas Risse, 'A European Identity? Europeanization and the Evolution of Nation-State Identities,' in *Transforming Europe. Europeanization and Domestic Change*, eds M. G. Cowles, J. Caporaso and T. Risse (Ithaca NY, 2001), pp. 198–216.

11   Hans-Joachim Knopf, 'English Identity and European Integration: A Case of Non-Europeanization?' (June paper and PhD proposal: European University Institute, Florence, 1997).

12   R. Bailey, *The European Connection. Implications of EEC Membership* (Oxford, 1983); Stephen George, *An Awkward Partner. Britain in the European Community* (Oxford, 1994).

13   Winston Churchill, 'Speech on 11 May,' House of Commons (1953): 513–895.

14   David Lyon, 'British Identity Cards: The Unpalatable Logic of European Membership?' *The Political Quarterly* 62/3 (1991): 377–85. Hans Schauer, *Europäische Identität und demokratische Tradition* (Munich, 1996). Petra L. Schmitz

and Rolf Geserick, *Die Anderen in Europa. Nationale Selbst- und Fremdbilder im europäischen Integrationsprozeß* (Bonn, 1996).

15   Stafford Cripps, 'Speech on 26 June,' House of Commons (1950): 1946.

16   Margaret Thatcher, 'Speech at the Conservative Party Conference,' *Financial Times*, 13 October 1990, p. 7.

17   John Major, 'Raise Your Eyes, There Is Land Beyond,' *The Economist*, 1993, p. 27.

18   See Patrick Wright, *On Living in an Old Country* (London and New York, 1985). Wright shows how during the Thatcher period there was a tension with the Conservative Party between the Tory tradition of paternalism and the New Right economic and moral libertarians.

19   See Daniela Engelmann-Martin, 'Arbeitsbericht für die Länderstudie Bundesrepublik Deutschland (Fünfziger Jahre)' (unpublished manuscript: European University Institute, Florence, August 1998); Thomas Risse and Daniela Engelmann-Martin, 'Identity Politics and European Integration: The Case of Germany,' in *The Idea of Europe*, ed. A. Pagden (Cambridge, forthcoming).

20   In the following, I use 'Germany' routinely for the Federal Republic, including the pre-unification period.

21   Simon Bulmer, *The Changing Agenda of West German Public Policy* (Aldershot, 1989); Peter J. Katzenstein, ed., *Tamed Power. Germany in Europe* (Ithaca NY, 1997).

22   Haas, *The Uniting of Europe*, p. 127.

23   William E. Paterson, *The SPD and European Integration* (Glasgow, 1974), p. 3.

24   Sozialdemokratische Partei Deutschlands, 'Politische Richtlinien,' Parteitag Hannover (May 1946).

25   Paterson, *The SPD; Detlef Rogosch, Vorstellungen von Europa. Europabilder in der SPD und der belgischen Sozialisten 1945-1957* (Hamburg, 1996).

26   Jürgen Bellers, 'Sozialdemokratie und Konservatismus im Angesicht der Zukunft Europas,' in *Europapolitik der Parteien. Konservatismus, Liberalismus und Sozialdemokratie im Ringen um die Zukunft Europas*, eds J. Bellers and M. Winking (Frankfurt, 1991), pp. 2–42; Rogosch, *Vorstellungen von Europa*.

27   See Thomas Banchoff, 'German Identity and European Integration,' *European Journal of International Relations* 5/3 (1999): 259–89; Gunther Hellmann, 'Goodbye Bismarck? The Foreign Policy of Contemporary Germany,' *Mershon Review of International Studies* 40/1 (1996): 1–39: Katzenstein, *Tamed Power*.

28   In contrast to both Soviet Communism and Anglo-Saxon 'laissez-faire' capitalism; see Bellers and Winking, *Europapolitik der Parteien*; Katzenstein, *Tamed Power*.

29   On the following see Klaus Roscher, 'Arbeitsbericht zur Fallstudie Frankreich' (Florence, 1998) [manuscript].

30   Erling Bjol, *La France devant l'Europe* (Copenhagen, 1966), pp. 172–73.

31   Socialist leader Guy Mollet, *Le Populaire* (1947).

32   MRP Leader Alfred Coste-Floret, 'Bilan et Perspectives d'une Politique Européenne,' *Politique Étrangère* (November 1952): 328.

33   Charles De Gaulle, 'Speech in Lille,' D.M.II (11 December 1950): 393.

34   François Furet, Jacques Juillard and Pierre Rosanvallon, *La République du Centre. La fin de l'Exception Française* (Paris, 1988); Claude Nicolet, *L'idée républicaine en France* (Paris, 1982); Christian Saint-Etienne, *L'Exception* (Paris, 1992).

35 Gregory Flynn, *The Remaking of the Hexagon: The New France in the New Europe* (Boulder CO, 1995); Vivien Schmidt, 'A New Europe for the Old?' *Daedalus* 126/3 (1997): 167–97.

36 Philippe Bauchard, *La Guerre des Deux Roses* (Paris, 1986); Henrik Uterwedde, *Die Wirtschaftspolitik der Linken in Frankreich. Programme und Praxis 1984-87* (Frankfurt, 1988).

37 François Mitterand, *Réflexions sur la Politique Extérieure de la France - Introduction à vingt-cinq Discours* (Paris, 1986), pp. 15, 104.

38 See Sarah Blowen, Marion Demossier and Jeanine Picard, eds, *Recollections of France: The Past, Heritage and Memories* (Oxford and New York, 2001).

39 See Flynn, *The Remaking of the Hexagon*.

NOTES ON CHAPTER 6

1 Jacques Derrida, *Spectres de Marx: l'état de la dette, le travail du deuil et la nouvelle Internationale* (Paris, 1993), p. 94.

2 Jacques Derrida, *Sur Parole: instantanés philosophiques* (Paris, 1999), p. 60.

3 Jacqueline Rose, *States of Fantasy* (Oxford, 1996), p. 3.

4 For concise articulations of the argument see Elizabeth Wright and Edmond Wright, *The Žižek Reader* (Oxford, 1999), pp. 122–23 and Slavoj Žižek, *The Plague of Fantasies* (London, 1997), pp. 27–30.

5 Žižek, *Plague*, pp. 64–65.

6 Žižek, *Plague*, p. 65.

7 Rose, *States*, p. 8.

8 Quoted by Dylan Evans, *An Introductory Dictionary of Lacanian Psychoanalysis* (London and New York, 1996), p. 157.

9 Rose, *States*, pp. 4–5. For further exposition of the value of the psychoanalytic notion of fantasy to political analysis see Yannis Stravrakakis, *Lacan and the Political* (London and New York, 1999), pp. 45–54.

10 '…le premier grand monument de la littérature française, le premier en date, et le plus riche, des poèmes épiques français, ou encore l'œuvre la plus connue du Moyen Age français, la plus belle des épopées nationales…Texte emblématique, texte des origines.' *La Chanson de Roland*, ed. Ian Short (Paris, 1990), p. 5. All references use this edition.

11 On Gaston Paris, see David Hult, 'Gaston Paris and the Invention of Courtly Love,' in *Medievalism and the Modernist Temper*, eds R.H. Bloch and Stephen G. Nichols (Baltimore MD and London, 1996), pp. 192–224 and particularly pp. 195–97 on the 1870 lecture. See also John F. Benton, '"Nostre Franceis n'unt talent de fuïr": the Song of Roland and the Enculturation of a Warrior Class,' *Olifant* 6 (1979): 237–58.

12 See Benton, '"Nostre Franceis n'unt talent de fuïr,"' pp. 249–50, note 3.

13 For biographical information on Bédier see Alain Corbellari, 'Joseph Bédier, Philologist and Writer,' in *Medievalism and the Modernist Temper*, pp. 269–85; Ferdinand Lot, *Joseph Bédier 1864–1938* (Paris, 1939); Per Nykrog, 'A Warrior Scholar at the Collège de France: Joseph Bédier,' in *Medievalism and the Modernist*

Temper, pp.286–307. I have unfortunately been unable to consult Corbellari's recent book on Bédier.

14   *Les Légendes épiques: recherches sur la formation des chansons de geste*, 4 vols (Paris, 1912).

15   See Simon Gaunt, *Gender and Genre in Medieval French Literature* (Cambridge, 1995), pp.24–25.

16   Joseph Bédier, *Les Crimes allemands d'après les témoignages allemands* (Paris, 1915); *Comment l'Allemagne essaye de justifier ses crimes* (Paris, 1915); *L'Effort français: quelques aspects de la guerre* (Paris, 1919).

17   For example, see Corbellari, 'Joseph Bédier,' p.280; Lot, *Joseph Bédier*, p.38; Nykrog, 'A warrior scholar,' p.292.

18   Joseph Bédier, *Roland à Roncevaux: the Romanes Lecture 1921* (Oxford, 1921), pp.5–6.

19   'Je ne crois pas qu'il y ait, dans le passé français, une date plus radieuse…elle sut aussi, la France des premières croisades, par dessus la diversité de ses dialectes et de ses patois, constituer cette belle chose, une langue littéraire et une littérature nationale assez particulière dès l'origine pour que nous y reconnaissions, qualités et défauts, les traits distinctifs de son génie, assez généralement humaine pourtant pour que les nations cultivées, et l'Angleterre entre toutes, s'en soient éprises et inspirées.' Bédier, *Roland à Roncevaux*, pp.6–7.

20   Bédier, *Roland à Roncevaux*, pp.18–19, 22.

21   Bédier, *Roland à Roncevaux*, p.23: 'Apprendre à aimer son propre sacrifice, n'est-ce pas une de ces choses divines?'

22   See the explicit conclusion: *Légendes épiques*, III, p.452.

23   'Interrogez au hasard l'un de nos vétérans sur ses plus lointaines impressions de la guerre. Immanquablement ce qu'il vous mettra sous les yeux, comme une naïve et touchante image d'Epinal, ce sera le souvenir d'un chef exemplaire, dont le plus souvent il aura oublié le nom: le capitaine, sabre haut, qui crie *En avant!*…C'était là notre caste militaire…pour les avoir vus si hardis au combat et dans la retraite si fermes et humains, nos soldats s'étaient donnés à eux…par eux nos soldats s'étaient reliés aux ancêtres…grâce à eux, ils retrouvaient intact, fidèlement gardé, leur propre patrimoine, le dépôt des vertus guerrières de leur race.' *L'Effort français*, pp.23–24.

24   *L'Effort français*, pp.34, note: 'Fidèles à notre grande tradition militaire, nous attachions une importance primordiale à la rencontre, au combat en rase campagne, énergique et rapide. Il était donc tout naturel qu'on regardât la tranchée avec une certaine méfiance, on peut dire aussi avec un mépris à peine dissimulé.'

25   *L'Effort français*, p.177.

26   Nine pamphlets were published by Armand Colin (Paris) in 1915; in addition to the two by Bédier cited in note 16 see: E.Durkheim and E.Denis, *Qui a voulu la guerre? Les origines de la guerre d'après les documents diplomatiques*; André Weiss, *La Violation de la neutralité belge et luxembourgeoise par l'Allemagne*; C.Andler, *Le Pangermanisme: les plans d'expansion allemande dans le monde*; E.Durkheim 'L'Allemagne au dessus de tout': la mentalité allemande et la guerre*; E.Lavisse et C.Andler, *Pratique et doctrine allemandes de la guerre*; R.A.Reiss, *Comment les Austro-Hongorois ont fait la guerre en Serbie: observations directes d'un neutre*;

Charles Seignebos, *1815-1915: Du congrès de Vienne à la guerre de 1914*. Judging by the fact that they were reprinted several times, translated into other languages including English, and provoked an international response, Bédier's pamphlets achieved the widest dissemination and notoriety: see Joseph Bédier, *German Atrocities from the German Evidence*, trans. B. Harrison (Paris, 1915) and *How Germany Seeks to Justify her Atrocities*, trans. J. S. (Paris, 1915); also Elis Wadstein, *Joseph Bédier's 'Crimes allemands': a critique* (Chicago IL, 1916).

27 Durkheim and Denis, *Qui a voulu la guerre?*, p. 61.

28 See the works cited in note 13 for biographical details.

29 For an excellent account of Lanson's career see Antoine Compagnon, *La Troisième République des lettres* (Paris, 1983).

30 Lanson particularly admired Bédier's one venture into modern literary history: *Etudes critiques* (Paris, 1903).

31 Quoted by Compagnon, *Troisième République*, p. 144.

32 'Pour tout dire, si l'écolier n'emporte pas avec lui le vivant souvenir de nos gloires nationales, s'il ne sait pas que ces ancêtres ont combattu sur tous les champs de bataille pour de nobles causes…s'il ne devient pas un citoyen pénétré de ses devoirs et un soldat qui aime son fusil, l'instituteur aura perdu son temps…Vous, enfants du peuple, sachez que vous apprenez l'histoire pour graver dans vos coeurs l'amour de votre pays. Les Gaulois, vos ancêtres, ont été des vaillants. Les Francs vos ancêtres, ont été des vaillants. Les Français vos ancêtres ont été des vaillants.' Cited by Pierre Nora in 'Lavisse, instituteur national: Le «Petit Lavisse», évangile de la République,' in *Les Lieux de Mémoire: La République* I, ed. Pierre Nora (Paris, 1984), pp. 247–89 (p. 282).

33 Cited by Benton, '"Nostre Franceis n'unt talent de fuïr,"' p. 238.

34 '"D'altre part est l'arcevesques Turpin:/ Sun cheval broche e muntet un lariz,/ Franceis apelet, un sermun lur ad dit:/ 'Seignurs baruns, Carles nus laissat ci;/ Pur nostre rei devum nus ben murir./ Chrestïentét aidez a sustenir!"'

35 'Ço dit li quens: "Jo n'en ferai nïent;/ Deus me cunfunde, se la geste en desment!"'

36 '"Jo i ferrai de Durendal m'espee,/ E vos, compainz, ferrez de Halteclere./ En tantes teres les avum nos portees,/ Tantes batailles en avum afinee!/ Male chançun n'en deit estre cantee."'

37 See Žižek, *Plague*, pp. 8–10 on the importance of intersubjectivity in fantasy.

38 See Žižek, *Plague*, pp. 16–18.

39 On *la jouissance de l'Autre* see, *inter alia*, Jacques Lacan, *Encore: le séminaire livre* XX (Paris, 1975), pp. 9–22 ('De la jouissance').

40 On this point see Benton, '"Nostre Franceis n'unt talent de fuïr,"' pp. 245–46.

41 Žižek, *Plague*, p. 32.

42 Peter Haidu, *The Subject of Violence: The* Song of Roland *and the Birth of the Modern State* (Bloomington and Indianapolis IN, 1993).

43 There are of course other copies of the *Roland* written in French, but today these are largely neglected. For overviews of other versions see William W. Kibler, 'The Roland after Oxford,' *Olifant* 6 (1979): 275–92, and particularly Cesare Segre, *La tradizione della «Chanson de Roland»* (Milan and Naples, 1974). For recent readings of other versions, see Gaunt, *Gender and Genre*, pp. 38–42 and Sarah Kay,

The Chansons de Geste in the Age of Romance: Political Fictions (Oxford, 1995), pp. 209–11.

NOTES ON CHAPTER 7

1   See Brian Graham, G.J.Ashworth and J.E.Tunbridge, *A Geography of Heritage: Power, Culture and Economy* (London, 2000).

2   Peter Vergo, ed., *The New Museology* (London, 1989), p. 1.

3   Anthony Smith, *National Identity* (Harmondsworth, 1991), p. 17.

4   See Ivan Karp, C.M.Kreamer and S.Lavine, eds, *Museums and Community: The Politics of Public Culture* (Washington DC, 1992).

5   For a recent German history of Schleswig-Holstein, see generally Ulrich Lange, ed., *Geschichte Schleswig-Holsteins von den Anfängen bis zur Gegenwart* (Neumünster, 1996). An impressive history in 8 volumes has been underway since 1939, see Volquart Pauls et al., eds, *Geschichte Schleswig-Holsteins*. A concise history is Franz de Jessen, ed., *Manuel Historique de la Question de Slesvig* (Copenhagen, 1906). For Danish studies, see H.V.Gregersen, *Slesvig og Holsten før 1830* (Copenhagen, 1981); Lorenz Rerup, *Slesvig og Holsten efter 1830* (Copenhagen, 1982).

6   The impressive cultural output of the Gottorp Court was highlighted in a large exhibition at Gottorp Castle in 1997, Gottorf im Glanz des Barocks, on the occasion of the 400th anniversary of Duke Friedrich III's birth. Artefacts from all over Scandinavia and Germany were brought together and give some indication of the splendours of seventeenth-century Gottorp. See the four-volume catalogue of the show edited by Heinz Spielmann et al., *Gottorf im Glanz des Barocks* (Schleswig, 1997). For a recent account of Gottorp Court culture, see Martin B.Djupdræt, 'Die Inszenierung der Gottofer Geschichte durch Jürgen Ovens. Der Zyklus von Historiengemälden aus Schloß Gottorf,' *Nordelbingen* 70 (2001): 25–49.

7   On the construction of Danish-Norwegian-Schleswig-Holsteinian state-patriotic ideas in the eighteenth century, see Thomas Lyngby, *Den Sentimentale Patriotisme* (Copenhagen, 2001), pp. 103–9.

8   Among the regular guests at Augustenborg was the writer Hans Christian Andersen.

9   Stine Wiell, *Flensborgsamlingen 1852-1864 – og dens skæbne* (Flensburg, 1997).

10   Franz de Jessen, *Manuel Historique de la Question du Slesvig 1906-1938* (Copenhagen and Paris, 1939).

11   Kim Furdal, *Fra preussiske landkommuner til danske sognekommuner. Kommunestyret i Sønderjylland fra 1867 til 1920'erne* (Aabenraa, 1999).

12   See note 6.

NOTES ON CHAPTER 8

1   There is a copious bibliography on the subject. See Kevin Walsh, *The Representation of the Past: Museums and Heritage in the Post-modern World* (London, 1992). For

general debates about the role of the museum, see the articles collected in Peter Vergo, ed., *The New Museology* (London, 1989); Sharon Macdonald and Gordon Fyfe, eds, *Theorizing Museums: Representing Identity and Diversity in a Changing World* (Oxford, 1996); Sharon Macdonald, ed., *The Politics of Display: Museums, Science, Culture* (London and New York, 1998).

2   *Cultural Trends* 30 (London, 1999).

3   See the UNESCO web pages devoted to Venice: http://www.unesco.org/culture/heritage/tangible/venice

4   On John Ruskin and Venice, see Denis Cosgrove, 'The Myth and the Stones of Venice: an Historical Geography of a Symbolic Landscape,' *Journal of Historical Geography* 8 (1982): 145–69.

5   Schama has pioneered a style of historical writing that not only gives authority to visual records, but also incorporates literary modes, such as personal recollection and first-person narrative, into the work. See for example his *Landscape and Memory* (New York and London, 1995). On the distrust of visual sources in history see Peter Burke, *Eyewitnessing: the Uses of Images as Historical Evidence* (London, 2001).

6   David Lowenthal, *The Heritage Crusade and the Spoils of History* (Harmondsworth, 1996).

7   Walter Benjamin, *Illuminations*, ed. H. Arendt, trans. H. Zohn (London, 1973), p. 215.

8   Donald M. Nichol, *Venice and Byzantium* (Cambridge, 1988).

9   Patricia Fortini Brown, *Venice and Antiquity: the Venetian Sense of the Past* (New Haven CT and London, 1996).

10   Fortini Brown, *Venice and Antiquity*, p. 16.

11   Nichol, *Venice and Byzantium*, pp. 182–83.

12   Fortini Brown, *Venice and Antiquity*, p. 29. On the use of painting as historical evidence see Patricia Fortini Brown, *Venetian Narrative Painting in the Age of Carpaccio* (New Haven CT and London, 1988).

13   Fortini Brown, *Venice and Antiquity*, p. 77–81.

14   Fortini Brown, *Venetian Narrative Painting*.

15   Lord Byron, *Childe Harold's Pilgrimage: A Romaunt* (London, 1853), Canto IV, verse 17.

16   Fuller documentation for this section of the argument may be found in Denis Cosgrove, 'The Myth and the Stones of Venice: An Historical Geography of a Symbolic Landscape,' *Journal of Historical Geography* 8 (1982): 145–69.

17   John Ruskin, *The Stones of Venice*, vol. 1 (London, 1851), p. 1.

18   John Ruskin, 'The Nature of Gothic,' in *The Stones of Venice*, vol. 2 (London, 1853), p. 188.

NOTES ON CHAPTER 9

Unless otherwise noted, all translations are my own.

1   Walter Benjamin to Florens Christian Rang, 18 November 1923, in Gershom Scholem and Theodor W. Adorno, eds, *The Correspondence of Walter Benjamin*

1910-1940, trans. M.R.Jacobson and E.M.Jacobson (Chicago IL and London, 1994), p.215.

2   Richard Muther, 'Ästhetische Kultur,' *Aufsätze über bildende Kunst*, vol. 2 (Berlin, 1914), p.154.

3   Thomas Nipperdey, 'Nationalidee und Nationaldenkmal in Deutschland im 19. Jahrhundert,' *Historische Zeitschrift* 206 (June 1968): 533. Nipperdey's essay remains the foundational text on German national monuments; it has been reprinted many times in studies on various aspects of monument production and provides a particularly useful articulation of the typologies of the national monument. On monuments and national identity in Germany, see also Reinhard Alings, *Monument und Nation. Das Bild vom Nationalstaat im Medium Denkmal - zur Verhältnis von Nation und Staat im deutschen Kaiserreich 1871-1918* (Berlin, 1996); Rudy Koshar, *From Monuments to Traces: Artefacts of German Memory, 1870-1990* (Berkeley CA, 2000); Karen Lang, 'Monumental Unease: Monuments and the Making of National Identity in Germany,' in *Imagining Modern German Culture: 1889-1910*, ed. Françoise Forster-Hahn [*Studies in the History of Art* 53] (Washington DC, 1996), pp.274–98; Antje Laumann-Kleineberg, *Denkmäler des 19. Jahrhunderts im Widerstreit. Drei Fallstudien zur Diskussion zwischen Auftraggebern, Planern und Öffentlichen Kritikern* (Frankfurt am Main, 1989); Ekkehard Mai and Stephan Waetzoldt, eds, *Kunstverwaltung, Bau- und Denkmal Politik im Kaiserreich* (Berlin, 1981); Ernst Mittig and Volker Plagemann, eds, *Denkmäler im 19. Jahrhundert* (Munich, 1972); Gavriel D. Rosenfeld, *Munich and Memory: Architecture, Monuments and the Legacy of the Third Reich* (Berkeley CA, 2000). From an expanding bibliography on monuments, memory, and nationalism, I note the following recent sources: Avner Ben-Amos, 'Monuments and Memory in French Nationalism,' *History and Memory* 5/2 (1993): 50–81; David Chidester and Edward T.Linenthal, eds, *American Sacred Space* (Bloomington and Indianapolis IN, 1995); Paul Connerton, *How Societies Remember* (Cambridge, 1989); Amos Funkenstein, 'Collective Memory and Historical Consciousness,' *History and Memory* 1/1 (Spring/Summer 1989): 5–26; John R.Gillis, ed., *Commemorations. The Politics of National Identity* (Princeton NJ, 1994); Richard Handler, *Nationalism and the Politics of Culture in Quebec* (Madison WI, 1988); Pierre Nora, 'Between Memory and History: Les Lieux de Mémoire,' *Representations* 26 (Spring 1989): 7–25; Nuala Johnson, 'Cast in Stone: Monuments, Geography, and Nationalism,' in *Political Geography: A Reader*, ed. J.Agnew (London and New York, 1997), pp.347–64; James Young, *The Texture of Memory: Holocaust Memorials and Meaning* (New Haven CT, 1993).

4   Nipperdey, 'Nationalidee,' pp.538–39. See also Wolfgang Hartwig, 'Bürgertum, Staatssymbolik und Staatsbewußtsein im Kaiserreich 1871-1914,' *Zeitschrift für Historische Sozialwissenschaft* 16 (1990): 269–95.

5   In 1887, Nietzsche wrote of the fog of nationalist rhetoric that lay over the new nation and, tongue-in-cheek, noted the possibilities of the commercialization of nationalism: 'I should like to know how many shiploads of sham idealism, heroic trappings and grand-word rattles…would have to be exported from Europe today before its air would begin to smell fresh again.

With this overproduction there is obviously a new opening for trade here; there is obviously a "business" to be made out of little ideal-idols and the "idealists" who go with them: don't let this opportunity slip!' Friedrich Nietzsche, *On the Genealogy of Morals*, trans. W.Kaufmann and R.J.Hollingdale (New York, 1969), p.159.

6   Eric Hobsbawm, 'Mass-Producing Traditions: Europe, 1870-1914,' in *The Invention of Tradition*, ed. E.Hobsbawm and T.Ranger (Cambridge, 1983), p.268. See also Michael Steinberg, *The Meaning of the Salzburg Festival. Austria as Theater and Ideology, 1890-1938* (Ithaca NY, 1990), where representation is considered 'constitutive rather than reflective of cultural and political identity and power.' (p.6).

7   Hobsbawm and Ranger, *The Invention of Tradition*. As Hobsbawm points out, the invention of traditions occurs more frequently under conditions of rapid social change. Therefore, the years 1870–1914 'saw them spring up with particular assiduity,' since 'new or old but dramatically transformed, social groups, environments and social contexts called for new devices to ensure or express social cohesion and identity and to structure social relations.' (p.263).

8   In addition to the network of Bismarck monuments, plazas, bridges, streets, mountain passes, as well as cities were named after Bismarck during this period. Bismarck, North Dakota, was founded in 1873, for instance. On the cult of Bismarck and monument production, see in particular Hans-Walter Hedinger, 'Bismarck-Denkmäler und Bismarck-Verehrung,' in Mai and Waetzoldt, eds, *Kunstverwaltung*, pp.277–314; Lothar Machtan, 'Bismarck-Kult und deutscher National-Mythos 1890 bis 1940,' in *Bismarck und der deutscher National-Mythos*, ed. Lothar Machtan (Bremen, 1994), pp.14–67; Volker Plagemann, 'Bismarck-Denkmäler,' in *Denkmäler*, eds Mittig and Plagemann, pp.217–52.

9   The term 'imagined community' comes from the provocative study by Benedict Anderson, *Imagined Communities. Reflections on the Origins and Spread of Nationalism* (London and New York, 1991) [originally 1983]. While Anderson discusses how the novel and the newspaper 'provided the technical means for "re-presenting" the kind of imagined community that is the nation' (p.25), he does not specifically examine the role of monuments in national identity formation. See also Kirsten Belgum, *Popularizing the Nation: audience, representation, and the production of identity in Die Gartenlaube, 1853-1900* (Lincoln, 1998).

10 Arthur Moeller van den Bruck, *Der preußische Stil* (Munich, 1916), p.165. On the question of monumentality for contemporary German architecture and monuments, see Peter Behrens, 'Was ist monumentale Kunst?' *Kunstgewerbeblatt* 20 (1909): 45–48; Robert Breuer, 'Die Wiedergeburt des Monumentalen,' *Deutsche Kunst und Dekoration* 14/2 (November 1910): 139–48; Barbara Miller Lane, 'Changing Attitudes to Monumentality: An Interpretation of European Architecture and Urban Form 1880-1914,' in *Growth and Transformation of the Modern City*, eds Ingrid Hammarström and Thomas Hall (Stockholm, 1979), pp.101–14; C.H.Reilly, 'The Monumental Qualities in Architecture,' *The Architectural Review* 32 (October 1912): 195–99; Fritz Schumacher, *Streifzüge eines Architekten* (Jena, 1907).

11 Richard Hamann and Jost Hermand, *Stilkunst um 1900* (Munich, 1973), p.349. Hamann and Herman's chapter on monumental art provides a rich introduction

to issues of monumentality, style, and national identity in turn-of-the-century German painting, sculpture, literature, and music.

12 I borrow the term 'national culture' from Ernst Gellner, *Nations and Nationalism* (Cambridge, 1983), p. 36. Gellner demonstrates how 'modern man is not loyal to a monarch or a land or a faith, whatever he may say, but to a culture.'

13 Detailed discussions of the various manifestations of the Bismarck cult may be found in Walter Hoffmann, ed., *Die Bismarck-Ehrung durch die Deutsche Studentenschaft* (Heidelberg, 1899); Hans-Walter Hedinger, 'Bismarck-Denkmäler und Bismarck-Verehrung,' in *Kunstverwaltung, Bau- und Denkmal-Politik im Kaiserreich*, eds E.Mai and S.Waetzoldt (Berlin, 1981), pp. 277–314; Werner Pols, 'Bismarckverehrung und Bismarcklegende als innenpolitisches Problem der wilhelminischen Zeit,' *Jahrbuch für Geschichte Mittel- und Ostdeutschlands* 20 (1971): 183–201.

14 *Hundert Entwürfe aus dem Wettbewerb für das Bismarck-National-Denkmal auf der Elisenhöhe bei Bingerbrück-Bingen* (Düsseldorf, 1911), p. 6.

15 *Deutsche Bauzeitung* 44/4 (12 January 1910), p. 24.

16 *Deutsche Bauzeitung* 44/4 (12 January 1910), p. 23. The selection of a site in the Rhine Valley must also be considered in the context of a popular Rheinromantik, or romance of the Rhine, which had been propagated by writers and poets from the end of the eighteenth century, and especially during the course of the nineteenth century. On this subject, see, for instance, the patriotically inflamed study by Heinz Stephan, *Die Entstehung der Rheinromantik* (Cologne, 1922).

17 'Wettbewerb Bismarck-National-Denkmal auf der Elisenhöhe bei Bingerbrück,' *Deutsche Bauzeitung* 45/53 (5 July 1911), p. 458. It should be added that the committee found the 'immediate vicinity of a larger city as well as the housing and transportation possibilities this offered' of importance in the selection of this site. H. [Albert Hofmann], 'Der Wettbewerb zur Erlangen von Entwürfen für ein Bismarck-Denkmal auf der Elisenhöhe bei Bingerbrück,' *Deutsche Bauzeitung* 45/14 (18 February 1911), p. 120. (This is part of a serial article by Albert Hofmann, editor of the *Deutsche Bauzeitung*, which continues through 1911. Unless otherwise noted, all references to articles by Hofmann, 1911, refer to the various instalments of this serial article.)

18 Brt. [Baurat] B, 'Betrachtung zum Wettbewerb für das Bismarck-National-Denkmal,' *Deutsche Bauzeitung* 45/4 (25 March 1911), p. 202.

19 Hofmann, 18 February 1911, pp. 120–21.

20 Paul Cassirer, 'Der Tempel des Bismarck,' *Pan* 2 (1911–12), p. 186. The jury included the painters Ludwig Dill (Karlsruhe) and Franz von Stuck (Munich), the sculptors Jos. Flossmann (Pasing), August Gaul (Berlin) and L.Tuaillon (Berlin), Max Klinger (Leipzig), the architects Theodor Fischer (Munich), Ludwig Hoffmann (Berlin), Hermann Muthesius (Nicolasee), Fritz Schumacher (Hamburg), the gallery directors Alfred Lichtwark (Hamburg), and Volbehr (Magdeburg), the conservator of the Rhine province Paul Clemen (Bonn), the scholars Max Dessoir (Berlin), Max Schmid (Aachen) and Count von Kalckreuth (Eddelsen bei Hamburg), and the industrialists Emil Kirdorf (Speldorf bei Mülheim an der Ruhr) and Walther Rathenau (Berlin). Alfred Lichtwark was selected as first president and Max Schmid

as the second president of the jury. The members of the jury also belonged to the artistic committee of approximately 36 members and to the executive committee of approximately 100 members. At the head of the monument committee sat the Oberpräsident der Rheinprovinz, Staatsminister von Rheinbaben. The industrialists Walther Rathenau and Emil Kirdorf were known as ardent Bismarck supporters. Their presence on the monument committee not only signalled this, it also, especially in the case of Kirdorf, ensured substantial financial support for the monument from the heavy industrial firms of the Rhine valley.

21 As reported in *Deutsche Bauzeitung* 45/29 (12 April 1911), p. 246.

22 See Max Schmidt, ed., *Bismarck-National-Denkmal. Katalog und Führer durch die Ausstellung* (Düsseldorf, 1911), as well as the designs illustrated in Deutsche Bauzeitung, 1911–12. The contestants were required to submit a 1:1000 site plan and a drawing in 1:500 dimensions. Additionally, they could receive a 1:500 model of the Elisenhöhe with which to construct site-specific models of their designs for 40 M. from the Düsseldorf firm of Zöbus and Eisenmeier.

23 Cited in Hoffmann, 18 February 1911, p. 122.

24 Michael Dorrmann, '"Wenn Bismarck Wiederkäme." Kunst, Ideologie und Rathenaus Engagement für ein Bismarck-National-Denkmal,' in *Die Extreme berühren sich. Walther Rathenau 1867-1922*, exhibition catalogue, Deutsches Historisches Museum, Berlin (Berlin, 1993), p. 103.

25 Alfred Lichtwark in Alfred Lichtwark and Walther Rathenau, *Der rheinische Bismarck* (Berlin, 1912), p. 10.

26 Eliza May Butler, *The Tyranny of Greece over Germany. A Study of the Influence Exercised by Greek Art and Poetry over the great German Writers of the Eighteenth, Nineteenth and Twentieth Centuries* (Cambridge, 1935).

27 Suzanne Marchand, 'Problems and Prospects for Intellectual History,' *New German Critique* 65 (Spring–Summer 1995): 94–95. See also her book, *Down from Olympus. Archaeology and Philhellenism in Germany, 1750-1970* (Princeton NJ, 1996).

28 In addition to general disapproval of the conception of the design, the Association of German Sculptors, Berlin, published a protest stating that the decision was unfair because Hahn had originally been slated as a member of the jury.

29 Lichtwark in Lichtwark and Rathenau, *Der rheinische Bismarck*, pp. 10–11 and passim. While Hermann Hahn had made a bust of Rathenau and had worked on various sculptural projects for the AEG, Michael Dorrmann does not believe that nepotism lay behind Rathenau's strong support of the Hahn and Bestelmeyer design. Rather, he attributes Rathenau's choice of design to his 'ausgeprägte Germanen-bewunderung,' to a 'bewunderten germanischen Rassenideals' represented in the statue of the young Siegfried. Dorrmann: 'Wenn Bismarck Wiederkäme,' p. 104.

30 Cassirer, 'Der Temple des Bismarck,' p. 187. See also Georg Biermann, 'Die Konkurrenz zum Bismarck-Nationaldenkmal,' *Der Cicerone* 3/3 (1911): 134.

31 Max Osborn in *Deutsche Kunst und Dekoration* 27/6 (March 1911): 444.

32 This was made patently clear by Hermann Muthesius, who, along with Max Dessoir, published *Das Bismarck-Nationaldenkmal* (Jena, 1912), a book written in response to Lichtwark and Rathenau's *Der rheinische Bismarck*. According to Muthesius, the unpopularity of the first-prize design did not rest on any lack of

understanding for its symbolic content but rather on the design's lyrical character and lack of heroicism. See p. 22 and passim.

33   Wilhelm Kreis in Hofmann, 2 November 1912, p. 771.

34   'Faust' was disqualified by the jury because, as they claimed, it failed to present a 'heroic' solution that fit into the landscape. Moreover, the cost of execution would have well exceeded the fixed sum of 1,800,000 marks. Hofmann, 12 April 1911, p. 246.

35   Like most inflated declarations of originality, Kreis's claim for the uniqueness of his design is disproved by the historical record: One need only mention the similarity of his design to the well-known Befreiungshalle in Kielheim, completed in 1863, to make this point.

36   Such a solution avoided the merely 'playful character' of a narrow tower in the landscape. Wilhelm Kreis, 'Nochmals zur Bismarck-National-Monument-Konkurrenz,' *Der Cicerone* 3 (1911): 219. The editor of the journal signalled to the reader the importance of Kreis's ideas, thereby lending further weight to this article. Kreis's essay was also printed under the title 'Denkmal und Landschaft,' in *Deutsche Bauzeitung* 45/22 (18 March 1911): 181–82.

37   Kreis, 'Nochmals zur Bismarck-National-Monument-Konkurrenz,' p. 219. Kreis adds that the effect is further intensified when the represented figure is seated rather than standing, thus bringing the entire form closer to the viewer and so working more immediately as a monumental unity.

38   Kreis in Hofmann, 2 November 1912, pp. 771–74. The greatest effect, however, is saved for the Pantheon in Rome (and thus by extension for Kreis's own memorial hall), whose 'interior is indescribable, but has the effect of the highest monumentality on us.' The mausoleum of Theodoric and the Castel del Monte had been reverently discussed and illustrated in *Deutsche Bauzeitung* in the early years of the century. See, for instance, *Deutsche Bauzeitung*, 40/50 (23 June 1906).

39   Dessoir in Dessoir and Muthesius, *Das Bismarck Nationaldenkmal*, p. 48.

40   Dessoir in Dessoir and Muthesius, *Das Bismarck Nationaldenkmal*, p. 48.

41   Biermann, 'Die Konkurrenz zum Bismarck-Nationaldenkmal,' p. 135. It is interesting to note that Kreis had submitted a virtually similar design for the 1902 Hamburg Bismarck monument competition. While Kreis had won favour at that time for the pure architectonic conception of his memorial hall, the jury felt that the 'almost gloomy seriousness of the interior, like the exterior, lead more to the impression of a mausoleum than to the memorial hall intended by the author.' In 1911, this 'mausoleum' was described as a 'kind of modern pantheon,' a description which also alludes to a funerary structure, yet one in which all 'gloomy seriousness' has been drained and replaced by a connotation of heroic apotheosis.

42   'Wettbewerbe,' *Deutsche Bauzeitung* 45/53 (5 July 1911), p. 459.

43   See the interesting report on this in *Deutsche Bauzeitung* 45/49 (21 June 1911), p. 418.

44   As reported in the section on competitions in *Deutsche Bauzeitung* 45/53 (5 July 1911), p. 459.

45   Only four votes were cast in favour of Kreis's reworked design for first place. The four jury members who voted in favour of the Kreis design were later revealed with considerable savour in *Deutsche Bauzeitung*. Muthesius, Dessoir, Schumacher and Clemen were praised for their decision not to support 'another weak

imitation,' and for this, 'the overwhelming majority of the nation was behind them.' 'Wettbewerbe,' *Deutsche Bauzeitung* 45/100 (16 December 1911), p.864.

46   H. [Albert Hofmann], 'Der zur Ausführung gewählte Entwurf für ein Bismarck-National-Monument auf der Elisenhöhe bei Bingerbrück,' *Deutsche Bauzeitung* 46/87 (30 October 1912), p.761. See the interesting report on the meeting of the executive committee in 'Wettbewerbe,' *Deutsche Bauzeitung* 45/98 (9 December 1911), p.844.

47   Kreis in Hofmann, 6 November 1912, p.786.

48   Kreis in Hofmann, 6 November 1912, p.786.

49   Tim Klein, 'Grundsätzliches zum Bismarck-National-Denkmal,' *Die Plastik* 2 (1911): 27. Klein adds (p.27) that 'a Bismarck national monument must not come from the fact of unity, but from a feeling of greatness.' Because such a feeling was currently lacking, it was impossible to erect such a monument at the present time, and so 'this Bismarck national monument will be a signpost on the way.'

50   Alexander Heilmeyer, 'Ausstellung der Wettbewerbs-Entwürfe zum Bismarck-National-Denkmal im Düsseldorfer Kunstpalast,' *Die Plastik* 3 (1911): 29.

51   Rathenau in Lichtwark and Rathenau, *Der rheinische Bismarck*, p.20. Rathenau refused to believe the majority of the nation really wanted the Kreis design. Instead, in analyzing how the competition went awry, he finds that 'their Bismarck' is no more than a 'rheinische Bismarck,' or the conception of Bismarck favoured by the majority of the citizens and industrialists of the Rhine valley.

52   Aby Warburg, 'Contemporary Art: Lederer,' in *Aby Warburg. An Intellectual Biography*, ed. E.H.Gombrich (Chicago IL, 1986), p.154.

53   Cassirer, 'Der Tempel des Bismarck': 187. On the monument as a shrine to a 'secular religion' of German nationalism, see the fascinating study by George L.Mosse, *The Nationalization of the Masses. Political Symbolism and Mass Movements in Germany from the Napoleonic Wars through the Third Reich* (New York, 1975).

54   Cassirer, 'Der Temple des Bismarck': 192–93.

55   Thomas Nipperdey, 'Nationalidee,' p.576.

56   Rathenau in Lichtwark and Rathenau, *Der rheinische Bismarck*, p.27.

57   Z., 'Das Bismarck-National-Denkmal bei Bingen am Rhein,' *Monatshefte für Baukunst und Städtebau* 17/7 (July 1933): 304.

58   Z., 'Das Bismarck-National-Denkmal:' 304.

59   Christoph Stölzl, 'Preface' in *Bismarck - Prussia, Germany, and Europe*, exhibition catalogue, German Historical Museum, Berlin (Berlin, 1990).

60   See Wolfgang Ernst, 'Augenblicke Bismarcks. Eine historische Ausstellung als ephemeres Denkmal' in *Mo(nu)mente. Formen und Funktionen ephemerer Denkmäler*, ed. M.Diers (Berlin, 1993), pp.283–97.

61   Podrecca, 'Preface,' p.18.

62   Podrecca, 'Preface,' p.18.

63   This point is underscored in a souvenir postcard for the exhibition in which Bismarck is shown at various stages of his life, along with members of his family, his cabinet and the goddess of victory. The *mis-en-scène* of this memento reminds one more of a suggestive advertisement for a sensationalist docudrama than a postcard for a didactic, historical exhibition.

64   Patrick Wright, 'Trafficking in History' (1985), reprinted in *Representing the Nation: A Reader. Histories, Heritage and Museums*, eds D.Boswell and J.Evans (London and New York, 1999), pp.115–50 (p.134).

NOTES ON CHAPTER 10

1   Simon Schama, *Landscape and Memory* (London, 1995), p.82.

2   Stephen Jay Gould, *Ever Since Darwin: Reflections in Natural History* (New York and London, 1979), p.231.

3   Wilfried Lipp, *Natur, Geschichte, Denkmal. Zur Entstehung des Denkmalbewußtseins der bürgerlichen Gesellschaft* (Frankfurt and New York, 1987), p.265.

4   Lipp, *Natur*, p.264.

5   See Friedrich Ludwig von Sckell, *Beiträge zur bildenden Gartenkunst für angehende Gartenkünstler und Gartenliebhaber*, reprint of 2nd ed. (1825) (Worms, 1982), p.197; see similar pp.130, 226.

6   Lipp, *Natur*, p.264.

7   Alexander von Humboldt, *Ideen zu einer Physiognomik der Gewächse* (Tübingen, 1806), p.14.

8   Von Humboldt, *Ideen*, p.13.

9   Von Humboldt, *Ideen*, p.13.

10   For Lange, natural gardens were determined not so much by ecology but by the physiognomic appearance of plants. In his concept of natural garden design, one goal was to use foreign plants that physiognomically fitted in with the native context in order to heighten and improve the beauty of nature by artistic means; see Gert Gröning and Joachim Wolschke-Bulmahn, 'Changes in the Philosophy of Garden Architecture in the 20th Century and their Impact upon the Social and Spatial Environment,' *Journal of Garden History* 9 (1989): 53–70 (55).

11   There were several elements to Lange's concept of natural garden design or the nature garden. The designer of a nature garden à la Lange was not permitted to use geometric and architectural forms; the design of the garden should be informal. The purpose of Lange's nature garden was not primarily to serve mankind; nature, especially plants and also animals, had equal rights. Native plants were favoured over foreign ones. Moreover, Lange interpreted the garden as part of the surrounding landscape, to which it was to be subordinated. The cutting of trees, shrubs and hedges was rejected in the nature garden as anthropocentric, a sign of human hegemony over nature. Instead, the laws of nature were to be followed and spiritually hightened, in order to produce an artistic display of nature in the garden.

12   Jost Hermand, *Old Dreams of a New Reich: Volkish Utopias and National Socialism*, trans. Paul Levesque in collaboration with Stefan Soldovieri (Bloomington IN, 1992), p.10.

13   Hermand, *Old Dreams*, p.14.

14   Willy Pastor, *Aus germanischer Vorzeit* (Berlin, 1907), Foreword.

15   Pastor, *Aus germanischer*, p.11.

16   Willy Pastor, *Die Erde in der Zeit des Menschen: Versuch einer naturwissenschaftlichen Kulturgeschichte* (Jena and Leipzig, 1904), p. 189.

17   See, for example, Joseph Strzygowski, *Die Landschaft in der nordischen Kunst. Bibliothek der Kunstgeschichte*, vol. 17 (Leipzig, 1922), p. 3; Joseph Strzygowski, *Der Norden in der bildenden Kunst Westeuropas. Heidnisches und Christliches um das Jahr 1000* (Vienna, 1926), p. 7.

18   In this context, see Malcom Quinn's discussion of the ways in which the symbol of the 'swastika,' which the archaeologist Heinrich Schliemann uncovered on artefacts at Troy was appropriated by a nationalist German ideology; *The Swastika: Constructing the Symbol* (London and New York, 1994).

19   Pastor, *Die Erde*, p. 128.

20   Heinrich Friedrich Wiepking-Jürgensmann, 'Germanische Ahnenlandschaften auf Insel Rügen,' *Die Gartenkunst* 49 (1936): 136–37 (137).

21   Pastor, *Aus germanischer*, p. 52.

22   See, for example, Willy Pastor, *Deutsche Urzeit. Grundlagen der germanischen Geschichte* (Weimar, n.d.), p. 283.

23   Regarding Lange's ideas about natural garden design see, for example, Gröning and Wolschke-Bulmahn, 'Changes in the Philosophy of Garden Architecture,' and Joachim Wolschke-Bulmahn and Gert Gröning, 'The Ideology of the Nature Garden. Nationalistic Trends in Garden Design in Germany during the Early Twentieth Century,' *Journal of Garden History* 12 (1992): 73–80. See also Willy Lange, 'Meine Anschauungen über die Gartengestaltung unserer Zeit,' *Die Gartenkunst* 7 (1905): 113–16 (114).

24   Willy Lange, *Gartenbilder* (Leipzig, 1922), p. 27.

25   Alois Riegl, *Stilfragen. Grundlegungen zu einer Geschichte der Ornamentik*, reprint of the 1893 edition (Munich, 1985), p. 3. The influence of Riegl on contemporary art history is demonstrated by W. Worringer's use of this passage in his book *Abstraktion und Einfühlung: Ein Beitrag zur Stilpsychologie*, 8th ed. (Munich, 1919), p. 22. See generally, Margaret Iversen, *Alois Riegl: Art History and Theory* (Cambridge MA, 1993).

26   Pastor, *Deutsche Urzeit*, p. 7.

27   Pastor, *Die Erde*, p. 190.

28   See, for example, Jens Jensen, *The Clearing: 'A Way of Life'* (Chicago IL, 1949).

29   Pastor, *Deutsche Urzeit*, p. 25.

30   For a discussion of the way in which an equivalent prehistoric site, Stonehenge, was appreciated in Britain, see Barbara Bender, 'Stonehenge – Contested Landscape (Medieval to Present-Day),' in *Landscape: Politics and Perspectives*, ed. B. Bender (Oxford, 1993), pp. 245–79.

31   Pastor, *Deutsche Urzeit*, p. 223.

32   Pastor, *Die Erde*, p. 55.

33   Hans Hasler was a student and ardent admirer of Willy Lange; in 1939 he published his book *Deutsche Gartenkunst* as a continuation and further development of Lange's ideas.

34   Jens Jensen, 'Park and Garden Planning,' Reichsminister für Ernährung und Landwirtschaft (ed.), *12. Internationaler Gartenbaukongreß Berlin 1938*, vol. II (Berlin, 1939), pp. 1003–12 (p. 1007).

35 Willy Lange, *Gartenpläne* (Leipzig, 1927), p.5.

36 Heinrich Friedrich Wiepking-Jürgensmann, 'Reichsehrenmal Tannenberg,' *Die Gartenschönheit* 18 (1937): 421–23 (p.421).

37 Wiepking-Jürgensmann, 'Reichsehrenmal Tannenberg,' p.421.

38 Wiepking-Jürgensmann, 'Über die Umwelt des deutschen Volkes,' *Die Gartenkunst* 50 (1937): 43–44 (43).

39 Hermand, *Old Dreams*, p.123.

40 See, for example, Mathilde Ludendorff, 'Verschüttete Volksseele: Nach Berichten aus Südwestafrika,' nos 11 and 12 of the *Schriftenreihe der Ludendorffs-Verlags-GmbH* (Munich, 1935), p.4.

41 Philip Rees, *Biographical Dictionary of the Extreme Right since 1890* (New York, 1990), p.239.

42 See Rees, *Biographical Dictionary*, p.239.

43 S.Platen, 'Ahnenstätte der Deutschvolkgemeinde Seelenfeld,' *Die Deutsche Revolution, Kampfblatt des Tannenbergbundes, Landesverband Nord* 1 (1932): 1–3 (3).

44 Rudolf Bergfeld, *Der Naturformgarten. Ein Versuch zur Begründung des Naturalismus im Garten* (Frankfurt/Oder, 1912).

45 *Stättenordnung für die Ahnenstätte Hilligenloh*, 23 August 1964.

46 *Stättenordnung*, 1964.

47 T.G.Jordan, *Texas Graveyards* (Austin TX, 1990), p.110.

48 For the history of the Sachsenhain (Grove of the Saxons) see in more detail Claudia Achenbach, 'Die ideologische Funktion der Landespflege in Deutschland - demonstriert an einem Projekt aus der Zeit des Nationalsozialismus,' master thesis at the Department of Landespflege, Technische Fachhochschule Berlin (Berlin, 1990), unpublished manuscript.

49 Schama, *Memory and Landscape*, p.82.

50 For a biography of Himmler, see Peter Padfield, *Himmler: Reichsführer-SS* (New York, 1991). For a discussion of the Ahnenerbe, see Michael H.Krater, *Das 'Ahnenerbe' der SS, 1933-1045: Ein Beitrage zur Kulturpolitik des Dritten Reiches* (Stuttgart, 1974).

51 See Wilhelm Hübotter, 'Steine - auch eine Art Landschaftsgestaltung,' *Garten und Landschaft* 66 (1956), pp.110–13.

52 See H.-H.Flohr, *Preface to Zehn Jahre Sachsenhain*, ed. Landesjugendpfarramt Hannover on the occasion of the Landesjugendtreffen (1960).

53 Hübotter, 'Steine - auch eine Art Landschaftsgestaltung,' p.112.

54 See, in this context, Reinhard Berkelmann, 'Der Sachsenhain bei Verden a. d. Aller,' *Die Gartenkunst* 50 (1937): 125–28 (128).

55 George Mosse, *Fallen Soldiers: Shaping the Memory of the World Wars* (New York, 1990), p.88.

56 Mosse, *Fallen Soldiers*, p.90.

57 Berkelmann, 'Der Sachsenhain,' p.125.

58 Berkelmann, 'Der Sachsenhain,' p.126.

59 Berkelmann, 'Der Sachsenhain,' p.128.

60 For a more detailed discussion of the Landscape Rules, see Gert Gröning, 'Die "Allgemeine Anordnung Nr. 20/VI/42" - Über die Gestaltung der Landschaft in

den eingegliederten Ostgebieten,' in *Der 'Generalplan Ost.' Hauptlinien der nationalsozialistischen Planungs- und Vernichtungspolitik*, eds Mechtild Rössler and Sabine Schleiermacher (Berlin, 1993), pp. 131–35.

61   See, Gert Groning and Joachim Wolschke-Bulmahn, '1 September 1939, Der Überfall auf Polen also Ausgangspunkt "totaler" Landespflege,' *RaumPlanung* 46/47 (1989): 149–53.

62   'Allgemeine Anordnung Nr. 20/VI/42 über die Gestaltung der Landschaft in den eingegliederten Ostgebieten vom 21. December 1942,' in E. Mäding, Regeln für die Gestaltung der Landschaft. Einführung in die Allgemeine Anordnung Nr. 20/VI/42 des Reichsführers SS, Reichskommissars für die Festigung deutschen Volkstums (Berlin, 1942).

63   W. J. T. Mitchell, ed., *Landscape and Power* (Chicago IL, 1994).

NOTES ON CHAPTER II

1   Introduction to 'The landscape approach of Bernard Lassus: Part II,' *Journal of Garden History* 15/2 (April–June 1995), p. 69. See also Bernard Lassus, *The Landscape Approach*, intro. P. Jacobs and R. B. Riley, afterword S. Bann (Philadelphia PA, 1998), where this introduction is reprinted (pp. 187–92). This comprehensive and finely illustrated volume provides a full record of Lassus's extensive work in gardens and landscapes.

2   See Julia Kristeva, *Proust and the Sense of Time*, trans. with intro. S. Bann (London, 1993), p. 10; quotation from Proust, *Remembrance of Things Past*, trans. T. Kilmartin (Harmondsworth, 1985), vol. III, p. 1095.

3   During the 1960s, Lassus alternated between the production of kinetic objects and environments ('ambiances') for exhibitions, and the fulfilment of large-scale projects involving mosaics and other coloured elements for schools and industrial locations. For the texts relating to this period, see Lassus, *The Landscape Approach*, pp. 13–23. An initial summary was provided in Stephen Bann, *Experimental Painting* (London, 1970), pp. 47–52.

4   For texts and images relating to the 'Glasses and Bottles,' see Lassus, *The Landscape Approach*, pp. 27–31.

5   See Lassus, *The Landscape Approach*, pp. 127–30 and plate 8 (three images).

6   See Lassus, *The Landscape Approach*, pp. 116–18, for the first project (1980), and pp. 121–24 for the second (1982).

7   See Lassus, *The Landscape Approach*, pp. 143–49.

8   See Lassus, *The Landscape Approach*, pp. 131–42.

9   See the statement 'Tactile Scale – Visual Scale,' (1961), in Lassus, *The Landscape Approach*, p. 43, and its further application in 'The Garden of the Anterior,' (1975), p. 110.

10   See Lassus, *The Landscape Approach*, pp. 164–67 and plate 13.

NOTES ON CHAPTER 12

1   Arthur C. Danto, 'The 1997 Whitney Biennial,' *The Nation* (2 June 1997).

2   See generally Ellis Shookman, ed., *The Faces of Physiognomy: Interdisciplinary Approaches to Johann Caspar Lavater* (New York, 1993); John Graham, *Lavater's Essays on Physiognomy: A Study in the History of Ideas* (Bern, 1980) [1979].

3   Tony Bennett, 'The Exhibitionary Complex,' *New Formations* 4 (1988): 73–102.

4   Carol Duncan and Alan Wallach have argued that art history is intertwined with the evolution of the public museum. The relationship between 'art' and 'artefact,' reflects an essentially hierarchical reading of culture. See, Duncan and Wallach, 'The Universal Survey Museum,' *Art History* 3/4 (December 1980): 448–69; Carol Duncan, *Civilising Rituals: Inside Public Art Museums* (London and New York, 1995); on art and the museum, see Andrew McClellan, *Inventing the Louvre: Art, Politics, and the Origins of the Modern Museum in Eighteenth-Century Paris* (Cambridge, 1994).

5   Although, as Douglas Crimp has argued, the heterogeneity of postmodern art might signal the demise of the museum and its concept of the 'archive.' See 'On the Museum's Ruins,' in *Postmodern Culture*, ed. H.Foster (London, 1985) [1983], pp.43–56.

6   See Michel De Certeau, *The Writing of History*, trans. T.Conley (New York, 1988) [1975].

7   Donald Preziosi, *Brain of the Earth's Body: Museums and the Fabrication of Modernity* (Minneapolis MN, in press).

8   Timothy Mitchell, *Colonising Egypt* (Berkeley CA, 1991) [1988]; Donald M.Reid, *Whose Pharoahs? Archaeology, Museums, and Egyptian National Identity from Napoleon to World War I* (Berkeley CA, in press).

NOTES ON CHAPTER 13

1   Ivan Vazov, 'Bulgarskii Naroden Teatur,' ('The Bulgarian Popular Theatre'), *Narodnii Glas* (*People's Voice Gazette*) 368 (12 February 1883), reprinted in Ivan Vazov, *Subrani Suchinenia* (*Complete Works*), vol. 19 (Sofia, 1979), p.154.

2   Todor Pavlov, *Luchi v Preizpodnjata. Pisma iz Zatvora. 1923 - 1929* (*Beams in Hell. Letters from Prison. 1923 - 1929*) (Sofia, 1947).

3   Pavlov, *Luchi v Preizpodnjata*, pp.61–62.

4   In Bulgaria it appeared as *Osnvni Vaprosi na Teoriyata na Poznanieto. Teoriya na Otrazenieto* (*Basic Problems of Theory of Knowledge. Theory of Reflection*) (Sofia, 1938).

5   Todor Pavlov, 'Georgi Bakalov kato Literaturen Kritik,' ('Georgi Bakalov as Literary Critic'), in *Etyudi, Studii, Statii* (Sofia, 1983) [1940], p.300.

6   Todor Pavlov, *Ivan Vazov, Po Sluchai 100 Godishninata ot Rojdenieto mu* (Sofia, 1950), pp.7–8.

NOTES ON CHAPTER 14

Primary Sources

Arbetet (daily newspaper), *Göteborgs Handels- och Sjöfartstidning* (daily newspaper), *Norrländska Socialdemokraten* (daily newspaper), *Dagens Eko* (radio news), Krigsarkivet (The Swedish Military Archive), Sveriges Riksdags Arkiv (The Swedish Parliament Archive).

1   Michael Landzelius, *Dis[re]membering Spaces. Swedish Modernism in Law Courts Controversy* (Göteborg, 1999).

2   Karl Molin, *Hemmakriget: Om den svenska krigsmaktens åtgärder mot kommunister under andra världskriget* (Stockholm, 1982).

3   *Göteborgs Handels- och Sjöfartstidning*, 21 October 1941, p.11; Molin, *Hemmakriget*, pp.123–32, 206–11.

4   Giorgio Agamben, *Homo Sacer. Sovereign Power and Bare Life* (Stanford CA, 1998), p.167.

5   Michel Foucault, 'Truth and Power,' in *Power/Knowledge. Selected Interviews and Other Writings 1972–1977*, ed. C.Gordon (Brighton, 1980), p.119.

6   See generally, Marija Anterić, 'Contested Heritage in the Former Yugoslavia,' in *Contemporary Issues in Heritage and Environmental Interpretation*, eds D.Uzzell and R.Ballantyne (London, 1998), pp.172–84; Pierre Bourdieu, *Distinction. A Social Critique of the Judgment of Taste* (London, 1984); Steven Connor, *Theory and Cultural Value* (Oxford, 1992); Brian Graham, 'The Past in Europe's Present: Diversity, Identity and the Construction of Place,' in *Modern Europe: Place, Culture and Identity*, ed. B.Graham (London, 1998), pp.19–49; Stuart Hall, 'Whose Heritage? Un-settling "The Heritage," Re-imagining the Post-nation,' *Third Text* 49 (Winter 1999–2000): 3–13; Barbara Herrnstein Smith, *Contingencies of Value* (Cambridge MA, 1988); Michael Heffernan, 'War and the Shaping of Europe,' in *Modern Europe*, pp.89–120; Briaval Holcomb, 'Gender and Heritage Interpretation,' in *Contemporary Issues in Heritage*, pp.37–55; Brian J.Shaw and Roy Jones, eds, *Contested Urban Heritage. Voices From the Periphery* (Aldershot, 1997); John E.Tunbridge, 'Whose Heritage to Preserve? Cross-Cultural Reflections on Political Dominance and Urban Heritage Conservation,' *The Canadian Geographer* 28/2 (1984): 171–80; John E.Tunbridge, 'The Question of Heritage in European Cultural Conflict,' in *Modern Europe*, pp.236–60; John E.Tunbridge and Gregory J.Ashworth, *Dissonant Heritage: The Management of the Past as a Resource in Conflict* (Chichester, 1996); David Uzzell, 'The Hot Interpretation of War and Conflict,' in *Heritage Interpretation Vol. 1: The Natural and Built Environment*, ed. D.Uzzell (London, 1989), pp.33–47; David Uzzell, 'Strategic Considerations and Practical Approaches to the Evaluation of Heritage Interpretation,' in *Contemporary Issues in Heritage*, pp.185–202; David Uzzell and Roy Ballantyne, 'Heritage That Hurts: Interpretation in a Postmodern World,' in *Contemporary Issues in Heritage*, pp.152–71.

7   See Iris Marion Young, *Justice and the Politics of Difference* (Princeton NJ, 1990), p.236.

8   Molin, *Hemmakriget*.

9   *Response to Interpellation 1999/2000*, 236.

10   *Response to Interpellation 1997/1998*, 106.

11   Not only expressed in the Communist press, but also by individual Social Democrats and on grounds of principle in some Liberal newspapers, notably *Göteborgs Handels - och Sjöfartstidning*.

12   David Held, *Democracy and the Global Order. From the Modern State to Cosmopolitan Governance* (Cambridge, 1995), pp.160–72.

13   Cornelius Castoriadis, *The Imaginary Institution of Society* (Cambridge, 1987), pp.101–8.

14   See Allan Pred, 'Pure and Simple Lines, Future Lines of Vision: The Stockholm Exhibition of 1930,' *Nordisk Samhällsgeografisk Tidskrift* (August 1992): 3–61.

15   For a general account, see *Yvonne Hirdman, Vi bygger landet*, 2nd ed. (Stockholm, 1990).

16   See Wilhelm M. Carlgren 'The Emergence of Sweden's Policy of Neutrality,' *Revue Internationale d'Histoire Militaire* 57 (1984): 11–33.

17   Göran Andolf, 'De grå lapparna: Regeringen och pressen under andra världskriget,' in *Nya fronter? 1943–spänd väntan*, ed. *Bo Hugemark* (Stockholm, 1994), pp.304–49; Kent Zetterberg, 'Presspolitik som säkerhetspolitik: En studie i statsmakternas presspolitik under det andra världskriget,' *Presshistorisk årsbok* (1993): 60–81.

18   The literature on these issues is extensive. See, in particular, Per G.Andreen, *De mörka åren. Perspektiv på svensk neutralitetspolitik våren 1940–nyåret 1942* (Stockholm, 1971); Maria-Pia Boëthius, *Heder och samvete. Sverige och andra världskriget* (Stockholm, 1992); Klaus-Richard Böhme, 'The Principal Features of Swedish Defence Policy 1925–1945,' *Revue Internationale d'Histoire Militaire* 57 (1984): 119–34; Wilhelm M.Carlgren, *Svensk utrikespolitik 1939–1945* (Stockholm, 1973); Louise Drangel, *Den kämpande demokratin. En studie i antinazistisk opinionsrörelse 1935–1945* (Stockholm, 1976); Janne Flyghed, *Rättsstat i kris. Spioneri och sabotage i Sverige under andra världskriget* (Stockholm, 1992); Martin Fritz, 'A Question of Practical Policies. Economic Neutrality During the Second World War,' *Revue Internationale d'Histoire Militaire* 57 (1984): 95–118; Yvonne Hirdman, *Sverges Kommunistiska Parti 1939–1945* (Stockholm, 1974); Karl Molin, *Försvaret, folkhemmet och demokratin. Socialdemokratisk riksdagspolitik 1939–1945* (Stockholm, 1974); Thorsten Nybom, *Motstånd–anpassning–uppslutning. Linjer i svensk debatt om utrikespolitik och internationell politik 1940–1943* (Stockholm, 1978); Niklas Stenlås, *Den inre kretsen. Den svenska ekonomiska elitens inflytande över partipolitik och opinionsbildning 1940–1949* (Lund, 1998); Maj Wechselmann, *De bruna förbindelserna* (Stockholm, 1995).

19   *Norrländska Socialdemokraten*, 18 April 1940, p.5.

20   Heléne Lööw, *Hakkorset och Wasakärven: En studie av nationalsocialismen i Sverige 1924–1950* (Göteborg, 1990), pp.413–18.

21   Ashley quoted in Gearóid Ó Tuathail, *Critical Geopolitics. The Politics of Writing Global Space* (Minneapolis MN, 1990), p.172.

22   Lööw, *Hakkorset och Wasakärven*, p.430.

23   Molin, *Hemmakriget*, pp. 122–23.

24   Molin, *Hemmakriget*, pp. 121, 157; Lööw, *Hakkorset och Wasakärven*, p. 419.

25   *Dagens Eko*, 1 January 2000.

26   Peter Wagner, *A Sociology of Modernity. Liberty and Discipline* (London, 1994), pp. 38–42, 73–88; Young, *Justice*, pp. 156–58.

27   On this process, see generally Tom Douglas, *Scapegoats. Transferring Blame* (London, 1995); Colin Sumner, *The Sociology of Deviance* (Buckingham, 1994); Stuart H. Traub, and Craig B. Little, *Theories of Deviance*, 5th ed. (Ithaca NY, 1999).

28   Michael Landzelius, 'The Politics of Spatial Imagery: Swedish Internment Camps in World War II,' paper presented at the 5th Conference of the International Association for the Study of Traditional Environments, 14–17 December 1996, University of California, Berkeley, USA; Michael Landzelius, 'Spatial Distortions of Democracy: Swedish Military Camps and the Abjects Within,' paper presented at the 4th 'Other Connections' Conference, 25–28 October 1999, American University of Beirut, Lebanon.

29   *Arbetet*, 9 September 1941, p. 5.

30   Mark Wigley, *The Architecture of Deconstruction: Derrida's Haunt* (Cambridge MA, 1993), p. 192. Among many other things, the 'Communist Threat' represented an alien internationalism that countered the strong nationalist sentiments of the period. See, in this context, Benedict Anderson, *Imagined Communities. Reflections on the Origin and Spread of Nationalism*, rev. ed. (London, 1991).

31   See, for accounts of such attempts and practices, numerous articles during the 1930s in *Social-Medicinsk Tidskrift*, as well as Gunnar Broberg and Mattias Tydén, *Oönskade i folkhemmet. Rashygien och sterilisering i Sverige* (Stockholm, 1991); Jonas Frykman, 'Pure and Rational. The Hygienic Vision: A Study of Cultural Transformation in the 1930s,' *Ethnologia Scandinavica* (1981): 36–63; Yvonne Hirdman, *Att lägga livet till rätta. Studier i svensk folkhemspolitik* (Stockholm, 1989); Landzelius, *Dis[re]membering Spaces*, pp. 313–96; Gunborg Lindholm, *Vägarnas folk. De resande och deras livsvärld* (Göteborg, 1995).

32   See Landzelius, 'The Politics of Spatial Imagery;' Landzelius, 'Spatial Distortions of Democracy.'

33   See, in this context, Julia Kristeva, *Powers of Horror. An Essay on Abjection* (New York, 1982); Richard Sennett, *The Uses of Disorder. Personal Identity and City Life* (New York, 1970); David Sibley, *Geographies of Exclusion. Society and Difference in the West* (London, 1995).

34   See Frank R. Ankersmit, *History and Tropology. The Rise and Fall of Metaphor* (Berkeley CA, 1984); Michel Foucault, *The Order of Things. An Archaeology of the Human Sciences* (London, 1970); Michel Foucault, *The Archaeology of Knowledge* (London, 1972); Hans Kellner, *Language and Historical Representation* (Madison WI, 1989); Reinhart Koselleck, *Futures Past. On the Semantics of Historical Time* (Cambridge MA, 1985); David Lowenthal, *The Past Is a Foreign Country* (Cambridge, 1985); Pierre Nora, 'Between Memory and History: Les Lieux de Mémoire,' *Representations* 26 (1989): 7–25; Peter Osborne, *The Politics of Time. Modernity and Avant-Garde* (London, 1995); Hayden White, *Metahistory: The Historical Imagination in Nineteenth-Century Europe* (Baltimore MD, 1973); Hayden White,

Tropics of Discourse. Essays in Cultural Criticism (Baltimore MD, 1978); Hayden White, *The Content of the Form. Narrative Discourse and Historical Representation* (Baltimore MD, 1987).

35   Held, *Democracy*, p.161.

36   Castoriadis, *The Imaginary Institution*, p.106.

37   Castoriadis, *The Imaginary Institution*, p.102.

38   Castoriadis, *The Imaginary Institution*, p.109.

39   Held, *Democracy*, p.268.

40   Tunbridge and Ashworth, *Dissonant Heritage*, p.21.

41   Henri Lefebvre, *The Production of Space* (Oxford, 1991), p.422.

42   Gilles Deleuze and Felix Guattari, *A Thousand Plateaus. Capitalism and Schizophrenia* (Minneapolis MN, 1987), p.12, italics in original.

43   Deleuze and Guattari, *A Thousand Plateaus*, pp.3–25.

44   Gilles Deleuze and Felix Guattari, *Anti-Oedipus. Capitalism and Schizophrenia* (Minneapolis MN, 1983), p.341.

45   Sergiusz Michalski, *Public Monuments. Art in Political Bondage 1870-1997* (London 1998), pp.205–10.

46   Steve Pile, 'Introduction: Opposition, Political Identities and Spaces of Resistance,' in *Geographies of Resistance*, eds S.Pile and M.Keith (London, 1997), pp.1–32.

47   David Sibley, *Geographies*, pp.5–11, 100–12.

48   Jacques Derrida's notion of 'différance' as a deferral of being has immediate bearing here, particularly as applied to the foundation of states in the inauguration of a new law, where 'this law to come will in return legitimate, retrospectively, the violence that may offend the sense of justice, its future anterior already justifies it.' 'Force of Law: The "Mystical Foundation of Authority,"' in *Deconstruction and the Possibility of Justice*, eds D.Cornell, M.Rosenfeld and D.Carlson (London, 1992), pp.3–65 (p.35). See also Deleuze and Guattari, *A Thousand Plateaus*, in which they argue that the lawful violence of the state 'consists in capturing while simultaneously constituting a right to capture' (p.448); as well as Agamben, Homo Sacer, who contends that: 'The particular "force" of law consists in this capacity of law to maintain itself in relation to an exteriority' (p.18), where this excluded exteriority can take the shape of life in 'the camp…the hidden matrix and nomos of the political space in which we are still living' (p.166).

49   See Castoriadis, *The Imaginary Institution*, p.135–56.

50   Michalski, *Public Monuments*, p.205, 207.

51   Gilles Deleuze, 'Whitman,' in *Essays Critical and Clinical* (London, 1998), pp.56–60 (p.58).

NOTES ON CHAPTER 15

1   Jay Winter, *Sites of Memory, Sites of Mourning: The Great War in European Cultural History* (Cambridge, 1995).

2   George L.Mosse, *Fallen Soldiers: Reshaping the Memory of the World Wars* (Oxford and New York, 1990).

3   Benedict Anderson, *Imagined Communities: Reflections on the Origin and Spread of Nationalism*, rev. ed. (London and New York, 1991), p. 9.

4   Gaynor Kavanagh, 'Museum as Memorial: The Origins of the Imperial War Museum,' *Journal of Contemporary History* 23 (1988): 77–97. See also Gaynor Kavanagh, *Museums and the First World War: A Social History* (Leicester, 1994).

5   Theodor W. Adorno, 'Valery Proust Museum,' in *Prisms*, trans. S. Weber and S. Weber (London, 1967), pp. 172–85.

6   George L. Mosse, 'National Cemeteries and National Revival: The Cult of the Fallen Soldiers in Germany,' *Journal of Contemporary History* 1/1 (1977): 1–20 (7–8).

7   Thomas W. Laqueur, 'Memory and Naming in the Great War,' in *Commemorations: The Politics of National Identity*, ed. J.R. Gillis (Princeton NJ, 1994), pp. 150–67 (p. 153).

8   David W. Lloyd, *Battlefield Tourism: Pilgrimage and the Commemoration of the Great War in Britain, Australia and Canada, 1919-1939* (Oxford, 1998).

9   Bob Bushaway, 'Name Upon Name: The Great War and remembrance,' in *Myths of the English*, ed. R. Porter (Cambridge, 1992), pp. 136–67 (p. 161). Bushaway argues that the commemorations were constructed so as to deny the mass of British society access to a political critique of the war. For a classic account of the ways in which the war 'has been remembered conventionalised, and mythologized,' see Paul Fussel, *The Great War and Modern Memory* (Oxford, 1977). See also Antoine Prost, 'Les Monuments aux Morts: Culte Républicain? Culte Civique? Culte Patriotique?,' in *Lieux de Mémoire*, ed. P. Nora, rev. ed. (Paris, 1997), vol. 1, pp. 199–223. Prost explores commemorative statuary to the dead of World War I in France within the context of the relationship between 'citizens,' municipalities and state.

10 See Mandy S. Morris, 'Gardens "For Ever England": Landscape, Identity and the First World War British Cemeteries on the Western Front,' *Ecumene* 4/4 (1997): 410–34; Michael Heffernan 'For Ever England: The Western Front and the Politics of Remembrance in Britain,' *Ecumene* 2/3 (1995): 293–323. On the importance of memorials in strengthening national identity in Germany, see Mosse, 'National Cemeteries and National Revival' and Mosse, *Fallen Soldiers*, p. 3.

11 Julia Kristeva, *Powers of Horror: an Essay on Abjection* (New York, 1982).

12 Elazar Barkan, *The Guilt of Nations: Restitution and Negotiating Historical Injustices* (New York, 2000), p. xvii.

13 On the proliferation of Holocaust memorial sites in the US, see Anson Rabinach, 'From Explosion to Erosion: Holocaust Memorialization in American Since Bitburg,' *History and Memory* 9/1–2 (Fall 1997): 226–55.

14 Michael Rowlands, 'Memory, Sacrifice and the Nation,' *New Formations* 30 (1996): 8–17. See also his chapter 'Remembering to Forget: Sublimation as Sacrifice in War Memorials,' in *The Art of Forgetting*, eds A. Forty and S. Küchler (Oxford and New York, 1999), pp. 129–45.

15 See Denis Cosgrove's discussion of heritage and *spolia* in Chapter 8.

16 Walter Benjamin, 'Theses on the Philosophy of History in Illuminations,' ed. H. Arendt, trans. H. Zohn (London, 1992), p. 248. See Jonathan Arac, 'The Struggle for the Cultural Heritage: Christina Stead Refunctions Charles Dickens and Mark Twain,' who compares Benjamin's observations to the assertions of André Malraux a few years earlier: 'A heritage is not transmitted; it must be conquered'

(1936), in *The New Historicism*, ed. H.A.Veeser (New York and London, 1989), pp.116–31 (p.116).

17   As compared to the 1914–1918 war, very few monuments were built in France to the dead soldiers of the disastrous 1870–1871 war; see Prost, 'Les Monuments aux Morts,' p.200.

18   Paul Gilroy, *Between Camps* (Harmondsworth, 2000), p.5.

19   Gilroy, *Between Camps*, p.8.

20   Gilroy, *Between Camps*, pp.2, 327–56.

21   Gilroy, *Between Camps*, p.6.

22   Gilroy, *Between Camps*, p.6.

23   Iris Marion Young, *Justice and the Politics of Difference* (Princeton NJ, 1990), pp.170–71.

24   'Nationalism,' writes Gellner, 'is not the awakening of nations to self-consciousness: it invents nations when they do not exist.' See *Thought and Change* (London, 1964), p.169. Maurice Halbwachs argued that collective memory is a social construct shaped by the concerns of the present; see *On Collective Memory*, ed. and trans. L.A.Coser (Chicago IL and London, 1992), p.22.

25   Eric Hobsbawm and Terence Ranger, eds, *Invented Traditions* (London, 1983); Anderson, *Imagined Communities*, pp.5–7.

26   Pierre Nora, 'Entre Mémoire et Histoire: Le Problématique des lieux,' in *Les Lieux de Mémoire*, pp.23–43. Translated into English as *Realms of Memory: Rethinking the French Past. Vol. I: Conflicts and Divisions*, ed. L.D.Kritzman, trans. A.Goldhammer (New York, 1996), pp.1–23 (p.7).

27   On memory as a fear of forgetting, see generally Forty and Küchler, *The Art of Forgetting*. For a critique of Nora's opposition between history and memory, see Dominick LaCapra, *History and Memory after Auschwitz* (Ithaca NY, 1998), especially Chapter 1.

28   Michel de Certeau, *The Practice of Everyday Life* (Berkeley CA, 1984), p.108.

29   More than 25,000 objects have been left by visitors at the memorial. These artefacts have inspired an exhibition at the National Museum of American History to commemorate the tenth anniversary of the Memorial in 1992, 'Personal Legacy: The Healing of a Nation.' For an interpretation of the offerings left at the Memorial, see Miles Richardson, 'The Gift of Presence: The Act of Leaving Artifacts at Shrines, Memorials, and Other Tragedies,' in *Textures of Place: Exploring Humanist Geographies*, eds P.C.Adams, S.Hoelscher and K.E.Till (Minneapolis MN and London, 2001), pp.257–72.

30   Thomas F.Gieryn, 'Balancing Acts: Science, Enola Gay and History Wars at the Smithsonian,' in *The Politics of Display: Museums, Science, Culture*, ed. S.Macdonald (London and New York, 1998), pp.197–228 (p.198). In the event, only the fuselage of the aircraft was displayed from June 1995 to May 1998. There is already a large bibliography on the Enola Gay; see Vera Zolberg, 'Museums as Contested Sites of Remembrace: The Enola Gay Affair,' in *Theorizing Museums*, eds S.Macdonald and G.Fyfe (Oxford, 1996), pp.69–82 and generally, Edward T.Linenthal and Tom Engelhardt, eds, *History Wars: The Enola Gay and Other Battles for the American Past* (New York, 1996).

31   James Young, *The Texture of Memory* (New Haven CT and London, 1993); see also Young's more recent study, *At Memory's Edge: After-Images of the Holocaust in Contemporary Art and Architecture* (New Haven CT and London, 2000).

32   As Barbara Stewart remarks: 'Shows on every imaginable aspect of September 11 are being planned at museums in New York, Washington, Chicago, Dallas and elsewhere.' See 'Forget Me Not,' *New York Times*, 9 March 2002.

33   Gordon A. Craig, *Germany, 1866-1945* (Oxford, 1978), pp. 434–68.

34   Barkan, *The Guilt of Nations*, pp. xxiii–xxv.

35   Martha Minow explores the wide range of responses to collective acts of violence and genocide in the twentieth century from Germany to Argentina and South Africa: see *Between Vengeance and Forgiveness: Facing History after Genocide and Mass Violence* (Boston MA, 1999).

36   Roy Foster, 'Is "Sorry" Enough?' *Independent on Sunday*, 18 July 1999.

37   See, however, Claudia Koonz, 'Between Memory and Oblivion: Concentration Camps in German Memory,' in *Commemorations*, pp. 258–80. Koonz argues that it was not until the 1960s that Germans engaged with their Nazi past. See also, more recently, Jeffrey Herf, *Divided Memory: The Nazi Past in the Two Germanys* (Cambridge MA, 1997), especially Chapter Nine, 'Politics and Memory since the 1960s,' pp. 334–72.

38   Ian Buruma, 'The Joys and Perils of Victimhood,' *New York Review of Books*, 8 April 1999. Buruma's article is discussed and quoted by Barkan in *The Guilt of Nations*, pp. xvii–xviii.

39   Catherine Bennett, 'Sorry, It's the Hardest Word,' *Guardian*, 28 September 2000.

40   In May 2001 the Pope apologized to Archbishop Christodoulos, the leader of the Greek Orthodox Church, for the fourth crusade, See Michael Binyon, 'Sometimes "Mea Culpa" is Just so Hard to Say,' *The Times*, 5 May 2001. See also Barkan, *The Guilt of Nations*, pp. xxviii–xxix.

41   'Californian Internment Camp Commemorated,' *New York Times*, 26 April 1992. For a discussion of Japanese-American camps, see Barkan, *The Guilt of Nations*, pp. 30–45.

42   Laura Peek, 'US Lawyers to Sue for Slavery Reparation,' *The Times*, 2 January 2001. The argument for reparation is taken up by Wole Soyinka in the first of his three essays collected in *The Burden of Memory, The Muse of Forgiveness* (Oxford and New York, 2000). See also Barkan, *The Guilt of Nations*, pp. 283–307.

43   Foster, 'Is "Sorry" Enough?'

44   See Desmond Tutu, *No Future Without Forgiveness* (London, 2000), Chapter 11, 'Without Forgiveness There Really is No Future,' pp. 206–30. Tutu prefaces his book with a quotation from George Santayana: 'Those who cannot remember the past are condemned to repeat it.'

45   Gilroy, *Between Camps*, pp. 26–27. See Kader Asmal, Louise Asmal and Ronald Suresh Roberts, *Reconciliation Through Truth: A Reckoning of Apartheid's Criminal Governance* (Cape Town, Oxford and New York, 1997) [1996], pp. 82–83, 132–33.

46   Tutu, *No Future Without Forgiveness*, Chapter 2, pp. 10–36, especially p. 24.

47   On the development of mass culture in Victorian Britain and the representation of the population as a social body, see Mary Poovey, *Making a Social Body: British Cultural Formation, 1830-1864* (Chicago IL, 1995).

48 See, for example, Neill Ferguson, ed., *Virtual History, Alternatives and Counterfactuals* (London, 1997).

49 Barkan, *The Guilt of Nations*, p. xvii.

50 Jean Améry, quoted in Gilroy, *Between Camps*, p. 25.

51 Gilroy, *Between Camps*, pp. 25–26.

52 See Tim Cole, *Images of the Holocaust: The Myth of the 'Shoah Business'* (London, 1999), p. 168.

53 Gilroy, *Between Camps*, p. 26. For an interesting article that explores Auschwitz as a contested place of memory, particularly the Catholic Church's symbolic appropriation of the camp, see Andrew Charlesworth, 'Contesting Places of Memory: The Case of Auschwitz,' *Environment and Planning D: Society and Space* 12/5 (October 1994): 579–93.

54 Clearly this vision of antagonistic group interests contrasts with the notion of 'public culture' described by Arjun Appadurai and Carol A. Breckenridge, where groups 'debate what culture is.' See 'Museums Are Good to Think: Heritage on View in India,' (1992) reprinted in *Representing the Nation: A Reader. Histories, Heritage and Museums*, eds D. Boswell and J. Evans (London and New York, 1999), pp. 404–20 (p. 407) and the Introduction to the present volume.

ACKNOWLEDGEMENTS

INTRODUCTION

I am grateful to Denis Cosgrove for his helpful comments on an earlier draft of this volume, and to Rebecca Peckham for her numerous suggestions. My sincere thanks to Erik Holm for his support, and to the many colleagues and friends who took part in the heritage debate, in particular Patrick Wright, Ludmilla Jordanova and Ivan Vejvoda.

CHAPTER 1

I am grateful to Nancy Duncan and Robert Shannan Peckham for their helpful comments on an earlier draft of this chapter.

CHAPTER 5

This chapter reports findings from a research project on 'Ideas, Institutions, and Political Culture: The Europeanization of National Identities' funded by the German Research Association (Deutsche Forschungsgemeinschaft). The empirical research was conducted by Daniela Engelmann-Martin, Hans-Joachim Knopf, Martin Marcussen, and Klaus Roscher. I am most grateful to them for their input.

CHAPTER 10

I would like to thank Robert Shannan Peckham for his editorial input in helping to render this chapter more accessible to an English-language readership.

CHAPTER 14

I would like to extend my appreciation to The Swedish Foundation for International Cooperation in Research and Higher Education (STINT) for generously funding part of this research.

INDEX